1·75

CELINE DION

✳ ACKNOWLEDGEMENTS ✳

Writing a book such as this is an incredible journey from start to finish, and along the path there are individuals who have played a vital role.

Thank you first and foremost to my collaborator Della Druick, who was a driving force behind this book; Mindy Laxer for her valuable input; my exceptional literary agent Susan Schulman and her co-agent in London, Meg Davis; and my dedicated Senior Editor, Doug Young, and copy-editor Kelly Davis, along with the superb team at Headline Book Publishing.

A heartfelt thank you to my husband David and my three sons Steven, Michael and Matthew, for their support throughout my arduous yet fascinating adventure in writing this biography.

Most of all, thank you to Celine Dion, for the wonderful gift she has given the world – her own special power of love.

– Lisa Peters

CELINE DION
The Complete Biography

BY LISA PETERS
IN COLLABORATION WITH DELLA DRUICK

HEADLINE

First published in 1999
by HEADLINE BOOK PUBLISHING

10 9 8 7 6 5 4 3 2 1

British Library Cataloguing in Publication Data

Peters Lisa
    Celine Dion - the power of love : the complete
    autobiography
    1.Dion, Celine 2.Women singers – Canada – Biography
    3.Singers – Canada – Biography
    I.Title

    782.4'2'166'092

    ISBN 0 7472 7393 6 hbk
    ISBN 0 7472 7394 4 tpb

Typeset by
Letterpart Limited, Reigate, Surrey

Printed and bound in Great Britain by
Mackays of Chatham PLC, Chatham, Kent

HEADLINE BOOK PUBLISHING
A division of the Hodder Headline Group
338 Euston Road
London NW1 3BH
www.headline.co.uk
www.hodderheadline.com

✳ CONTENTS ✳

She stood on stage, over 70,000 fans cheering and chanting 'Celine . . . Celine . . . Celine.' They screamed, they cried. One look at that vast sea of people and Celine was home. It didn't matter where she was in the world. The stage was her home – a place she had always yearned to be, ever since she was five years old, standing on the kitchen table, singing her heart out.

On stage she felt powerful. Off stage, it was a different story. 'When I sing, I take myself seriously,' Celine has said. 'I am like an actress and I have confidence in myself. But when I leave the stage, I become the fourteenth child of a big family.'

As the youngest in a large French-Canadian family, she grew up surrounded by love. But at only thirteen she was plucked from the nest and her life would never be the same again. Years of sacrifice and harsh self-discipline were the price Celine paid for superstardom. 'The years flew by,' as she said, 'without my having the time to live them.' She would never truly be able to return to the life she once cherished, nestled in the warmth of a family that was poor in possessions but rich in love.

Celine's success brought her all the material possessions any woman could ever want – mansions, enough designer clothes to last a lifetime, a thousand pairs of shoes – and her life seemed like a fairytale. But with the glory came the pain of years of sacrifice that have marked her life forever.

For decades she was driven by ambition – the vision of 'always going higher and always going farther'. Then came *Titanic*, the film that swept her into a new dimension of success. She was now the most popular singer in the world. With ninety million albums sold, and enough trophies and awards to fill the *Titanic* itself, Celine had realized her dream of worldwide fame and glory. But was she truly happy?

What of the triumphs and the tragedies, the lost adolescence, the years when she was forced to hide the identity of the true love of her life, and the many sacrifices she had to make? It has been a life of courage, pain and, above all, passion that she has lived on her way to becoming the hottest singing sensation on the planet – a true ambassador of song.

By the time she was thirty Celine could already say: 'I gave my life to music. There is nothing more beautiful than the sound of applause, the love of the public. For that – for the public – I am ready to make all sacrifices . . . It's what I live for.'

Yet Celine had other desires – things she dreamed of that most people take for granted. Music had always been the power of her love, but there was more in her heart. A love for her family and mentor-manager that knew no equal. A love she would do anything for.

This is the remarkable story of Celine Dion.

'I Was an Accident'

'Thirteen brothers and sisters encouraged me. I'm the fourteenth, the baby of the family, and they call me "the accident". I have to say they call me the accident because my parents had twins and after thirteen they said "Enough, enough." Six years later, I was happy to be here.'

— CELINE DION

They say that Celine Dion was born under the right star. Divine providence had its way and this unexpected fourteenth child 'accidentally' found her way into the world, changing the lives of everyone around her. At first Maman and Papa Dion reeled at the notion of yet another child. But, after an arduous pregnancy, the birth became a joyous occasion for the whole family. Now there was a fascinating new 'living doll' for her thirteen siblings to play with.

The Dion family lived in the small rural community of Charlemagne, Quebec, the kind of city that you adopted right away – or it adopted you. It was only 30 miles northeast of Montreal but it was so different from the bustling metropolis that they could have been on different planets. Charlemagne was a small French-speaking Catholic town, with large families and a big heart. It was not uncommon to have nine or ten children and quite normal to have Christmas celebrations with over a hundred people – all family – by the time you added in all the cousins, aunts, uncles, grandchildren, grandparents, and in-laws.

'Small town, big family,' as Celine puts it. The Dions *did* have the most kids in town, but that wasn't the only thing that set them apart. They were a different type of family – a family that lived and breathed music.

Maman played the violin and Papa the accordion, and at weekends they often performed at weddings and parties to help make ends meet. The Dions' guitars, drums and piano were important fixtures in their home, and touched the lives of each and every one of their children. As Maman recalls: 'Music came with the bib.'

When Celine was born, on 30 March 1968, she was no exception, her 8½-pound bundle of warmth a sharp contrast to the frigid Canadian winter. Earlier that morning, as Therese Dion looked out at the falling snow, she felt the first of those all too familiar contractions. There was a song on the radio, a beautiful French melody that temporarily distracted her from the pain. All day long the French tune *'Dis-moi Céline'* ('Tell Me Celine') played in her head. 'What a perfect name for my baby,' thought Maman. It was only fitting that this child with the golden voice was to be named after a song. Celine was born into a family where the language was music.

Celine was born six years after what Therese and Adhemar Dion thought were their last offspring, the twins Paul and Pauline. Maman and Papa had decided then that they would not have any more children, but this didn't stop Celine from making her way into the world. As she later recalled, 'Thirteen brothers and sisters encouraged me. I'm the fourteenth, the baby of the family, and they call me "the accident". I have to say they call me the accident because my parents had twins and after thirteen they said "Enough, enough". Six years later, I was happy to be here.'

In 1968, the year Celine was born, the Dions already had a full house. Besides the six-year-old twins Paul and Pauline, there was Manon (eight), Linda (nine), Ghislaine (ten), Daniel (twelve), Jacques (thirteen), Louise (fifteen), Michel (sixteen), Liette (eighteen), Claudette (twenty), Clement (twenty-one) and Denise (twenty-two). Her eight sisters and five brothers surrounded the new baby, with a passion for music that was somehow capable of replacing whatever the family lacked in their small, poverty-stricken home.

'From as far back as I could remember,' Celine reminisces, 'singing was most important.' At a young age she wanted success. She yearned to be on the greatest stages of the world. Celine wanted the glory and she wanted to be like her parents – artists. 'I was almost born on stage,' recalls Celine. Her love of music had a lot to do with a family background deeply embedded in musical tradition.

Tradition lies at the very heart of Quebec, Canada's largest province. Over 80 per cent of its inhabitants are French-speaking and the vast majority belong to the Roman Catholic Church. The province was named when French explorer Samuel de Champlain heard the native Indians refer to it using the Algonquin Indian word *kebec*, which means 'the place where the river narrows'. In 1608 de Champlain founded Quebec city as a permanent European settlement. However, in 1759, at the battle of the Plains of Abraham, France lost this settlement to Great Britain. And thus began Quebec's age-old quest for cultural independence and its fierce love of tradition. The province is composed of a mosaic of basically French-speaking towns and villages, each with a neighbourhood church and a neighbourhood school, where everybody knows everybody and families are always big.

Celine's mother, Therese Tanguay, was born on 20 March 1927, the sixth in a French-speaking family of nine children that included five boys and four girls. The Tanguay family farmed the lush pastures of Sainte-Anne-des-Monts, a stretch of land on the Gaspasian coast in Quebec that benefited from the rich soil of the St Lawrence River Valley. Therese has fond memories of these years: 'Once you spend your childhood on a farm . . . those years remain the most beautiful of your life.'

The Tanguays had little, yet wanted for nothing. Maman recalls, 'The most beautiful gift of my life was a violin ordered by my father from a department store catalogue.' Her father had nicknamed her *Petite*, which means Little One, and he adored the soothing quality of her playing. That violin became her most treasured possession and her constant companion. It was an instrument that had always featured in Quebec's musical tradition, adding a special atmosphere when used to accompany storytelling ballads.

By the early 1940s, farming was becoming more difficult; the Second World War broke out and Quebec factories expanded to manufacture war supplies. Therese's father, Achille Tanguay, sold the farm in search of more lucrative opportunities and found work 800 kilometres away in the city of La Tuque in Quebec. It was a difficult move for Therese's mother, Antoinette, and for all the children. The clean air of Therese's childhood was suddenly replaced by the acrid smell of steel factories. Therese found a job as a nurse's aid at a local hospital but she remained terribly homesick.

One summer night in 1944, her eldest brother Henri, (who was working at an aluminum factory) met a man who had grown up in their home town. His name was Adhemar Dion. He had been born in Sainte-Anne-des-Monts, the oldest in a family of five boys and two girls. His parents, Charles-Edouard and Ernestine Dion, turned out to be childhood schoolfriends of Therese's parents – amazingly, they had also moved to La Tuque and lived only a few streets away.

There had to be a reunion! The next day was Saturday, and Therese and her family went off to visit the Dion family. Her parents insisted that she bring her violin. After all, in Quebec there could never be a gathering without music! She shyly moved the bow up and down, all the while stealing glances at Adhemar. He was twenty-one, slim and tall, with an elegance about him. And those eyes! Therese was instantly mesmerized. Her robust frame was crowned by short auburn hair, which framed jovial cheeks and eyes that lit up when she smiled at him. Adhemar soon joined in with his accordion and everyone sat in a circle in the living-room, joining in spontaneously with the high-spirited tunes and folk melodies. Therese and Adhemar played on through the night, striking an emotional chord, falling in love.

Ten months later, on 20 June 1945, they were married at the Saint-Zephirin Church in a double wedding ceremony. Therese's brother Valmont had decided to get married as well. After the wedding the four newlyweds took the five-hour train ride to Quebec city for their honeymoon. The whole city was celebrating – it was 1945 and the war was over! The two newlywed couples spent four glorious days there. Just as their honeymoon ended, Therese and Adhemar were walking hand in hand when she gazed over at a woman pushing a pram.

'How many children do you want, Adhemar?' she ventured.

He looked sullen. 'It's not that I don't like children, Therese, but we have our whole lives ahead of us.'

His reply didn't please her. In her world, the happiness of a couple was often judged by how many children they had. If they had only known then how truly filled with happiness their lives were to be.

By Christmas time, Therese was pregnant. They had barely celebrated their first wedding anniversary when, at nineteen years of age, she gave birth to their first child, a girl named Denise, on 15 August 1946. Even though she worked as a nurse's assistant in a hospital at the time, she would not see a doctor, preferring to give birth at home. The following year, on 2 November 1947, Therese gave birth to their first son, Clement. Thirteen months later, on 10 December 1948, there was another daughter, Claudette. Liette was born on 8 February 1950.

In the post-war years factory production began to slow down and work was scarce. Adhemar had to leave the factory and find work in forestry. Money was tight and Therese and the four small children were often on their own, as Adhemar had to work fifteen-day stints. Winter nights were long and music was the only thing that could fill the endless hours. Maman could not only play violin, but guitar and mandolin as well, and the children loved it when she played.

Then a friend convinced Adhemar to go to Montreal, where there was rumoured to be work in construction. Adhemar knew that he had to do something to make a better life for Therese and his young brood. So he took his toolbox and set off alone. He found work immediately. Montreal was becoming a boom town and everywhere things were expanding.

This was also true of the Dion family, for Therese soon found herself pregnant once again. Adhemar had asked Therese to join him in Montreal but she didn't like big cities. So he found a three-room apartment for the family in the small town of Charlemagne, less than an hour's drive away. Everyone spoke French and the rural region was inviting, but the move was stressful. They were cramped and the apartment was damp from the endless laundry hanging from the make-shift clothesline in the kitchen. Therese spent all her time washing diapers – the thick cotton ones were a real nuisance to hand-wash. Then, on 18 August 1952, she gave birth to their fifth child, Michel.

Even though all their children were blessed with good health, these were very difficult years. To make matters worse, Adhemar lost his job. He then found work for a manufacturer, where he had to tear rags apart all day long. It didn't matter what he had to do to make a living. He always said he 'preferred having a hard time at work than a hard time at home'.

Adhemar desperately wanted to buy a house. But he made only 65 cents an hour and there were all those mouths to feed. How could he afford it? Yet he was a man of stubborn conviction – he decided to walk the hour distance across the bridge to and from work to save the 20-cent bus fare each day. With every extra penny going into their savings, the Dions managed to put aside 7 dollars a week. Miraculously, they had 400 hundred dollars in the bank after a year.

They looked for land and found it in the heart of Charlemagne. It was a strange coincidence that Charlemagne became their home because the Dions could trace their ancestry back to the French emperor Charlemagne, whose descendant, Catherine Baillon, arrived in Quebec city in 1669 (as one of 1000 women recruited by Louis XIV as spouses for colonists in Quebec). Her eventual grandchildren married into the Dion family.

There may have been a hint of nobility in the family line. But, for Therese and Adhemar, there were bills to pay. Having bought the land, they had no money left to build the house. They asked the local suppliers for credit and, being a warm, friendly town, everyone advanced them their building materials. But who was going to actually *build* the house? *They* were. Adhemar and Therese built the house by hand. They did everything – from the foundations up. Maman recalls: 'The neighbours couldn't believe seeing me there, along with my husband, climbing ladders, and carrying beams.'

Less than a year later, they moved into their house. Home, at last. They had more space – and it was a good thing, because there were more children on the way. The Dions already had five children, which would have been enough for Therese, who confides, 'I really only wanted five kids. My husband – he didn't want any!'

The Dion children were a lively bunch. But, when things became a little too rambunctious, Adhemar didn't take out the belt. He took out the accordion. The folk songs had a calming effect on the children, who drank in the music like water.

Therese and Adhemar had five more children within the next six years. In June 1957, by their fourteenth year of marriage, they already had ten children. Louise was born in 1953, Jacques in 1955, Daniel in 1956, Ghislaine in 1958, and Linda in 1959. One year later in 1960, Manon was born. This time, the home birth was difficult. Manon was in a breech position and it was a frightening experience for the family.

In between having babies the Dions moved once again – this time to another home only minutes away, on Notre-Dame Street, across the road from a food market. The house was bigger, but still modest with barely enough space for all the kids. But the warmth of their small home kept out the chills of growing up poor – it was 'big' in love.

The focal point of the house was the basement. There, the children found themselves in another world. Musical instruments and microphones filled the room, providing an escape from the mundane struggle of everyday life. Between washing the dishes, Therese continued to play the violin and Adhemar the accordion. The whole family joined in these impromptu jam sessions, strumming, singing and dancing to their hearts' content. The music was a mixture of traditional and contemporary songs. The drums banged out the rhythm. The piano played incessantly. When they weren't creating melodies, the eleven children used to watch television, each sitting on one of the thirteen steps leading to the basement. They used to tease their parents, saying, 'If we have more brothers and sisters you will have to lengthen the stairway!'

In April 1962, at the age of thirty-five, with eleven children to take care of, Therese was on the verge of giving birth once again. But there were problems. Her legs had become terribly swollen and the risk to her health was too great. After eleven home deliveries, she would have to give birth in a hospital this time. It was a wise decision. This time, a huge surprise was in store. In only a few hours, she gave birth to not one, but two babies! She and Adhemar were in total shock, never having suspected that she was carrying twins. After all, Therese had never even been to see a doctor during the pregnancy.

Twins Paul and Pauline came into the world weighing a healthy 6 pounds, 7 ounces and 6 pounds, 4 ounces. But when Maman Dion returned with the twins, life was hectic. Manon, Linda and Ghislaine were still toddlers in diapers as well. Mealtimes involved food preparation on a grand scale – the dishes were a gargantuan task. But the music those children played. 'By our fourteenth wedding anniversary, there were thirteen children – all guitarists, singers, drummers, composers, choir singers and entertainers. A nice number,' says Maman.

At this point Maman Dion made an important decision. With thirteen children in the house, she felt that she had done her duty as a good Catholic. 'I decided that it was enough,' she explains. 'I must tell you . . . I am a strong believer. I always followed the directives of the Church. There was no question of taking the birth control pill either.'

So Maman Dion did her own form of family planning, with a calendar. But Therese was shocked to find herself pregnant once again – at forty years old!

Therese didn't want to believe it. She was sure there was some mistake. 'But I had to get used to the idea and this child I was carrying,' she recalls.

Maman Dion was about to give birth in the same year that two of her eldest daughters were getting married. She confesses: 'I was almost ashamed. I had the feeling that on the street people pointed at me. Luckily, we didn't go out much!'

They spent their evenings at home. After all, where would they go with all those children and hardly any money? 'But we loved it this way,' Maman recalls. 'We spent our evenings as a family, making music. The children were musicians and everyone knew how to sing. I can say that we were never bored. There was rarely a family as close and united as ours.'

Therese awoke on Saturday morning, 30 March 1968, with labour pains. Adhemar had already left for work. The French song 'Dis-moi Céline' ('Tell Me Celine') that she heard on the radio that morning was playing itself over and over in her head as she picked up her suitcase and left for the hospital. At the age of forty-one, she knew it would be too risky to give birth at home. Many hours later, Therese was holding a healthy 8½-pound baby in her arms. She named her Celine, the morning's tune still on her mind.

Adhemar looked lovingly at his wife and the new baby and wanted to do something special. He had the perfect idea. A gift. That old violin of hers, the one her father had given her, was worn with use. Adhemar gave Therese a new violin to mark Celine's birth – a gesture that said far more than words.

Celine – an accident of fate? Her destiny had just begun.

CHAPTER 2

'I Want to Sing'

*'I did my first show at five years old. When I heard the applause,
I knew that singing would be my life.'*

— CELINE DION

The gang of wide-eyed kids that crowded around Maman when she first brought Celine home from the hospital were euphoric about their new living doll. From the moment they laid eyes on the plump, cherub-faced baby, with hazel eyes and a mop of dark hair, they were in love. They had all anxiously awaited her arrival — well, almost all. The twins Paul and Pauline hadn't expected her until she was brought home on the day of their sixth birthday. 'For me, she was like a surprise baby. I wasn't even aware of Maman's pregnancy!' recounts Paul.

Baby Celine's thirteen brothers and sisters could be divided into three groups: the oldest ones; Denise, Clement and Claudette who were in their early twenties and were no longer living at home; her adolescent siblings: Liette, Michel, Louise and Jacques; and the twelve and under group: Daniel, Ghislaine, Linda, Manon, Paul and Pauline. For them, Celine was about the best toy a kid could have.

Everyone wanted to help take care of her. Each night they took turns giving her the bottle, giving her a bath or changing her diaper. As Maman put it: 'Never was there ever a baby as spoiled!'

Her oldest sister Denise was always calling her *Mon Petit Bébé*. As the oldest sibling in the family, Denise was already twenty-two years old when Celine was a baby and had been married for several years. She was pregnant with her first child. Sadly, she lost the unborn baby girl after eight-and-a-half months of pregnancy. She lived very close to the Dion house. So, when Maman Dion came to visit, she often brought Celine with her, wrapped in a fluffy pink blanket.

'You already have thirteen children . . . Let me raise her!' Denise urged. But, even though Denise was old enough to be a second mother to Celine, no one could replace Maman. Therese was an extraordinary mother to her fourteen children. She was always there to console, to iron and to fix – 'A woman who saw to everything and didn't leave anything to chance,' as Denise puts it.

From the start, Maman Dion and Celine had a special closeness because all the other children were already at school when she was born. Maman held her tightly in her arms, adoring her little 'accident of fate'. In return, Celine worshipped her. 'She's my idol,' explains Celine. 'She's the most incredible artist because she can do whatever she wants with her hands. She is very, very talented. She cooks, she can sing, she plays violin, and she raised fourteen kids. That's something!'

Her mother's hands always had the power to soothe, even though they were red and calloused from all those hours washing dishes. And the beautiful music that Therese could make with those hands! Meanwhile Papa Dion struggled from job to job, trying to ensure that there would be enough money to go around. His shoulders were now slightly stooped, his hair receding. But he was a jovial man and fiercely proud of his family.

Celine's siblings happily continued to spoil and pamper her. Louise, who left school to help out at home, used to invite her friends over and Celine was always the centre of attention. 'We played with Celine as if she was a doll and we changed and re-changed her clothes all the time.'

Celine was pushed in a doll's pram by Ghislaine, accidentally pricked with a diaper pin by her sister Linda, rocked and sung lullabies to by Clement, bathed in bubbles by Louise, and tucked in at night by Linda.

Most of the Dion children had nicknames, and some had more than one. Celine was called *La Puce* which means Pet; Paul was called *Popol* which means Mama's Boy because he was always following Maman around the house; Clement was called *Le Kid*, a name always assigned to the oldest boy and handed down. Louise was *Loulou*; Liette was called *La Souris*, which means The Mouse because she put her fingers in her mother's cakes and also because she got her fingers caught in a mousetrap; Ghislaine was *Gigi*; and Pauline was *Paupau*, and then later nicknamed *Olive* because she grew like an olive branch.

Celine had a small round face and the warmth of her heart was reflected in her large brown eyes, which seemed to come alive when she heard the music which emanated from below.

'My fondest memories were of hearing my brothers and sisters playing instruments in the basement,' recalls Celine and even at a very young age she was extraordinarily determined. 'I want to sing and I want to be a singer!' she boldly announced.

Maman was a bit discouraging. In later years, Celine had her own insights about this. 'Maman had thirteen kids and everyone wanted to be in showbusiness and everyone wanted to sing.' Maman must have thought, 'Please, let this child do something normal.' But all Celine wanted to do was sing.

'At our house we sang,' said Claudette. 'The voices and harmonies were our way of speaking and communicating. Our way of being happy was through music.' It was the thread that wove them together.

Her sister Manon also recalls that, as a child, Celine was very sensitive. 'We sang melodies to her in gentle harmonies and Celine cried, as if she found this almost too beautiful. It's because of her great sensitivity that at her professional debut (years later) she couldn't contain her tears, even in public.'

Young Celine was also a dreamer. She talked very little, preferring to live in her own world and play with her dolls. She was quiet, patient and gentle. As Manon recalls, 'She never took up more space than she needed.'

Maman and the other children never took their eyes off Celine – there was always someone to watch over her. But tragedy struck only a few months after Celine's second birthday. It was a beautiful day and Celine was outside making sandcastles in the garden. Maman was close by, showing some of the boys how to trim the hedges. There was a food market across the street and suddenly Celine looked up and saw a woman with blonde hair pushing a pram. Maybe it was her sister Denise, who also had blonde hair and had just had a baby? Inquisitively, Celine wandered off and made her way across the road. Her mother and brothers never noticed her leave.

Celine instantly saw that the woman was not her sister. 'You should go home,' said the woman. Celine crossed back across the street but for an instant she was hidden from view by a truck, and a car which was going a little too fast struck her as it left the market. The woman with the pram screamed, but it was too late. 'I heard the brakes screech and then a deep thump,' Maman painfully recalls.

Celine lay motionless. Everyone was horrified.

'Oh, my God,' prayed Maman. 'Let nothing happen to her.'

Michel ran to her and saw her body on the ground. Horrified, he gently picked her up and carried her in his arms.

At the Sainte-Justine's Children's Hospital, the doctors worked frantically, and found that Celine had a serious skull fracture. She was in intensive care. Everyone was sick with worry and Maman was beside herself. 'That night I prayed my strongest ever.' For twenty-four hours Celine stayed in intensive care and then, miraculously, she completely recovered.

She was sent home from the hospital after only two days. As Celine recuperated at home, the only scars left were the terror and anguish her family had experienced which would remain engraved in their memory forever.

Barring that incident, Celine had a relatively normal childhood, except for one thing. She couldn't get her mind off singing.

At three, little Celine perked up her ears and listened to the music coming from the basement. Her older brothers and sisters had formed a band and practised regularly. She wanted to join them.

'Maman, I want to sing and I won't take no for an answer,' she insisted, mustering all the tenacity of her three years. But no one paid much attention. They were all singers, and it was normal for Celine to want to be part of it. As long as she didn't get in the way.

At four, Celine followed her seventeen-year-old brother Jacques to the basement, where he was practising on his guitar. 'Can I have the microphone?' she begged Jacques, who at the time hadn't noticed anything exceptional about Celine. Dismayed, Jacques cried out, 'Maman! Come and get Celine!'

It was when Celine was five years old that she finally got her chance to perform. One day, she climbed up on the kitchen table, and, surrounded by her family, who gave her a pencil to use as a microphone, Celine started to sing a French song called 'Les Cerisiers sont Blancs' ('The Cherry Trees are White'), a song sung by Quebec star Ginette Reno. Celine surprised everyone. It was as if her family was hearing her for the first time.

That incident on the kitchen table changed everything. 'When I heard the applause I knew that singing would be my life,' says Celine.

Her family soon discovered that Celine already had a surprisingly good vocal and musical talent. In fact – she was astonishing.

'She was already well ahead of us, and we were in our twenties,' observed Clement, the oldest brother in the family. 'She even started coming down to the basement to tease us.'

'It's not like that! You're making a mistake!' Celine claimed, at only five, directing her comments to Clement as he rehearsed with the others.

As she grew older, she tagged along everywhere. Celine was always running alongside Clement, begging him and the older ones to take her with them when they went to perform. 'You have to believe that she had it in her blood,' says Clement.

Celine's brother Michel was a singer with ruggedly handsome good looks. He had left home when Celine was only three and was on the road during most of his twenty-year singing career under the name of Michel Saint-Clair. While he was under contract, working in a neighbouring town, Celine insisted that she come along to hear him. She always had a special relationship with Michel who, as her 'godfather', always seemed to be there to watch over her.

One day, when she was five years old, Celine finally got a chance to perform in public. It was 18 August 1973 – a day Celine will never forget. 'My first show was at my brother Michel's wedding. This was the first time I went up on stage before people. I remember the song I sang: "Du fil, des aiguilles et du coton" ("Thread, Needles and Cotton").' From that moment on, she laid claim to the microphone.

In fact, as far back as Celine can remember, singing was the most important thing for her. She already saw herself on the greatest stages in the world. She wanted the glory. And her role models – her brothers, sisters and parents – gave her inspiration.

To make ends meet, Therese and Adhemar continued to accept jobs performing at weddings, church halls and small provisional tours. Therese played violin, Adhemar was on the accordion, their son Clement played the drums, and Jacques was on the guitar.

'Here I was at five years old and I started to tour with them also,' recalls Celine.

'I'll never forget her show,' says Celine's sister Linda. 'She was only five and sang at a hotel in a neighbouring town. Our parents accompanied her. There were even publicity shots, which advertised: "A young singer of five years old from Charlemagne gives a show of popular songs." '

The hall was packed! Celine commanded the stage, and after she sang there was thunderous applause. From that day on, she had the audience in the palm of her hands.

She became known as *La P'tite Québécoise* – The Little Quebeccer.

When Celine was five years old, her parents took her to another club where they performed. Ghislaine was the drummer and received 60 dollars for the weekend. Papa put Celine on stage to sing. And, according to Ghislaine, 'Believe it or not, people put 10-dollar bills at her feet to encourage her. I couldn't believe it. Ten dollars was a lot at the time. I had a meagre 60 dollars for the whole weekend as a drummer and this little kid of five was getting big bills.' Ghislaine laughs as she remembers: 'I was actually never really jealous of her. I loved her too much for that.'

Celine already had a vast repertoire. She loved watching singers perform on television – and she could impersonate them all. One of her greatest idols was Barbra Streisand. Celine adored her voice and the way Barbra performed and would sing along with her in front of the television. She didn't understand a single word of English, but music transcended all language barriers. Celine 'felt' the song.

Apart from the world of showbusiness, there were many sides to young Celine. She loved to have fun during the long snowy winters in Charlemagne. Papa made the children a skating rink behind the house where they spent many blissful hours.

'In the summer, she had her own swimming pool in the yard, a splashpool containing at most 2 feet of water, but she found a way to fill up buckets and ran after us to splash us, bursting into laughter,' remembers Clement.

'Celine was very expressive,' recalls her sister Liette. 'She showed her joy easily at happy events and was so emotional that she was easily driven to tears as well.' It was a family trait. 'We are all "criers" in my family,' laughs Liette. Tears of joy, tears of sadness – for Celine tears were the easiest way to show her emotions.

At six years old Celine continued to find a way into her siblings' music. But her drive to be a star sometimes caused problems for her brother Daniel. He was talented and, at eighteen, had also set his sights on a musical career. 'Dan', as he was known, had composed a musical soundtrack on piano for a group. But he knew that Celine was in the habit of going through the older brothers' and sisters' music in the basement.

'Celine, don't touch the tapes downstairs,' warned Dan. A few days later the people at the recording studio called Dan to tell him that on the master tape, there was not his composition, but the voice of a six-year-old girl! The producers were pressed for time and had to choose someone else's composition, and Daniel lost the contract. Many years later he would laugh about this story but at the time he didn't find it very funny!

This was by no means the only mischievous thing Celine did as a child. One day when she was seven years old she hid her brother Paul's entire hockey card collection – and then offered it to him as a Christmas present!

Celine had a very comical side to her and loved to 'ham it up' in front of the camera. The little girl with the crooked fringe and long flowing hair would pose for pictures wearing a feather boa around her neck, a big hat and a cigarette holder. Celine loved dressing up – sometimes she left the room and would come back transformed into a fairy princess. She went through just about everything in Maman's memory chest, including long pearl necklaces and shawls belonging to her grandmother. Celine often dressed up in her older sisters' petticoats and dresses, planted herself on top of the kitchen table and sang, imitating one of her favourite stars. According to her sister Pauline, 'Celine already had the style of a diva.'

In later years Celine said that if she hadn't been a singer, she would have liked to have been a model. 'I love posing,' confesses Celine, reminiscing about her early childhood. Even at this young age, Celine already had a passion for shopping and loved her trips out with her older sisters, even if they were only to gaze at dresses they could not afford. She was happiest with her family – and completely depressed when it came to school.

Despite her first-grade photo showing a grinning Celine in a pretty plaid dress – with her warm eyes glowing – when it came to school

Celine usually had nothing to smile about. School was a foreign place for her, something that took her away from her family and her dreams.

School aside, 'Celine was an easy child to raise,' according to Maman. Except when it came to eating. She was always a finicky eater, and Maman, an excellent cook, had to use a lot of culinary creativity to get Celine to take any interest in eating. But, like any child, she had her favourite foods and adored going out with her siblings for spaghetti or Kentucky Fried Chicken.

As she grew Celine remained a very generous child, a quality which stayed with her right through to adulthood. Celine had the character-istics of both her parents. She was sensitive, like Maman, but she also had her father's nerve and courage, and his great sense of humour. Yet, while Adhemar was a direct man who saw things one way, Maman and Celine could be fairly diplomatic and usually tried to please everyone.

Celine never liked to be alone. She loved being with her brothers and sisters and even slept in the same bed as three of her sisters when she was young. Later, when her brother Daniel left home, she had her own room for the first time. But she surrounded herself with Barbie dolls – fourteen dolls to be exact (probably because there were fourteen children in the family) and many had the names of her big sisters. Every night Celine cuddled them, then laid them down comfortably before she herself went to sleep. She even performed in front of them.

There was no question about it – Celine was always happiest when she was singing. Papa had great insight into Celine as a child: 'I had the impression that, in her head, she thought music and sang all the time.' In fact, it seemed as if she was *only* happy when she was singing. By the time she was seven years old, Celine was performing regularly in a series of twenty-minute mini-shows. It was all Celine could talk about and Maman was concerned. 'Nothing else interested her. I was afraid. I told her: "It's finished, we'll stop everything. You will go to school, study well, and you'll make a good secretary!" '

CHAPTER 3

It Was More Than a Dream

'I always hated school. I'll always remember the school bell. I was so anxious to leave that world.'

— CELINE DION

Could it be that Maman really wanted Celine to be a secretary? To go to school, day in and day out – a world she felt she didn't belong in? As the years passed, Celine's passion for music grew ever stronger, as did her disdain for anything that took her away from it.

'I always hated school,' Celine admits.

This was something she came to regret in later years, when she realized that her lack of education meant she lacked the right tools with which to express herself. She knew that she made a lot of grammatical mistakes in French and was not at ease writing. But she admits that, although school is very important, it's not for everyone, and it definitely wasn't for her.

'Celine detested school,' recalls her sister Claudette. 'Often, at night, Celine insisted on singing just one last song with us before going to sleep. I drove Celine to school so that she could rest as long as possible, getting there just before the bell rang. This is something that happened until Celine was in the fourth grade.'

Persuading Celine to go to school was not easy. Some mornings were harder than others. 'She had the impression that we didn't understand her,' as Claudette puts it. 'It was like we were asking her to lose track of her dream of singing to enter a situation she didn't like. Already, at this stage, Celine felt different from the others.'

When Celine was nine years old, life in the Dion household suddenly changed dramatically. Papa and Maman bought a restaurant-bar called *Le Vieux Baril* (The Old Barrel) in the city of Le Gardeur, Quebec, less than a mile away from their home. Maman found herself behind the counter of the restaurant while Papa tended the bar.

At first, business wasn't very good. Then Maman and Papa had a brainwave. They would transform it into a piano bar. A piano would add life to the bar and Paul was the perfect person to play it. At the age of fifteen, he was enormously talented, his fingers working magic on the ivory keys. Soon the restaurant became very popular. The clientele was mostly made up of workers from manufacturing plants in the region. The Dions opened very early in the morning for breakfast, saw a busy lunch, and then after four o'clock they focused on the bar area, where Paul was a star.

Celine was overjoyed when she found out that Paul was playing at their parents' club. But she had an even better idea. She would sing there as well! She couldn't wait to tell Maman her great plan. 'Can I go there? I will only sing two or three songs and then I'll come back home,' Celine begged. It was the most wonderful opportunity – a real microphone and a real audience.

But Maman was adamant. Celine was too young to go to a bar, even if it was owned by her father. Celine sulked. She became depressed and introverted. This wasn't the Celine they knew. Finally, Maman relented and allowed Celine to come to the restaurant. But there was one condition: Celine had to stay in the kitchen and not go into the bar area.

One evening, despite Maman's warning, Celine went out into the bar and sang anyway. Maman was furious! Celine gave a mini-recital and the patrons loved it. But Maman was not amused. She sent Celine to the kitchen and told her to stay there, shaking her finger at her. But Papa was torn. 'Mother, let the little singer sing another song. The customers want to hear her!'

Maman responded: 'Father, it is late enough for the little one.'

Eventually, Maman ended up giving in. Did she really have a choice? Maman watched her daughter as she sang again that night. Celine imitated the great stars, with the same gestures and emotions. There was no holding her back. She knew that Celine needed an audience. 'It was perhaps this night,' says Maman, 'when Celine received a long standing ovation, that I admitted that the destiny of my daughter was already outlined. Celine would be an artist.'

As the years went by, Celine's parents would always remain at her side and close to her heart, even if distance separated them. Maman was her best friend, her 'idol', and she gave Celine the confidence to scale the heights she had always known she would reach. Adhemar called himself, 'her number one fan'.

Celine was soon the star attraction at *Le Vieux Baril*. 'People started calling to ask if Celine would be singing on Saturday evening,' recalls her sister Claudette. Before long, customers would book in advance to hear 'that little girl'.

Papa remembers, 'By the time she was eleven years old, she filled up my bar.' She was the girl with the golden voice. For Celine, it was her biggest thrill.

As she recalls, 'It's really from that moment that I felt the need to say something that I felt inside me. When I sing, I open my door to people. When I'm on stage in front of so many people, I need to connect with them.'

Celine might have been 'in tune' with her audience at the bar, but at school . . . she was definitely out of key. 'She knew the hit charts a lot better than her schoolwork,' says Claudette.

School remained an alien environment for Celine, who never felt comfortable there. 'I'll always remember the school bell. I was so anxious to leave that world. To get rid of my homework and run to *Le*

Vieux Baril in the hope that my mother would let me sing.' Celine often stayed there until the wee small hours. As Celine recalls, 'The bar closed at four o'clock in the morning and I fell asleep on the edge of the counter. My father came to wake me, saying: "It's the last call and there is someone who wants you to sing." The next day I had a stomach ache and I was really too tired to go to school.'

Even when Celine wasn't performing at the bar, she was always anxious to get home. 'I would come running home as fast as I could from school. I couldn't wait to come back to the basement to hear my brothers and sisters rehearse every day,' she remembers. 'I told Maman that all I dreamed about was singing.'

Maman knew that Celine could go far. Since the others were all grown (even the twins were eighteen by now) and Celine had demonstrated so much potential at such a young age, Maman decided to try and take care of Celine's career.

'My mother wanted us all to be stars,' explains her sister Ghislaine, who had also dreamed of being a singer. 'But with Celine she had the time. She decided to make one of us at least really happy.'

When asked in later years if she thought that she was the most talented one of all her siblings, Celine replied, 'I am the luckiest one.' Things could have been different. There could have been a war of egos, a painful atmosphere of jealousy and envy. But there wasn't. Instead, 'I was encouraged,' recalls Celine. Together, the family shared everything. Celebrations. Secrets. Sadness. Joy.

Celine always had a lot of sisters and brothers to talk to and Claudette recalls that they were very close. 'Despite the seventeen years that separated us, we confided in each other because we both had the same ambition: to sing. We would both elaborate on dreams together and I found Celine to be older in character than her age. Even though Celine was very young, she was interested not only in song, but in what was happening in my marriage and my role as a mother,' says Claudette.

This incredible bond with her siblings brought Celine moments of great happiness – and also moments of intense pain. Being so close, especially to her sisters, when one of them had heartache, Celine would suffer too.

When Celine was only nine years old she experienced the greatest sadness of her young life. Her sister Liette's baby daughter Karine was diagnosed with cystic fibrosis and the pain of watching Karine struggle with the illness stayed with Celine forever. It was rare for someone so young to take on so much grief.

For Celine, music was the easiest way to express her emotions. She often found herself composing songs with her brother Paul. Even then, her lyrics showed her deep sensitivity and passion, in songs about love, pain and tears.

The emotional Celine was never without her dream. She admits, 'Singing was all I ever wanted to do.' And she wanted to succeed 'big time'. She went to her first concert to see Stevie Wonder, whom she adored. She stood practically the whole time, singing alone and applauding, despite the fact that she still only understood French.

When Celine listened to singers like Aretha Franklin, Janis Joplin and the Bee Gees, the words didn't seem to matter. Only the music mattered. 'Once I sang "What a Feeling" (from the movie Flashdance) and everyone was clapping and dancing – and I didn't understand a word of what I was singing at the time,' she remembers.

Celine gained more confidence in her singing with each performance. Even at home her voice was never silent. In the shower, when she discovered the marvellous echo that amplified her voice, she thought to herself: 'Maybe one day I'll record an album in the bathroom!'

People begged her to come to neighbouring towns to sing. Maman was protective of Celine – she wasn't ready to give her daughter away. What's more, Maman didn't believe Celine was ready because she didn't have any original songs of her own, but only sang the songs of other singers.

But Celine was persistent, even relentless. As she recalls, 'I grew up telling her, every single day, "Mom, I want to sing." And one day Maman told me: "Celine, I want you to sing, but I want you to do it professionally. I don't want you to perform in clubs. I want you to sing your own songs." '

Celine remembers it vividly. 'Naturally I didn't have any of my own repertoire so my mother said, "I'll write a song for you!" '

Maman had a plan. There was a song in her head. Maman loved to write little songs from time to time and this one came easily to her. One night, she sat down in a corner of the kitchen and wrote the first verse which began with the phrase, 'Ce n'était qu'un rêve' (It was Only a Dream). This became the title of the song.

The following day Maman asked her son Jacques, who was a talented guitar player, to help her. One night he came to the house and hummed a tune for Maman's song. They couldn't wait for Celine to hear it.

Celine was in the kitchen, washing the supper dishes – a task she did not seem to mind at all. In fact she found it relaxing and usually hummed the whole time. Maman and Jacques told her that they had written a song for her and she eagerly walked over to the living room to hear it. She listened quietly, and then shrugged her shoulders. 'I don't like the chorus,' was all she said.

The words stung. 'Instead of criticizing, it would be better if you helped us!' Maman responded angrily.

Celine went back to the kitchen and resumed washing the dishes. Maman thought that was the end of that. But minutes later Celine emerged. 'She had the most beautiful smile,' recalls Maman. Celine had rewritten the chorus. As she sang, Maman and Jacques were flabberghasted. That was it! It was perfect.

As Celine and Jacques worked together to complete the song, he quickly realized that Celine had matured. Suddenly he saw his sister with new eyes. She was not a baby any more, but a professional. 'It was without a doubt the most intimate moment that I ever experienced with Celine,' explains Jacques. 'As we worked on the song, she told me what she liked and what she didn't and why she wanted to change a passage. She already knew exactly what she wanted. I could imagine Celine on the greatest stages in the world, acclaimed by the crowds.'

They recorded the song on a cassette, in the kitchen. As Jacques accompanied her on his guitar, Celine's powerful voice filled the room. The song about a dream was no longer just a dream.

Celine couldn't wait to perform it at *Le Vieux Baril*. 'Celine sang the song again and again. Each time there was a standing ovation,' Maman says proudly. After one performance, someone suggested that she send the cassette of the song to a manager or a producer.

It was true. Celine needed a manager. Maman and Papa could only do so much to help her. And soon they thought that they had found the right person. A manager by the name of Paul Levesque had been involved with Celine's brother, Michel Saint-Clair, in a series of performances called *Le Show*. Levesque managed several rock groups, such as Mahogany Rush, and in later years a pop singer named Luba. He was young – only twenty-eight – with a penchant for sports cars, and a flamboyant, wild manner. Yet he had achieved a certain success, if mostly on the rock scene. At first sceptical about managing her career, Paul soon saw tremendous potential in Celine, and Maman and Papa decided to agree to a five-year management contract with him, beginning on 5 December 1980. He recorded a demo of Maman's song in a studio, along with two other original songs.

But it wasn't easy. The world was not yet clamouring for Celine and Paul Levesque could not seem to get a recording contract for her. What's more, he wanted Celine to spend more time at school. Months passed and for Celine it was all taking too long. Maman and Papa were growing impatient as well. Finally, Paul Levesque sent Celine's demo cassette to a producer he knew in Montreal – René Angelil.

'My mother had heard the name René Angelil on a lot of records,' recalls Celine. 'She knew him from the time he sang with the group

Les Baronets [The Baronets].' But above all, she knew that he managed many big stars in Quebec, including her favourite singer, Ginette Reno, whose career had seen great success. The cassette was sent off with red adhesive tape adorning the package like a ribbon. Maman believed that red brought good luck. They needed it. At the moment Celine's career was going nowhere.

CHAPTER 4

Meeting the Mentor

'I would simply like to say that, in life, nothing is impossible,'
— RENE ANGELIL

It was a cold day in early January 1981 and René Angelil was not in a good mood. Outside, a storm was brewing and he sat in his office, depressed and on edge. He had just spent the saddest Christmas of his life. His star client, Ginette Reno, had ended their partnership. And it was a real blow. She was a French music veteran who could belt out a ballad like nobody else. René had helped her win fame and her most successful album, *"Je ne suis qu'une chanson"* ("I am But a Song"), had been the best-selling record in Quebec. He had accumulated many debts and now there was no money coming in. He had spent so much time building up Ginette's career and what did he have to show for it? Nothing.

Celine's cassette sat on his desk. There was a note enclosed with the cassette: 'This is a twelve-year-old with a fantastic voice. Please listen to her. If it pleases you, call us at this number. The song was written by her mother.' He was unmoved by the note. He would be turning thirty-nine on 16 January and he had no money, no hope.

He thought longingly of the sixties when he had played in a trio that performed Beatles songs – in French! His group was called *Les Baronets* and at the time he was a real heart-throb for French teenage girls in

Montreal. He had been a dashing figure, with a charming smile and penetrating dark brown eyes. But there was no sparkle in his eyes now.

Twenty years later, he was ready to quit the music business forever and go to law school. It wasn't what he wanted, but the music business just wasn't for him any more. Celine's tape lay there, among all the bills. He just didn't care.

Suddenly the telephone rang. 'Bonjour Monsieur,' said the voice at the other end. It was Celine's brother Michel. It had been a while since Celine's manager, Paul Levesque had forwarded her demo tape to René and they had not heard back from René Angelil yet. Something was wrong.

'Yes,' René answered.

'You are Monsieur Angelil?'

'Yes,' came René's reply again.

'You didn't listen to the cassette sung by my sister,' said Michel. René was speechless. 'Because, if you had, Monsieur, you would have called right away.'

At Michel's urging, René promised to play the cassette. He was reluctant because he had also managed the career of another Quebec child star, René Simard, and that was not something he wanted to do again. Besides, he was through with music. But a promise was a promise.

René Angelil finally listened to the tape and had the surprise of his life. 'Michel was right!' he confirmed. 'There was this voice . . . this fantastic voice.' The girl was astounding. 'Not only was the music extraordinary, but the voice . . .' René couldn't believe that a girl who was only twelve could sing with such power. He had to meet her and see for himself.

He called the Dion home immediately and spoke to Maman. 'I would like to meet your daughter as soon as possible. Today would even be the best time,' he said.

Despite the winter storm raging outside, Maman and Celine left straight away and arrived at his office three hours later.

René greeted them and liked Maman immediately. She was full of confidence and did most of the talking. But as he gazed at Celine he was surprised. She was not at all as he had imagined her. She didn't seem to match the voice on the tape. The girl who stood before him was skinny, awkward and gangly. She was terribly shy and hardly opened her mouth. And, when she did, he saw a mouthful of crooked teeth!

René recalls: 'You wouldn't say she was a cute child. But she had these incredible brown eyes. And her talent!' René wanted to make sure she could sing as well in front of him — a stranger, in an unfamiliar place — with no music to accompany her. René looked at Celine and spoke gently to her. He saw that she was painfully shy. 'I would like you to sing your song for me, right here in this office.' Thoughts raced through Celine's head. She liked him. He was tall and handsome and there was a gentleness about him. 'The way he talked to me was so respectful. Not like a baby.'

Celine kept looking at Maman. Sing for him? Right there, without music . . . without anything. 'But I always sing with a microphone,' Celine said meekly. She looked at her mother again. René took a pen from his desk and handed it to her. '*Voilà!*' he said. 'There's your microphone. Sing into it. Close your eyes and imagine that you are a great star on stage in front of a thousand spectators.' It wasn't hard — Celine imagined it all the time. She pretended that there were musicians all around her and she was performing in a huge concert hall. She only had to close her eyes and she was there on stage. She started to sing '*Ce n'était qu'un rêve*' acappella. She gave it everything.

After she was finished, Celine first looked at Maman, who met her glance with a nod. As she looked back at René, Celine saw that he had tears in his eyes. Seeing his reaction, Celine gazed over at Maman and gave her a wink. She knew all about tears.

René had goosebumps listening to her voice. 'So full of feeling, and older than her years,' he thought. She had a voice that came from deep inside. She was unbelievable for a twelve-year-old. René was mesmerized. She was ten times better in person than on the cassette.

He had worked with a lot of talent in his role as impresario, but he had never heard anything like her voice before. 'From the start, I realized that Celine not only had an extraordinary voice, but that she was also a very special person,' recalls René. He saw that she had a rare talent. He imagined all that they could achieve together with her marvellous gift. His whole career had been going downhill but maybe this child of twelve was going to change all that. Was it possible?

He felt that destiny had called him to accept the biggest challenge of his career. His mind was racing. He wanted to do a brand-new studio recording of 'Ce n'était qu'un rêve'. He would work out everything with Celine's manager Paul Levesque. 'We'll do a single and, if it goes well, we'll continue,' René told Celine and Maman. There was a lot to be done. He wanted to work with her for two months and see if she had the self-discipline to become a star. He knew the sacrifices that lay ahead of her and he had to be sure she was ready to make them. If she was, he gave her a promise: 'Just give me five years and I'll make you a star.'

Maman was elated, but she turned to René and said, 'I must warn you, the mother goes with the daughter!' And, for many years to come, Maman would keep her promise.

René's involvement was the real catalyst. Whereas Paul Levesque had perhaps taken things at too slow a pace, René was a man of action and he wasn't going to sit still for a minute. Now things were going almost too quickly. 'The dream started but it was so fast. Everything was fast, fast, fast,' says Celine. But for René there was no time to lose.

'I knew very early that the development of her career would be the biggest challenge of my life,' he recalls. 'For me, an incorrigible gambler, there was no question of doing things halfway. I staked everything on one bet, telling myself, "Either it will work or not." It's as simple as that.' René was no stranger to Las Vegas casinos and he knew how to push a winning streak when he saw one. He would risk everything to see where it would take him with this soon to turn thirteen-year-old prodigy. But René knew that it would take money. 'When you target an international career, you have to have the means,' he emphasized.

However, René was not exactly in the best of financial positions. The ending of his professional relationship with Ginette Reno hurt him a great deal. In fact he had to declare bankruptcy. And it was very difficult for him to start again in business. He was also married and had three children to support: Patrick, who was thirteen (from René's first marriage), and two children, Jean-Pierre, aged seven and Anne-Marie, who was four, with his second wife Anne-Renée. But he would have risked anything to gamble on Celine.

'To launch Celine's first record, I had to mortgage my house. But I really believed in her. In twenty years of this profession, I had never seen a raw talent as considerable as hers.' The next day, after reaching an agreement with Paul Levesque, René immediately started work in his new role as Celine's producer. He booked the studio to record 'Ce n'était qu'un rêve' professionally, with new arrangements and a full line-up of musicians.

But René wanted full control in order to fulfil the promise he had made to Celine. And he was starting to lose faith in Celine's manager Paul Levesque. He wanted to be the one to make all the decisions and he started to take on more and more responsibility. Paul Levesque took a back seat. René was the one in the driver's seat.

René knew that for Celine, as a Francophone singer, it would be important to succeed not only in the primarily French-speaking province of Quebec, but in France as well. René wanted his friend, the great Parisian songwriter Eddy Marnay, to hear Celine's cassette. Eddy had written songs for many international stars. He had worked on a French album with Barbra Streisand, and had also composed songs for Nana Mouskouri and the legendary French ballad singer Edith Piaf.

René anxiously awaited Eddy Marnay's visit to Montreal the following month. René played the new tape for him and saw Eddy react in the same way as he had himself. Eddy had tears in his eyes at the end of the song, and said, 'It's a voice that comes from heaven.' Eddy was astounded at the depth of emotion possessed by someone so young. For both René and Eddy, Celine was now under their wing and there was no bigger priority than her.

Eddy stayed up all night writing a song for her. He even had a title, inspired by the celestial qualities he had heard in Celine's voice, and called the song, 'La voix du Bon Dieu' (The Voice of the Good God). He wrote not only the lyrics, but the music as well. Eddy was a sentimental, caring man and Celine adored this fatherly Frenchman, whom she later called her 'showbusiness godfather'. As she explains: 'He was a very great friend in the deepest part of my heart. The things that he wrote for me, are the things that I feel – that I live. He got to know my friends and my family. He knows me very well. When I sing a song, it's good to *feel* it, instead of singing a song that has no meaning.'

Meanwhile, as René recalls, everyone believed that he was completely crazy. He loved gambling, but this roll of the dice was a big one – even for him. 'Everything was staked on one child! Maybe her voice wouldn't change, but she was skinny and not pretty. She cried constantly, even in front of cameras, and when she smiled, it was a catastrophe! Terrible canine eye teeth.'

Her mother consoled her. 'If you sing well, if you feel good about yourself – it's you who will have the last word.' And the public willingly adopted her: voice, teeth, tears and all.

René wanted Celine to have as much exposure as possible, and that meant television. He went all out to get her on the powerful Michel Jasmin show, which was like a Quebec version of Johnny Carson's *The Tonight Show*, broadcast in French throughout the province. Michel Jasmin's talk show, featuring an impressive roster of entertainers, had one of the highest ratings in Quebec. The untested young singer had never appeared on television before, and this would be a coup for the show. It was agreed! Celine would appear on the show on 19 June 1981, less than three months after her thirteenth birthday. It was an invaluable opportunity for Celine to be known throughout Quebec. René felt unstoppable. He had found a new beginning in Celine.

For Celine, it was one of the best things that had ever happened. She had already watched the show so often that she felt she almost knew Michel Jasmin. 'After hearing the news, I fell into my mother's arms and we both cried. It's stronger than we are – we are a family of criers,' admits Celine.

However, Celine soon started worrying about being on the show, and it wasn't her singing that scared her – she had nothing to wear. She went up to her room, emptied her closet and found . . . absolutely nothing. The family had so little money that Celine usually wore hand-me-downs that made her look like a ragamuffin. She started panicking.

'Don't worry, I'll make you a dress,' consoled Maman, 'A pink dress, your favourite colour.' For three nights Maman sewed and sewed. The pink dress was gathered tightly at the waist, with a wide belt, and a full skirt. Celine was no different from any other young girl – she loved wearing a dress that twirled when she turned around. And the accessories Maman bought her! Pink silk stockings and shoes that were dyed pink to match her dress.

Celine went to bed early the night before the show. She was a strong believer in a good night's sleep, not only for her voice but for her appearance as well, and could easily sleep twelve to sixteen hours a night! But tonight she tossed and turned, asking herself how the other girls in her school would react to seeing her on television.

The next day, Papa accompanied Celine and Maman to René's office, and from there they went to the television studio. René knew everyone! He had participated in shows when the station had first gone on air, before Celine was even born. She had a dressing room and it was the first time she had her make-up professionally done. Suddenly Celine felt beautiful. It was an experience that would have an effect on her for the rest of her career.

Celine changed into her pink dress, and during the rehearsal she was shown where to stand and how to follow the camera (something she would do a thousand times in years to come). The technicians said everything was fine, but René, ever the perfectionist, told her that she had made an error. She had looked up at the monitor. 'You must never do that,' he told her. At least it was only a rehearsal.

When it was almost time for the actual performance, there was one thing Celine *had* to do before she went on. Celine was very super-stitious. She explains, 'When something very important is happening to me, I must touch wood. But the room behind the studio which we waited in until I went on only had plastic, steel and glass. I looked for even the smallest piece of wood and then started to panic. But I found a pipe in an ashtray and I touched it. Then I wasn't afraid any more.'

It was showtime! Michel Jasmin introduced her: 'This night is very, very special, in the sense that the young lady that we will present to you is only thirteen years old and has a magnificent voice. You be the judge. Here is Celine Dion!' Suddenly she found herself on the set where she was welcomed by a standing ovation. Just before she sang she was so shy she thought she would die. Then she performed 'Ce n'était qu'un rêve' and held out the single to the audience. Celine was surprised to see all her family and many relatives at the show. They were a group of almost forty. Seeing them warmed her heart, and she cried.

Pierre Daigneault, a saxophone player who was a member of the Michel Jasmin show band, remembers her performance vividly. 'We all took notice of her and said "Wow!" She was shy and very emotional – but what talent! I'll never forget the richness of her voice for someone so young.'

The song had gone well, but now it was time for the interview. 'Singing was one thing, talking was another,' recalled Celine at the time. As powerful as she felt on stage, Celine could not overcome her shyness and would have been much happier if René had done all the talking. But interviews were to be a part of her life and she had to overcome her fear of them. According to René, 'As much as she conveyed emotion in her songs, she was cold and stiff when she had to answer questions from interviewers on television and radio.' Celine gave only brief answers to every question – and couldn't wait for the interview to be over. But the song had been magical!

In the days after the show, her song was number one in the charts in Quebec. Celine was a new sensation. Even if she herself thought she had sounded too nasal in her television singing debut, and even if some journalists poked fun at her shyness and her tears, the public had been astounded by her vocal power. She was a child star, well on her way to a life where she would reach new heights – both personally and professionally. Years later, Celine confessed: 'When I made my debut on the Michel Jasmin show at thirteen, I already knew I would perform on the largest stage in Montreal.'

CHAPTER 5

Not Your Average Teen

'Who will be able to love me for me? I don't even know who I am myself. No, I don't have an easy life. They say that I am full of many persons inside myself.'

– CELINE DION

I f Celine was a star after the Michel Jasmin show, it was a mixed blessing for her. At school, the other girls teased her unmercifully. There was no mistaking their envy and jealousy. Celine was terribly unhappy. Her sister Claudette says, 'My heart went out to her.'

'High school was difficult for Celine,' recalls Denise. 'Children are often cruel to each other and they played nasty tricks on Celine simply because she was written up in newspapers or seen on TV.' Celine was very sensitive to this, and her difficulties touched the Dion family a great deal.

There were also problems to correct – like her pointed teeth that looked like a vampire's when she smiled, a slightly nasal tone when she hit certain notes, her painful shyness, and the tears that seemed to well up at any moment. But helping Celine to overcome these obstacles would have to wait. Meanwhile, there was no time to lose in building her career.

After Celine's success on her first talk show and the success of her first single, it seemed that she was up and running. But René didn't want

41 *

her career to take off like a burst of fireworks, and then disappear into oblivion.

He had the risky idea of coming out with not one but two albums at the same time. This was an especially bold move, considering that Celine had yet to record even her first album. It was a gamble. And it would take money. René began knocking on doors. He went to see Denys Bergeron, the general director of Trans-Canada Records in Montreal and explained his situation. René told him he needed 50,000 dollars. Impressed with Celine's hit single, it was an easy decision for Bergeron and the record label endorsed her. 'I was saved,' René later remembered. As a gambler, coming out with two albums was like doubling the stakes. If he was wrong, they would lose everything. If he was right, it would arouse the curiosity of the record industry and journalists, and the pay-off could be tremendous.

René thought that one of the albums should be call *La voix du Bon Dieu* (The Voice of the Good God), named after the song Eddy Marnay had written for Celine. In addition to the hit single, there were several other songs written by Maman and Celine, along with some older tunes. On the album cover, a serene Celine looked slightly upwards (to the heavens) while her long dark-brown wavy hair cascaded halfway down her back.

The second album, was called *Céline Dion chante Noël* (Celine Dion Sings Christmas) and featured songs for the festive season. In four sessions, Celine recorded nineteen songs for the two albums. Her self-discipline was astounding and she drove herself harder than anyone else. The session musicians had never seen anyone work at such a tireless pace – at only thirteen!

On 9 November 1981, at the Hotel Bonaventure in Montreal, they launched Celine's first French Album and only weeks later, in time for the Christmas buying period, they launched the second album. Newspapers all over Quebec carried articles about Celine. In the Montreal French-language newspaper *La Presse*, a journalist called her 'the new Judy Garland'. Celine was the girl with the angelic voice – the girl every grandmother loved. She had even written a song about grandmothers with Maman and Jacques. During the Christmas period alone they sold 30,000 copies of the two albums. Over time, *La voix du Bon Dieu* would become a gold record in Canada, with sales of 50,000 and the Christmas album would sell a total of 25,000 copies.

At this point, René decided to take full control of Celine's career. When it came to choosing between Paul Levesque and René Angelil – there was no contest. René had befriended the family and they believed in him. René Angelil had a proposal for Celine and Maman Dion. 'They should work together and allow him [René] the flexibility and the trust to make the decisions for her career.' That was effectively the end for Paul Levesque – though he would retain a small percentage of royalties for the next few years.

René was at the helm now (where, in a sense, he had always been from the first day he laid eyes on Celine). 'When I trust someone, I give them my life,' Celine has said. René was everything – her mentor, her manager and her friend. And now her career was in his hands.

René had started a record production company to promote Celine. He created the company, TBS Productions Inc, with his wife Anne-Renée, who was no stranger to showbusiness, although she had retired as a performer. She was a pretty blonde who, like Celine, had started singing at a young age and had toured everywhere in Quebec along with her mother. Anne-Renée had been on television and made numerous records. No one could better identify with what Celine was going through at thirteen than her. She was also sensitive and was the only one René felt could help Celine overcome her tremendous shyness. 'Celine's shyness was like a sickness and it gave a false image of her.'

Anne-Renée performed a miracle with Celine. Pierre Daigneault, one of Celine's musicians at the time, recalls, 'It was Anne-Renée who taught Celine everything – how to talk, how to dress, and how to speak to interviewers.'

When Celine talked of Anne-Renée in those early years, she referred to her in the most loving terms, 'A woman who I adore. When I met René, I was a shy, timid girl, introverted and clumsy. During more than three months we worked together, Anne-Renée showed me how to get rid of my greatest fears. She completely changed me. Today, I can talk to anyone, and I have no barriers or shyness. What I love about Anne is that she understands that I am only a teenager and sometimes it is hard to only be with adults.' Celine missed being with friends, and already realized that she could never have a 'normal adolescence'.

There was a new challenge for René — he wanted France to fall in love with Celine too. In Paris, Eddy Marnay and a well-known record producer from Paris, Claude Pascal, had approached the powerful Parisian record company Pathé-Marconi and it didn't take long to convince them to come out with a single of 'Ce n'était qu'un rêve' under their label in France. This was only the beginning. By now Eddy Marnay had started composing lyrics for songs to appear on Celine's third French album, this one to be recorded partially in Paris. The album was named *Tellement j'ai d'amour* . . . (I Have So Much Love . . .). The title song Eddy had written was about Celine's deep love for Maman. The album cover would show Celine at her most angelic, in a white frilly blouse, with her hair back and flowing past her shoulders. The album cover also included Celine's dedication of her love to Maman.

Celine, Maman, René and Anne-Renée left for Paris on 2 July 1982 to record three songs for the album. The rest of the songs on the album would be recorded back in Quebec the following month. The day she left for Paris, Celine received the first stamp on a passport that would one day read like a scrapbook of her life. It was also her first plane ride and Celine panicked when the flight attendant went through the life-saving procedures. 'Why are they doing that?' she asked nervously. René calmly explained that it was just an exercise, but Celine replied, 'If they do that it's because they are not sure about their plane!' Everything was new for her, and she reacted with child-like wonder.

Celine was thrilled by Paris. She loved the Champs-Elysées and drank in the new experience with the thirst of a fourteen-year-old who had led a very sheltered life until then.

The French record company Pathé-Marconi had booked one of Europe's finest studios, the Studio Family Song. And René was amazed at Celine's ability to be as relaxed in a studio in Paris, as back home in a studio in Quebec. In the studio, Celine offered her ideas on arrangements, a result of all the years she had spent playing music with her older sisters and brothers. Interviews may have intimidated her, but music did not. The stage and the studio were her home.

As she recorded, her eyes were fixed on her mother. When Celine finished singing, Maman was crying.

Two weeks later, back in Quebec, Eddy called René to tell him that record producer Claude Pascal had sent a copy of the song 'Tellement j'ai d'amour pour toi', as France's entry, to the organizers of the Thirteenth Annual Yamaha World Popular Song Festival to be held in Japan, one of the most important festivals in the world. (Each year, record companies and producers from all over the world send almost two thousand songs to Japan and the jury picks out twenty finalists.) René was quietly confident. After all, one of his past protégés (the young Quebec talent René Simard) had won the medal in 1974.

But the excitement had only begun. Celine's third French album was launched in September – and album that would double the sales of her first two albums combined. It was only a few weeks after the album release that Eddy called to speak to Celine and told her that she had been chosen, out of 1,907 candidates from forty-nine countries, to participate in the Yamaha World Popular Song Festival in Tokyo – an event that would be televised for 115 million people in Japan!

Celine was shocked when she heard the news.

'No, it's not true . . . it's unbelievable. I must ask my mother,' she stammered, bursting into tears. She hung up the phone and turned to Maman. 'Tell me, Maman. You'll go with me? You won't let me go alone?' Maman knew nothing of the plans yet, but one thing was certain, her daughter wasn't going out of the country without her. Soon René was on the phone to Maman. 'Do you speak Japanese?' he asked. Maman was thrilled.

They left for Tokyo at the end of October. The flight was long and Celine didn't sleep at all. She tried to look through magazines, but they were all in English and she still couldn't understand a word. She listened to music on the headphones for so long that her ears started to ache! Finally, they arrived in Tokyo and Celine was amazed at the crowds of people in Western dress. She had expected to see them all wearing kimonos!

They were also joined in Tokyo by Ben Kaye, a pleasant, charismatic man, who had managed René when he was in the group *Les Baronets*. Ben was still a music associate of René's and had been involved in helping him with Celine's career as well. Although René towered above his friend, Ben was a giant of a 'behind-the-scenes' man for Celine and René.

In the next few days, Celine would have a chance to rehearse with the fifty musicians who were there to accompany every contestant. Finally, it was time for the semi-finals at Budokan Hall, the famous sports hall and sanctuary of sumo wrestling, with seating for 12,000 people. Ten semi-finalists would make it to the finals that Sunday.

Each contestant was given a number and they gave Celine the number five, which in Japanese is pronounced 'go'. When she finished her song she received a standing ovation but she had to wait until the next day to find out if she had made it. She was frustrated. There were great artists competing, like B.J. Thomas, who had sold over ten million records in the US with his song 'Raindrops Keep Falling on My Head', as well as fellow Canadian Bryan Adams. At last, all the results were given out – but in Japanese. All Celine heard was 'go', her lucky number five, she cried and cried.

They gave the finalists new numbers for the competition and, by coincidence, Celine's number was five once again. (Five would be her lucky number for the rest of her life.) Celine touched wood quickly, believing that it would bring her luck.

At the final competition, wearing an angelic white dress, Celine sang the song from her very soul, grasping the microphone as if it were a torch, closing her eyes with emotion. The judges deliberated for two hours, and then convened for the various trophies. One by one, they handed out awards, starting with the least important. Eventually only Celine and one other remained on stage. The suspense was unbearable, then finally they announced the winner of the Grand Prize of Song – a Mexican performer, Yoshio. Celine was dismayed. But suddenly the host turned towards Celine and pointed to her. There had been a tie. Celine had also won the gold medal! Once again, tears cascaded down her cheeks. Her triumph in Japan was an important milestone. For Maman, it would always remain one of the most moving moments in Celine's career.

When Celine arrived at the reception for the winners, she admits she 'wasn't a beautiful sight'. She had cried tears of hapiness all evening. 'My eyes were all red and swollen,' she recalls. During the gala, they announced that a special prize would be awarded, the Orchestra Leader's Award for the artist who the musicians most appreciated. Celine won again! It was not just that Celine was talented. She was also modest and sensitive. She had 'heart' and 'compassion', traits that would always remain with her. Celine stayed an extra week, at Yamaha's request, to do a special concert for the Ministers of Government. The concert was held at the other end of Japan, at Nemu Nosato, where she and her entourage were rapidly transported to another world – of small houses with Japanese gardens. They were treated like royalty and Celine sang four songs in front of 600 people. They thought they were in paradise. It was more than a dream now.

All the publicity that surrounded Celine after the Yamaha World Popular Song Festival had a huge impact on the release of her third album *Tellement j'ai d'amour . . .* It had sold 25,000 copies in the following weeks, but, although the record was doing well in Canada, it wasn't yet a success in France. As a French performer, it was important for Celine to succeed in both Quebec and France. Now there was a huge musical extravaganza in Cannes, France, called the MIDEM, which stands for the *Marché International du Disque et de l'Édition Musicale* (International Market of Records and Music Publishing), which would offer Celine the exposure she needed to give her career some momentum in France. Claude Pascal, who continued to take care of her business in France, convinced the organizers of the MIDEM to invite Celine to perform at the great record fair. Her recent trophy in Japan had helped spark interest in her and Celine was chosen to represent Canada, as the Newcomer of the Year in France.

Celine loved the Mediterranean charm of Cannes. As she approached the massive building where the MIDEM was held, Celine was thrilled to see giant posters of herself outside. On 24 January 1983, Celine performed in front of 3,500 people, singing the song, 'D'amour ou d'amitié' (Of Love or Friendship). The audience, composed of record industry pioneers, gave her a long standing ovation. Reporters from RTL, one of the most important radio stations in France, were covering the show and when they saw the reaction of the audience, they insisted their disc jockeys play her record. Soon all the other radio stations followed suit.

Celine stayed on in France, because she had been invited to appear on the Michel Drucker talk show in Paris, called *Champs-Élysées*. It was the number one weekly show in France, watched by 14 million European television viewers in France, Switzerland, Germany, Italy, Spain and Belgium. She was to appear on the show on 29 January 1983.

In her hotel room, the night before the taping, Celine slept sixteen hours straight. But when she awoke, she was a bundle of nerves. When Celine was nervous, she kept singing songs in her head, which helped her relax. She tried to think of nothing else.

There was a great deal of pressure on her to perform well on the French talk show. 'Don't forget Celine, you are the best. Don't be afraid, here you are at home,' consoled René. But Celine could hear nothing but the pounding of her heart. Michel Drucker announced her as the girl who had been a revelation in Cannes at the MIDEM. 'Remember this name: Celine Dion.'

Then Celine sang '*D'amour ou d'amitié* – and triumphed. She had an instant affinity with the dashing Michel Drucker and, after her appearance on the show, her records started flying out of the shops in France.

Back in Montreal, in May 1983, Celine realized another dream, when she performed for the first time at Place des Arts, the city's most celebrated concert theatre. She was accompanied by the Metropolitan Symphony Orchestra at a gala to raise funds for cystic fibrosis research. Her niece Karine was now six years old and, as Celine remarked, 'It's rare that at six years old a child could possess such wisdom and such lucidity.' She loved Karine with all her heart and, at fifteen, Celine had already taken on the challenge to help find a cure for the illness, as 'godmother of the Quebec association'.

By now Celine's once simple life had changed dramatically. She was constantly travelling back and forth between Paris and Montreal for recordings and promotional appearances. It seemed as if Celine was spending more time on planes than on the ground. She worked almost all the time.

In July 1983, Celine did a series of five one-hour shows throughout major centres in Quebec which broke all attendance records. One of the most sensational of Celine's early shows, was at the spectacular venue, Man and His World, the site of the famous World's Fair, Expo '67, in Montreal. The event took place on 30 July 1983, in front of 45,000 people and would be televised in French across Quebec in September.

As something totally unique for this show, Celine was to sing on a floating stage in the middle of the artificial lake of La Ronde, the theme park at the fair. Celine's family alone had reserved fifty seats. When she went to climb in the small boat that would take her to the platform, she was terrified. 'I was afraid,' she recalls. 'There were *sooooo* many people.'

The floating platform had a complete orchestra and, according to one of the musicians, 'It was an incredible sight, watching Celine on the floating stage. We were all worried that she would get electrocuted, there were so many wires!' Celine would always remember this performance.

On 7 September 1983, Celine was back on the Michel Jasmin show and he had a surprise for her. He presented her with her first gold record in Canada, marking the sale of over 50,000 copies of her album *Tellement j'ai d'amour . . .* Meanwhile, her single *'D'amour ou d'amitié'* had exceeded sales of 500,000 in France, and Celine was the first Canadian to have a gold record there!

From the very start of her career, Celine amassed an amazing collection of trophies, awards and gold and platinum records. Yet none touched her as deeply as the music awards she received back home in Quebec.

Celine started winning trophy after trophy for her work as a Quebec artist at Quebec's French milieu equivalent of the Grammy Awards in the US, the ADISQ – (*L'Association du disque et de l'industrie du spectacle du Québec* which stands for the Association of Recording and Show Business in Quebec). The trophy handed out at the ADISQ is called the *'Félix'*, honouring the artist Félix Leclerc, a legendary Quebec writer, composer and performer. In 1983, Celine won four awards. These included Best Newcomer of the Year, Best Album of the Year, the Most Successful Artist Outside Quebec and Female Artist of the Year – all when she was only fifteen years old!

But, amidst all her success, there remained one problem – school. Celine spent her grade nine year in a private school, to give her the flexibility to fit her studies around her demanding recording schedule. But she remained terribly unhappy. She confided in a favourite teacher because she couldn't talk to schoolfriends since many of them were jealous. Many girls didn't even talk to her any more and felt that Celine thought she was a big star, which hurt her a lot. By the end of the year, Celine had been spending so much time out of school that she finally decided to abandon her studies altogether.

In later years, Celine rolled her eyes when a television interviewer brought this up. She responded sarcastically, 'Yes, I know two plus two is four.' But the fact was that she hated being in school – and those days were now over.

All she wanted to do was sing. 'I was going to school because I had to. Every time I went to school I did not get involved in the activities or play with other kids . . . all the normal things. I was always on the stairway in the school singing. I couldn't study correctly. I was always dreaming. And then the teachers started to send letters to my parents. Then they sent someone to my home because they thought I wasn't normal. They thought I was an abused child.' Nothing could have been further from the truth but Celine understood why the teacher was worried.

As Celine describes it, 'I was not involved. I didn't want to do any activities at school. I just did what they wanted me to do. And then I couldn't wait to go back home. I wanted to do the dishes with my mom. I wanted to cook with her. I wanted to hear my brothers and sisters play instruments in the basement of the house.'

Maman continued to follow Celine throughout her engagements, as she had done from the time Celine was twelve. 'Since the other children were at least six years older than Celine, I decided to be fully involved in Celine's career in the early years.' On radio and television shows, and at a multitude of performances, Therese was her constant companion. 'I gave myself the job of educating Celine about everything.'

Celine practised all the time, and when she wasn't working on her singing style, she was working on her looks. 'At fifteen, we corrected, in a few months, that which should have taken three years. The orthodontist tightened her teeth so much that she had nausea all the time, which cut her appetite and also gave her the violent migraines that robbed her of her precious sleep,' recalls Maman.

Celine's greatest strength on the career side, her total self-discipline, was also the greatest cause of her personal solitude. She had to put aside everything, friends, boyfriends, and all the usual adolescent experiences, so that she could keep climbing professionally. 'I don't want people to think I'm miserable,' she says. 'I have the life I always wanted to have. I'm surrounded with these wonderful people. But personal friends to go out with – buddies – I do not consider that I have friends like that.'

Instead, Celine treasured the times when she could have fun with her family. One summer, when she was fifteen, she went with them to a lakeside chalet. Wearing monster costumes and accessories, Celine, Pauline and the son of the chalet owner put together a mini-show of 'Thriller', by Michael Jackson, who was one of Celine's favourite singers. Celine loved horror movies! The whole performance was filmed and they had a great souvenir of the holiday.

Celine's fascination with Michael Jackson was shared with most teenagers at the time. Little did she know that their paths would cross in the future. Many years later, Michael Jackson gave Celine his legendary black fedora from the 'Billy Jean' music video, which he autographed for her. He wrote a special note, 'To Celine With Love 1998 . . .!' She never asked him what he meant by 1998 since, at the time that he gave her the hat, it was still the early nineties. Maybe he thought that 1998 would be a great year for her!

In September 1983, at the age of fifteen, Celine's fifth French album *Les chemins de ma maison* (The Paths to My Home) was launched simultaneously in Canada and in France. The title reflected how lonely Celine was at times, and the fact that, no matter where she was in the world, she would always find her way back home.

It was a very 'sweet sixteenth' year for Celine in 1984, when she sang in front of Pope Jean-Paul II during his visit to Montreal for the Annual Celebration of Youth. The Quebec clergy had chosen her to perform and Celine sang the song *'Une colombe'* ('A Dove') in front of the Pope and 65,000 young people at the Montreal Olympic Stadium on

11 September 1984. As she sang, Celine couldn't help her tears. She cried excessively during this performance, and the image of 'The Crying Dove', penned by some Quebec journalists, would stay with her for a long while.

And the French albums kept on coming. In 1984 her sixth French album was released, *Les plus grands succès* (Greatest Hits) and her seventh album, *Mélanie*, came out on 15 October, featuring a title song about a child with an incurable illness. Celine had already recorded seven albums by the time she was sixteen, and won more Quebec music awards for Best-selling Album and Female Artist of the Year.

But these events appeared to unsettle Celine's original manager, Paul Levesque. He suddenly resurfaced, in November 1984, suing them for what he felt would be a fairer settlement. A final 'undisclosed' amount put an end, once and for all, to any claims Paul Levesque had with respect to Celine's career. She was all René's.

Celine not only had a manager. She had much more. She had what the press would call the architect of her career – her 'good genie'. When asked about love, Celine said that there was no one in her life. But there were rumours that behind the simple, innocent young girl was another Celine, more complicated, and in love – for a long time – with her manager.

When asked to explain her relationship with René, Celine had this insight: 'This is false. People don't understand. I knew René when I was twelve years old.' Celine had an analogy to try to illustrate her feelings for René. 'Imagine a child who dreams of going to Disneyland. Someone arrives, takes you by the hand and says: "This pleases you, my little one? Come, I'll take you! Do you want ice cream also? Chocolate mousse?" And after, he looks straight into your eyes and asks you, "Do you want more?" '

As far as romance was concerned, Celine didn't have enough time for friends, let alone boyfriends. However, there was one exception. Her sister Claudette recalls that at sixteen Celine fell in love with the boy next door. Unfortunately, her constant trips to Europe made the relationship difficult, and the boy found another girl. 'She told me that she expected it, that she understood,' adds Claudette, 'But I'm sure this still caused sadness.' Celine was a romantic, but love seemed to elude her. 'Who will be able to love me for me?' she wondered. 'I don't even know who I am myself. No, I don't have an easy life. They say that I am full of many persons inside myself.'

Celine was back in Paris again from early November to early December 1984 where she had a contract for a five-week period at the Olympia in Paris. Maman was by her side. 'I was always behind the curtains,' she recalls. 'I didn't want to watch Celine from the audience. I wanted to feel that I was on stage with her. At the Olympia . . . every night, for five weeks, I was hidden behind a door, my nose in the doorway.' Maman was her constant companion. She did Celine's hair, ironed her dresses, she was her close friend and companion in the hotel rooms.

While they were in Europe, René arranged a trip to Rome where they had a private benediction with the Pope. For Maman, it was one of the most touching moments of her life. 'I was very moved. I've met a lot of people in my life but the Pope is an unforgettable person. In meeting him, I felt the strength of his presence.'

But the journalists had a field day with 'whiter than white' Celine. They made fun of her – and even tormented her with satires. Good or bad, at sixteen Celine was on magazine covers throughout Quebec, as well as Paris, and, despite the orthodontic work, the photos still revealed pointed and crooked teeth. Several teeth in particular, were jagged. Her eyes showed some fatigue with bags underneath. But Celine put on a brave face and told magazine interviewers: 'Success, it's twice as beautiful as I thought. I was sure . . . that there would be high and lows. I haven't felt the lows.'

But other teens she knew, at the impressionable peer-orientated age of sixteen, reacted differently to her now and sometimes made her feel isolated. Her friends were her 'team' but even that circle was now smaller. René and Anne-Renée's marriage had crumbled in 1985, and ended, the following year, in a bitter divorce. Some believed that René's attention to Celine's career had taken up all his time. Others speculated that Celine was madly in love with him. Emotions ran high, but that did not stop two more albums from being launched that year, her eighth French album, *Céline Dion en concert* (Celine Dion in Concert) and her ninth album *C'est pour toi* (It's for You). And that year René and Celine set up a (perfectly named) new company – Feeling Productions. The company would take care of the business aspects as well as tours and promotions.

In the first four years of her career, from 1981 to 1985, Celine had recorded nine albums in the French language. She had earned several gold records and won a gold medal at the Thirteenth Yamaha World Popular Song Festival in Tokyo. She was 'Newcomer of the Year' in Cannes, and had five more Quebec music awards at the age of seventeen, which brought her total up to eleven music awards by 1985. Celine had already performed at the Place des Arts in Montreal, at the Olympia of Paris and had sung before the Pope!

Yet all this success didn't prevent Celine from stopping her career at the end of her seventeenth year. She was about to turn eighteen. It was time for a change.

CHAPTER 6

Celine Transformed

'I was sick of my image . . . I was fed up with being seen as a crying child.'

– CELINE DION

At seventeen Celine had a lot going for her but there was one big problem – she hated the way she looked. As she approached her eighteenth birthday, her appearance seemed like a terrifying obstacle.

The little-girl, child-star image was one that she had outgrown. The angelic robes may have helped her succeed at thirteen, fourteen, fifteen and sixteen but now she hated them. In later years, Celine looked back at photographs of herself as an adolescent and grimaced. Pointing at a picture of herself, she said: 'I don't know, there's a lot of things I don't like, right here.' She motioned to an area around her nose and laughed: 'My nose is a little big and I have small lips.' Another time Celine commented, 'When I look back at the start of my career . . . those clothes were *awful*.' During her professional debuts, it's certainly true that she had a lot more talent than tailoring.

In her early adolescence, Celine kept her long hair off her forehead, making her face look more elongated. Her eyebrows were very thick and her dresses were bland, appealing to an elderly fan base. She wore little make-up and matronly, over-sized clothes, sometimes accentuated with an old-fashioned brooch. Celine was not exactly in tune with teenage fashions. Indeed, it was almost as if she was out of sync with her own generation.

The problem wasn't only the 'angelic' white garments and 'old maid' style smock dresses that she was so often seen in. It was more than her crooked, pointed teeth. It was also her frequent emotional outbursts that made local comedians ridicule her and the media scrutinize her, even though her voice was beyond reproach. Whether they were tears of joy or tears of sorrow, crying came almost as easily to Celine as singing.

She had sung the song about a dove for the Pope but it was 'The Crying Dove' that they now called her. It was an image Celine hated. 'I was fed up with being seen as a crying child,' Celine recalls. 'I really had the desire for a change.'

When people had made fun of her looks before, she had always been comforted by her mother's philosophy: 'If you feel good in your own skin, if you feel good about yourself, then that's the only thing that matters.' Now, five years into her career, it wasn't enough. The right image mattered a great deal – enough to stop her career.

When Celine complained of being locked in a little girl image, even René – despite the gruelling schedule of recording sessions and performances he had envisioned – advised her to disappear from public view for over a year. Eighteen months to be exact. Celine needed a break and record sales had dropped for her last two French albums. It was time to change her image.

Celine was about to undergo a dramatic transformation, a metamorphosis. During this period, 'I wasn't seen too often in public,' she remembers. 'I didn't perform in shows and I didn't do a lot of television. I found this difficult because I love working before and *for* the public.' It was like a blackout.

Nevertheless, brilliant career orchestrator René kept material coming to the public. While Celine was 'away' he re-released a selection of many of her French hits in an album (her tenth) called *Céline Dion – Les chansons en or* (Songs of Gold) for her eighteenth birthday.

But Celine accepted that it would be wise to disappear from people's memories for a while. 'I still had the image of the well-behaved little girl that all parents wished to have. This touched me a lot, but at a certain moment, a girl feels that she simply needs to be treated like a woman.' Celine felt that if she continued to evolve under public scrutiny they wouldn't accept this change in her. 'They were too used to a certain image of me. It was necessary for people to forget me for a little while.'

'One and a half years without giving concerts was really difficult,' she admits, but she tried to use the time for 'self-improvement'. During her eighteen-month 'sabbatical', Celine took singing and dancing lessons and perfected her singing skills for her next album, confident that she had made the right decision to take time off at the moment when it was most important to make the change from 'girl' to 'woman'.

At this time Celine suffered a great deal of dental surgery and had her teeth capped. She had her hair permed and cut, her eyebrows plucked and her make-up changed, and she replaced her childish wardrobe with figure-hugging outfits and spiked heels.

She resurfaced as a bolder, more fashionable, more confident Celine. Her hair was cut and she wore skin-tight dresses with plunging necklines. She traded her white cotton frocks for leather and sequins. Celine's new look was a complete turnaround – suddenly she was a 'vamp', with long tousled hair, wearing a leather bomber jacket over a sexy, low-necked dress.

Celine wanted to cause a reaction. She wanted to amaze, if not seduce. Not too much – just enough. Her new image might have lost her a few grandmotherly fans but it certainly won over the fifteen to thirty-five age bracket. Celine now chose bold shades of red or black. She still wore white sometimes but her ensembles were sensuous rather than innocent. She changed daily to reflect her mood: 'I wear black when I feel strong, white when I feel romantic, and when I feel full of love, I wear red.'

She appointed a costume designer who created stage clothes that were glitzy and risqué – but not too much. She had left the public eye as a child, and returned . . . a woman.

It was around this time that Maman Dion decided she would no longer be able to accompany Celine on all her tours. Papa Dion was alone at home and, as Maman explains: 'I realized that we had the chance to grow old together and this was our choice. Since Celine was well surrounded, I left her career in the hands of René. We had already seen the success that they knew together.'

When she resurfaced, in November 1987, at nineteen-and-a-half years old, magazine covers show a drastically different Celine, wearing jeans and a leather jacket, her hair cut to above shoulder length. She became fixated on clothes, owning thirty-five bathing suits and just as many pairs of sunglasses. Celine also started to show a weakness for high-heeled shoes.

Yet, despite her new look and new confidence, not everything had changed. Celine remained easily moved to tears and continued to feel very lonely at times. 'It's true that I haven't had the chance to go dancing in discotheques, or go to the movies with pals,' she explained, 'but I don't miss it because I've never known what that was.' She tried to make sense of her pain. 'Showbiz is beautiful,' she said. 'We are applauded by thousands of people, but at night after the show, René drives me home. My parents are asleep and I am all alone. Sometimes, I burst out in tears.'

Celine was a romantic. She described herself as a passionate girl, who loved gallantry and chivalry. She needed to belong to someone. But she was young. There was plenty of time.

Meanwhile, René negotiated a recording contract with the Canadian arm of American-owned CBS Music, which later became part of the massive Sony family. The time off had not only given birth to a new Celine, but a new French album that was 'more rock and less smock' with daring lyrics, such as the song 'Lolita' about a young girl in love with an older man.

Her eleventh French album, *Incognito*, was launched in 1987. It was her greatest success yet, and would go on to sell half a million copies – her first platinum record.

Incognito – it was a perfect name. To have one's identity concealed . . . it reflected what she had undergone during the past eighteen months. In 1987, Celine arrived back on the scene with a new look, a big recording contract, and a whole new pop emphasis.

CHAPTER 7

In Unison with the World

'There isn't an artist who doesn't dream of triumphing in New York.'

– RENE ANGELIL

Celine was in unison with the world. She was chosen to compete in the Thirty-third Annual Eurovision Song Contest, one of the largest competitions in the world. The event was to take place on 30 April 1988, and Celine represented Switzerland with a song called *'Ne partez pas sans moi'* (Don't Leave Without Me) by two Swiss songwriters. But in the weeks that led up to the competition Papa gave Celine some disturbing news. He had noticed that Maman was not herself any more. She was pale and weak. Yet she still hadn't seen a doctor and Papa – he just didn't know what to do. Barely twenty, Celine found she had to take control, all the while fighting her worst fear – of one day losing her best friend, and her idol, who was over sixty now. Celine made an appointment with a Montreal cardiologist. The doctor took one look at Maman and immediately hospitalized her. She had emergency quadruple bypass surgery the same day. It was a terrible scare for the family. According to Maman, Celine had saved her life.

It was particularly hard for Celine to see her mother, who had always been so strong, suddenly so weak. Afterwards, Maman spent twelve days in a convalescent home. While Maman recuperated, Papa seemed lost without her. And Celine saw how much her parents needed each other.

Celine had been so busy, promoting *Incognito* in Quebec with a gruelling series of forty-two concerts, that she had hardly noticed how things were going with her parents.

As she rummaged around at her parents' home, getting everything ready for Maman's return, she was shocked to see the way they lived. Her career had been escalating, and there was more money coming in than ever before. Celine had already purchased a house for her parents in an area called Laval, 20 miles north of Montreal. Yet Maman lived the same way she always had, watching every penny and buying only things that were low-priced or on sale, even when she had to order something from a restaurant. Celine made a vow that her parents should never want for anything again. She had the house redecorated, breaking down walls, opening up the space, as Maman had always opened her heart to Celine.

'I don't ever want to see my parents deprive themselves of anything in life,' she says. 'They have done everything in their existence to permit fourteen children to be happy and I want to focus on them and give them back, in my way, all the love they gave to me.'

Celine noticed that her parents were closer than ever after the operation. In the years when the house was filled with children, she 'never saw them show a lot of affection towards each other. When you have to run a family of fourteen children, you don't have time to hug each other all day. I have discovered the love they have for one another and I understand why their marriage gave birth to such a beautiful family. They have plenty of love.' A love that Celine missed desperately when she was away.

Only weeks after this scare, Celine had to go to Dublin for the Eurovision competition, where she would be seen by 600 million television viewers.

At the Eurovision, Celine was a sure-fire bet for René Angelil – literally. When René found out that people were betting on who would win, he wanted to join in. Not only because he had a passion for gambling, but because he was so sure that Celine would triumph. She wasn't the favourite at the Eurovision contest: the odds were three to one against. 'Imagine,' said René, 'I could stake on Celine.' He emptied the contents of his pockets. He had £400 – about 800 dollars.

Celine won the Grand Prize at Eurovision and cried and cried. But René was laughing. Not only was his protégé a gold medal winner, but he had won $2,400 on his wager. 'She's never let us down,' said René. After winning the Eurovision gold medal Celine sold 200,000 records in Europe in only two days. She was bombarded with invitations.

On their triumphant return home, they had made headlines everywhere. One article read: 'A hell of a duo: he bets, she sings . . . they both win!'

A *duo?* Celine and her manager mentor were conquering the world together. Along the way, something happened. They fell in love.

When newspapers started referring to them as a duo, it was because that was exactly what they had become. In every way. Celine and René were in love. There was only one problem. They were secret lovers. At the time, Celine was only twenty, and René, forty-six. What would the public think? What would her parents think?

Celine would have been happy to 'tell the world' but René was mortified.

Their love remained hidden from public view, carefully disguised. It was never a lover's kiss that the public saw, but an innocent peck on the cheek appropriate for a manager/star relationship. For now. After two failed marriages, René, it seemed, had found his destiny in Celine, in more ways than one. For Celine's part, she was totally enamoured of the man who was her career architect, her good genie.

'He is the only one I will listen to without questioning anything, with my eyes closed,' she confessed.

For René, Celine's wishes were his commands. He was ready to orchestrate anything she wanted.

There was one wish Celine and René shared. It was no secret that they yearned for a career in the United States. But Celine had still only recorded French songs. After eleven albums containing over a hundred French songs, Celine still couldn't speak a word of English. Her last French album *Incognito*, produced by CBS Music, had sold half a million copies. Now the time had come to take a walk on the English side. It was a gamble, but René was determined that Celine should become a star in the States and he started to set things in motion. 'It was all little moves,' agrees Vito Luprano, then artistic director of Sony Music in Montreal. 'The progression happened little by little through a series of successful advances.' And those advances meant targeting the American market as well as English Canada and, ultimately, the world.

When Celine understood that she had the possibility of an American career, she went to the Berlitz school in Montreal for English lessons, where she immersed herself in intensive study. After all, Celine never did anything by halves!

Little by little, she began to understand English. And it was time well spent for Celine would make just about any sacrifice for her career. 'If I needed to do algebra in order to sing better,' she says, 'I would do it.' Celine had sung English songs before, but had never understood what she was singing. During the two-month course – from nine to five each day – Celine learned to speak and comprehend English. It was a costly investment – today these lessons at Berlitz cost well over 10,000 Canadian dollars for two months of private instruction. But it was a move that would repay her a thousand times over.

The experience was so fascinating for Celine that she even incorporated it in later concerts as part of her friendly banter with the audience. She described how hard it was for her to learn to pronounce 'h' or, as she exaggerated to her audience, 'hhhhhhh—ach'. The tendency in going from French to English was to leave out the 'h', saying 'im', for example, instead of 'him', and 'appy' instead of 'happy'. But Celine made the transition and she was very, very, *hhhhh-appy* about it. As she recalled years later, 'I felt it was important to learn English to communicate around the world.'

She may have been broadening her audience but Celine was still loved by French Canadians. At the age of twenty, she won three more Quebec music awards for her work on *Incognito*, and won the popular vote in Quebec for the Metro Star Young Artist of the Year for performers under the age of twenty-five.

It was at this time that the Canadian Academy of Recording Arts invited Celine to sing one of her songs from the French-language album *Incognito* at the 1988 Juno Awards – the Canadian equivalent of the Grammy Awards. René accepted but insisted that she would sing in English. The organizers wanted Celine to sing in French. But, as beautiful as the French lyrics were, René felt that the audience needed to hear how capable Celine was of singing in English. What's more, René found that the English audience was sometimes nonplussed by Celine's French songs. 'I've seen the reaction before, and my artist was not going to sing before a blasé audience,' attested René. 'I translated one of the songs from *Incognito* and we called it "Just Have a Heart". Celine stole the show.'

Just to put his 'foot in the door', René had originally inserted a small clause in his contract with CBS that a sum of 25,000 dollars would be devoted to the production of an English album.

Was this a joke they asked? 'Twenty-five thousand dollars? You'll do nothing with this,' they laughed. But at every opportunity, René kept revising the clause, bumping it higher and higher. When Celine sang 'Just Have a Heart' the reaction she received enabled him to negotiate 300,000 dollars. By the time Celine entered the recording studio in 1989 for her first English album *Unison*, sources said that the amount had escalated to a million dollars, the largest budget ever for a Canadian artist.

Celine was confident about fulfilling her American dream. 'I've waited for eight years. At thirteen years old, I dreamt of a worldwide career, particularly in the United States, and I've worked very hard in getting there. It will work. I am certain. It will work because it is what I want most in the world.'

Her career had advanced steadily, but Celine felt she was still the same girl – 'Two feet on the ground and my head in the right place.' Confidence was her greatest ally, and the strength of her self-belief came from within, from her family, and from René.

'She has a talent rarely seen. Personally, I've never seen a similar artist. Nothing is impossible with Celine. An incredible voice, an extraordinary woman, and an exceptional talent. In all, Celine is the simplest, most gentle person you could meet. She's completely changed my life,' admitted René.

Her voice was also on top form. Celine had been taking singing lessons for the past five years and her vocal chords were stronger than ever. In addition, the CBS company surrounded her with some of the most talented people in the music industry. One of the song-writers and producers on the *Unison* album was fellow Canadian David Foster, an enormously celebrated composer and producer who had already written and produced for a star-studded line-up of clients, including Barbra Streisand and Lionel Richie. In addition, he had done an outstanding job of meshing together the voices of Natalie Cole and her late father, Nat King Cole, for the album *Unforgettable*. He was completely astounded by Celine's voice.

Also collaborating on the album was Andy Goldmark, who had produced songs for the Pointer Sisters, and Christopher Neil who had produced for Tina Turner.

Celine made several visits to Malibu in 1989 to record her first English album, *Unison*, renting a house near Zuma Beach. There she discovered the chic, trendy world of Rodeo Drive, where Rolls Royces and Mercedes lined the street. She made the most of this new experience, spending time there with René. And, from their first meeting, a wonderful relationship evolved between her and David

Foster, one that was destined to get ever stronger.

'I've seen so many cases of talented singers who perform well on stage but are without soul in the studio. With Celine, emotion is always there. She really loves her work and it's a pleasure to direct her,' says David Foster, who first heard Celine sing at the Canadian Juno Awards in 1988 and was immediately won over by her vocal power and energy. 'Honestly, I was overwhelmed,' he recalls from his studio in Los Angeles. 'I don't remember the last time that an artist impressed me as much. She has a raw talent and is well-polished at the same time. A stunning voice, and she sings in tune and in pitch which is more rare than we think.

'Working on this project to launch Celine's career in the States was especially important to me because it was rare for me to work with someone who was not already a public persona,' Foster has said. 'I had no doubt that she would be able to win over everyone who came her way.'

At that time, René Angelil was already recognized as the remarkable orchestrator of her career. David Foster witnessed what he described as an, 'almost never-seen devotion to an artist from a manager.' With good reason.

Celine was on magazine covers everywhere, under such banner headlines as 'Celine ... The American Dream'. And she loved every moment of it. Not only was her career going well, but she had two lucrative deals for product endorsements, one with a department store chain, and the other, a six-figure deal with Chrysler Canada. Later she would sign up to do a campaign for Diet Coke. She now owned two houses: the one that she already shared with her parents, and a spectacular half-a-million-dollar second home, nestled in the Laurentian mountains, an hour's drive from Montreal. The magnificent all-white country home had been bought – appliances, furnishing and all – back on 1988, when she was twenty. Celine shared the house with her parents, a cat named Isis and two white doves. It overlooked the ski resorts and it was a change of venue that did her a world of good.

According to Maman, 'Celine bought the house in the Laurentians for the simple reason that it was the ideal place to rest and get back her energy. It's here that [even in later years] Celine could forget the demands of her profession.' Relax? Yes, the word *was* in her vocabulary – here she could kick off those three-inch heels. Her parents adored the country house – going back to their city home only to get clothes now and then. Said Maman, 'Knowing how happy we were there, Celine invited us to live in the house permanently.'

The house was a spectacular vision of white – like the winter snow on the mountains that surrounded it. Even Celine's room was a peaceful haven, reflecting the utmost sobriety and simplicity. It had high ceilings, big windows, and walls that were all white – devoid, for the most part, of ornaments or paintings. The only exceptions were two big laminated black and white photos of Marilyn Monroe – a legend, according to Celine. One day she too hoped to be remembered like Marilyn.

Celine had given her mother a free hand in decorating, but there was only one rule. 'Celine didn't want any photos of herself on the walls. She didn't want to see her face everywhere around the house, even though she was rarely there. She detested this,' according to Maman.

But in Maman's room, she had a painting of Celine anyway. 'It's me that makes the rules for my room!' declares Maman

'Celine is constantly out of the country,' reflects Maman. 'It's strange to see her empty room. I am the first to rejoice in her success on the international music scene, but this gives me the sadness of not seeing her more often. When she is in Quebec, she makes it a priority to spend several days of rest here. Celine always feels the need to be among us.'

Despite her homesickness, Celine had an almost alarming drive to succeed. 'I see myself BIG!' she said. 'With bodyguards like Michael Jackson. I imagine crowds, where everyone fights to touch even a small piece of my clothes. It's exciting and scary. I want to climb on the stage and be known everywhere. That's all.'

The *Unison* album was launched on 2 April 1990 in Montreal. The songs on this first English album were sensational – her English singing impeccable. The album featured ten songs, and the cover showed a black and white close-up of Celine, with her hair wild, looking sultry yet innocent. One of the star songs of the album, 'Where Does My Heart Beat Now' was soon in Top Ten charts everywhere. It would become Celine's signature song on the soon-to-be experienced American talk-show circuit.

'There isn't an artist who doesn't dream of triumphing in New York,' said René Angelil. But Celine was still virtually unknown in America, despite the wide recognition she had received in Canada and certain parts of Europe. In Montreal, on 6 September 1990, Celine was just about to start a press conference announcing that the *Unison* album would be released in eighteen countries on 11 September. It was fifteen minutes before the press conference when the telephone rang. René answered the phone.

It was Glen Bruman, responsible for press relations for Epic Records, a division of CBS, where Celine was under contract. Glen was a key person involved in the promotion of Michael Jackson and, now, Celine Dion.

'Hi, Mr Angelil,' said Glen. 'We presented Celine Dion's dossier to the researchers of *The Tonight Show*. They saw her video and heard her songs. They flipped!' he exclaimed, hardly able to conceal his excitement.

At the other end, René listened intently. *The Tonight Show* wanted Celine to appear in two weeks' time, on 21 September. It was the number one talk show in the United States.

It would be guest talk-show host Jay Leno who would be interviewing her, and naturally they wanted Celine to sing a song, said Glen. Phil Collins would also be on the show that night.

René couldn't believe his ears! The moment they had been waiting for had come. He knew it.

'There was just a little problem,' Glen mentioned cautiously. Celine and her musicians did not have work permits for the United States. It could take three weeks to get all the paperwork they needed.

René was shocked. He wouldn't let any tangle of red tape deprive

Celine of her chance of a lifetime . . . performing in front of 30 million television viewers. She had worked so hard for this.

But the next day René had his work cut out for him. Dealing with American Immigration wasn't easy. Lawyers, letters . . . nothing seemed to help. The voice at the other end of the telephone always said the same thing, 'Celine Dion? Could you spell her name please?' He was spending endless futile hours attempting to get a temporary work permit for Celine – not to mention the work permits needed for all her musicians.

René was flustered and he didn't fluster easily. He took pride in his superb organizational skills – he usually had every detail worked out in advance, and he loved it when everything went like clockwork, or a perfect chess game. But this time it seemed that Celine was the pawn and bureaucracy was about to checkmate her American career.

Finally René called an official from the Canadian Federal Government in Ottawa and asked for his help. At last the work permits arrived, just a few days before the show was to be recorded. Celine barely had time to pack!

When they arrived in California, a fleet of limousines greeted Celine and her troupe. But she barely had time to enjoy her first taste of true luxury. The whole drive to their hotel in Beverly Hills, Celine nervously listened (for the umpteenth time) to René's advice.

'All the rehearsals are important in this show, Celine,' explained René, who prided himself on his vast knowledge of the music and entertainment industry. He had done his homework. 'I know that usually you keep your best for the final recording. Here, it doesn't happen this way. All the rehearsal stages are important. From the first sound check, the producers follow everything from behind the scenes in the control room. They judge the artist from the first try.' He turned to a pensive Celine and gently encouraged her, 'So don't hesitate to do your maximum and go to your farthest level possible, right away.'

At the studio, everything happened exactly as René had foreseen.

The musicians were in place, and if Celine trembled with stage fright only René knew it.

As she rehearsed 'Where Does My Heart Beat Now' everyone stood gaping at the pure power of her voice and the emotion in her performance. The song was not yet finished and already the show's associate producer Freddy De Cordova was pulling René by the sleeve. 'I have never heard anything like it. I want her back as soon as possible,' begged an enthralled Freddy. 'And the next time, it will be Johnny Carson himself who will be hosting the show. What do you say about 8 October?'

René beamed inwardly. He knew that he had won the first round of his American epic.

'The 8th?' René responded. 'Impossible. Celine is starting a Quebec tour.'

'That is no problem, Mr Angelil. We'll set the date that is most convenient for you.'

'OK. Tell me, what is your best viewing day?' said René, in perfect form as Celine's career architect.

'Thursday.'

'Perfect. We'll be there Thursday, 15 November.'

Several hours later, it was time for the actual taping. Celine gave the performance of her life, singing 'Where Does My Heart Beat Now'. The audience was transfixed. It was not just the ballad that over-powered them, it was Celine's style – the highly charged emotional gestures that would be her trademark for ever. Celine always said that to sing a song, you had to 'feel the song'. Her emotion was genuine and the gripping ballad showcased her amazing five-octave range and extraordinary vocal power. There was pure silence from the audience until the end of the song, when they burst into thunderous applause. René knew that Celine could go very far but this time she had surpassed herself.

The night America discovered her she wore a short black long-sleeved dress and pendant earrings. Her hair flowed down her back, wavy and parted from the right. One song was enough to put America in the palm of her hand. Jay Leno held up her album *Unison* and said, 'She's a huge star up in Canada, especially in Montreal, and she's made her first appearance here on American television tonight. Her name is Celine Dion and you'll hear a lot more from her.'

Afterwards, Celine was in a daze as she took the flight home. 'I was really in the clouds,' she reminisced. 'I didn't have the time to realize what had happened to me. Everything went so fast.'

It was only two days later, when Celine saw a taped recording of the show, that she understood the full impact of her performance on *The Tonight Show*. She watched the tape, almost in amazement. Surprised, she said to herself: 'It's true, I did it!'

Now the proverbial ice was broken and Celine made a remarkable entry into the American and European hit charts. The album quickly went gold, with 500,000 copies sold (as certified by the Recording Industry Association of America). In time, sales would escalate to two million copies. This one English album would out-sell all Celine's previous eleven French albums combined.

The door to the United States was wide open and Celine had taken the first big step towards her American dream. 'It's my profession . . . it's my life.' She said. 'I always want to go farther, always higher. Go until the limits.'

Then Celine reflected and revised her wording. 'No . . . there *are* no limits!' But in the meantime, she was cautious. 'I'm not the only singer there. And there is talent everywhere in the world. I have patience. I have time to become the best.'

eline Dion aged 14. The start of an ternational career soon brought her to cord and perform in Paris. Her life would ever be the same again

Aged 23, Celine shocked the audience at a Quebec music gala by appearing in this androgynous look

The 16 members of the Dion family

The home in Charlemagne, Quebec, where Celine grew up. Today it is a small renovation store

Rene Angelil took on Celine's career the moment he heard her sing. Beside Celine is Maman who accompanied her everywhere in the early years

Already a teen star in Paris, Celine took time out to sign autographs for adoring fans

Celine, aged 13, at her first television appearance on the popular Michel Drucker show in France, called *Champs Elysées*

Celine at the end of her sixteenth year. She poured emotion into her songs, and was easily moved to tears during a performance

Celine transformed! She took eighteen months off to transform her image and came back with this new look aged 19

At only 16 years old, Celine performed for the Pope and her largest audience yet – 65000 youths at the Celebration of Youth Festival in Montreal's Olympic Stadium

eline and her parents in September 1994. Her father was her number one fan and her other was her 'idol'

line's first English album, *Unison*, was nched in 1990 and was a huge success, th over two million sales worldwide

Celine holding up her *Colour of My Love* album - a huge hit across the world. Celine officially announced her love for her manager at the time of the album's release

On December 17, 1994, Celine had the fairy tale wedding of her dreams. She named wedding dress 'Age of Innocence' and wore a heavy, 20lb headdress made up of 200 Bavarian beads. The tiara was sewn on to her hair

The bride and groom – Celine, aged 26, and Rene Angelil, aged 52, tie the knot

Celine and Rene Angelil

Will Smith and Celine at the 1991 American Music Awards.

Celine on stage wearing black leather pants and high-heeled boots

Celine, sleek and slender, performs in France in October, 1995 with yet another new look: lighter hair

Celine's 'Cher' look

CHAPTER 8

Silence is Not Always Golden

'I imagined that I was completely mute for life . . .'
– CELINE DION

B ecoming the best wasn't easy. Exhaustion was taking its toll on Celine. In one concert, in Sherbrooke, Quebec, less than a month after her appearance on *The Tonight Show*, Celine was on her third song when suddenly . . . silence. She had completely lost her voice. There was nothing but silence. A horrible fear gripped her soul.

Her voice was everything to her.

She had to leave the stage right in the middle of the concert . . . and she remained mute for three weeks. She had acute laryngitis, and she was exhausted. Celine had a forced rest where she would not utter a word. She communicated only through signs. Even the telephone receiver was equipped to signal the people calling. It wasn't the first time. Several years before, Celine had developed acute laryngitis during the course of her punishing schedule, and had to remain silent for fifteen days. 'I didn't even answer the telephone,' she recalls.

One of her greatest fears is that of harming her voice. Exhausted by a series of performances and promotional appearances in November

1990, one morning a pale and worn-out Celine awoke with a burning sensation in her throat. When she was advised to stop speaking – this time for five days – she again took the doctor literally, communicating with René and other family members only be means of sign language or notes scribbled on paper.

Her vocal cords were tired and irritated, and although they could always operate on her nodules Celine was terrified that an operation would change her voice forever. So she opted for a vow of silence instead. Absolute silence.

This was a very painful experience. And Celine explains what a difficult period it was for her: 'After a few hours without talking, I started telling myself stories . . . I imagined that I was completely mute for life. I was afraid and I cried.' When Celine was finally able to talk again, but at this point in her career she began a self-imposed discipline of remaining mute before and after performances and recordings – sometimes for two or three days at a time, just to rest her voice.

'These three-day periods are René's favourite times,' jokes Celine.

When Celine's throat problems continued to plague her in 1991, she went to see Dr Gwen Korovin, noted ear, nose and throat specialist of New York, who had treated Barbra Streisand, Luciano Pavarotti, Cher and even Frank Sinatra. The walls were covered with photos and thank you letters from celebrities.

At the doctor's, Celine would sit patiently, undergoing the torturous process of having a camera inserted down her throat. This was done regularly, just to be sure that her throat was in perfect working order, or to check on a past infection. She had to be completely calm for this, and keep her throat open and relaxed. It was easy for Celine to do – but not for some of her backing singers in later years, as Celine insisted on taking care of their vocal cord health as well.

If anyone cared about protecting her voice – it was Celine. She was harder, and more disciplined, with herself than any doctor could have been. Celine explained that keeping her voice in top form was what was expected from her. 'They pay me fortunes to sing – so taking care of my voice is the least I can do.'

Celine has a rigorous daily regime of singing exercises and warm-up exercises to stretch her vocal cords – a process that takes about half an hour. At the time, she also had to have at least twelve hours of sleep to be able to cope with all that was expected of her during the day. She practised and exercised, both body and soul, to reach ever greater heights.

Celine did her voice training exercises with an intensity that was astounding. She made all the sacrifices: she didn't drink, didn't smoke, and rarely ate meat. She ate small portions, and a lot of pablum (a nutritious, easily digestible babyfood cereal).

Every day, except when her doctor advised against it, she did the vocal exercises, that her singing teacher, a very old Parisian woman named Tosca Marmor, had prepared for her and put on a walkman. They were strange operatic-type voice exercises. In the morning, she talked little and in a very low voice, because Madame Marmor had told her that she mustn't force her voice in the morning.

Celine had a unique way of breathing while doing her vocal exercises and people overhearing her in the next hotel room at night would think the sounds emanating from her room were a little sensual. Some critics had once accused Celine of sounding rather nasal in the early years of her career. Whether Celine took this to heart or not (she says she doesn't read what the critics have to say), her vocal exercises and other forms of training paid off as her voice continued to improve, in terms of richness, clarity and stamina.

Recalls her sister Ghislaine, who used to sing as a backing singer in Celine's shows, 'After every show, we did what they called 'the vapours' or steam to humidify our vocal cords. Ordinarily, we put our heads over a bowl of very hot water and breathed in the steam. This time, Celine had the idea of sitting comfortably in the bathroom and running the shower with very hot water. All was well until, because of the heat and the humidity, the ceiling tiles started to become unglued and fell down almost on top of our heads. We laughed like crazy.'

But if Celine's naturally comical nature was the source of a lot of laughs from time to time, her meticulous attention to the health of her precious vocal cords was deeply serious. She had to have things just right at performance time. According to her brother Michel, who began working as assistant to the director of her tours, 'Before she arrives, I have to make sure that the temperature is ideal in her dressing room to ensure that her voice will not be affected.' Michel remarks, 'Even when we go out for supper together, during the time under the code of silence that she imposes on herself, since Celine does things to the maximum, she doesn't say hello.'

Interviewers waiting for her after a performance had to be quick. Usually, within a half-hour to an hour after a performance, she would stop talking and become totally mute until the next day at noon. She was once in the middle of doing an interview in her dressing room after a performance. 'Hurry up,' Maman had warned the journalist. 'Soon she won't be talking any more.' True to her word, when the time came, Celine wouldn't utter another word. She did continue the interview but communicated by making signs or by writing down her answers on a paper napkin.

It might make life awkward. Yet Celine often enjoyed these periods of silence. 'It gives other people a chance to talk to me. I just listen,' she says. Celine protected her voice at all costs and with a seldom-seen spirit of determination. Her self-discipline was remarkable.

CHAPTER 9

I'll Cry if I Want To

'I am a girl who is strong on stage, but once the curtain closes I feel like a little girl who is very weak and feeble. I don't believe I can ever unwind anywhere else like I can on stage.'

— CELINE DION

Celine had it all, it seemed. She had the proverbial world at her feet and was now considered an international star, something she had always yearned for.

'Where Does My Heart Beat Now' was a huge success and was constantly played on American radio. By 5 January 1991, it took its place in the charts and stayed there for twenty-four weeks, reaching fourth position on the *Billboard* Hot 100 Singles, and first position in Adult Contemporary Music in the *Radio and Records* magazine hit list. That month Celine had already made her third appearance on *The Tonight Show* in less than four months. In February, Celine joined Michael Bolton, Cindy Crawford, Wayne Gretsky, Whoopi Goldberg and many other celebrities who took part in the recording of the song and the video of 'Voices That Care', dedicated to the American soldiers fighting in the Gulf War. She had also been a presenter at the American Music Awards.

In May, Celine had important promotional tours in the Japanese cities of Tokyo, Osaka, Nagoya and Fukuoka, and on 19 June 1991 she celebrated her tenth anniversary in showbusiness with a massive concert at Montreal's Forum concert hall.

With the release of Celine's new English material, her popularity started to spread to the rest of Canada; while in Europe she was already scheduled to appear in Holland, Germany, England, Spain and Belgium, plus Asia. In the United States, it was as if Americans had just discovered her, even though at twenty-three she had already been singing professionally for ten years.

'It's a lot easier to generate an interest after having a hit in America,' said René. Celine's songs were played in over seventy stations in the United States, with over a million listeners per station, and starting to rival the success of Whitney Houston.

Yet life in the fast lane took its toll, and periods of serious depression sometimes overshadowed her life like a dark cloud. That cloud frequently resulted in floods of tears when journalists and interviewers asked her questions about happiness, love and her personal life.

The sacrifices were her own choice. But it wasn't easy. As Celine said, 'I do not have a normal life.'

The pressure on her was enormous. The transition from French to English, the time away from home, the sacrifices she was making . . . it was all much more painful for Celine than most people realized. At the time of her first English album's release, she had the same nightmare, six nights in a row. 'In the dream,' said Celine, 'I was on the ledge of a high-rise, with police cruisers and ambulances swirling below me. As a police officer moved closer in to grab me, I jumped and felt myself falling through the air. I awoke just before I was about to hit the ground.'

Celine cried. And cried. And cried. As she watched music specials of herself on television, she realized that what they said was true – she did cry very often.

In one series of television appearances, however, her tears were intentional. Celine made her acting debut starring as Elisa Trudel in a four-part television series called *Des fleurs sur la neige* (Flowers on the

Snow), the true story of an abused child. The series aired on a French-language television station in March 1991.

In the series, Celine played a young girl subjected to cruel treatment by her mother, her father, her mother's boyfriend, her foster family and, eventually, her boyfriend. The show echoed the growing awareness in the nineties of emotional, physical and sexual abuse, and Celine was acclaimed for playing such a difficult role.

But it was an exhausting experience. One evening, after a taping, Celine was so tired that she lost control of her car on the highway, going off the road and across the median. She emerged without serious injury but it was quite a scare. That night she spoke to René who was in Las Vegas. She begged him never to leave her alone again and he promised. But, with their hectic lifestyle, it was a promise that was difficult to fulfil.

In March 1991, on what should have been a wonderful twenty-third birthday in Paris, one of the most romantic cities in the world, throat problems plagued Celine and she was confined to bed, suffering from acute tonsillitis.

'I still always feel like crying,' confessed Celine less than a month later.

She described herself as feeling old, despite her mere twenty-three years. This was, according to Celine, 'The result of a life which had unravelled very quickly, without my having the time to live it. I am someone who is very emotional and my emotions have taken a blow.'

Her schedule was hectic, to say the least. This was a typical month in her life: 13 April, Philadelphia; 16 April, Washington, and an afternoon interview with USA Today; 17 April, New York; 18 April she recorded Good Morning America, which was aired on 19 April 1991. After the recording she left for Connecticut and returned to New York the same night; 19 April, Los Angeles, where she took some sun for two days; 22 April, she recorded a TV show; 23-24 April, she was in Kansas City; 25 April, Atlanta; 26 April, New York; 28 April, Pittsburgh; 29 April, Chicago; 30 April, Minnesota. On 1 May she returned to Montreal for a press conference, then back to New York the same night, then off to Nashville for a big performance; 4 May another show in LA; 5-16 May, Japan; 19 May, her Quebec tour began. When did Celine have time for herself?

The loneliness of not being with her family and the added pain of having to keep her love for her manager René Angelil a secret made a heavy load for such narrow shoulders.

She still did not admit that she was in love with René, a man twenty-six years her senior. Instead, she said that she considered René, who was about to turn fifty, like a father, brother, friend and confidant. He was her strength, the man who had been by her side since she was twelve. But the romance was a taboo subject. 'When we kept our love a secret and we would go to a restaurant for an intimate meal together, I would touch his hand and then see someone who might be looking, and I would have to turn away. It was really hard. It ruined the evening for me.'

While she may have confided in René or Maman or some of her siblings from time to time, for the most part Celine suffered her pain silently. She didn't want to burden her family, or René, with the sadness she felt. So she had no shoulder to cry on. 'I keep a lot of things inside me,' she says, 'even if I know it's not something I should be doing. By doing a lot for other people, my way of encouraging others is like therapy for me.' She didn't want other people to cry for her. She had made her choice and never regretted it, but she did find it difficult sometimes.

Celine pushed on and on. Her sister Ghislaine had been singing backing vocals for her, but after four years the arrangement was no longer working. Ghislaine was less reliable and definitely not as disciplined as Celine. It was in everyone's best interest for her to stop singing with the tour. Instead of gaining peace of mind from having a family member with her, this had only caused added stress for Celine.

Yet, after she no longer sang with Celine, Ghislaine remarked on what a beautiful time it had been. 'When we worked together we were really close to each other. I really loved the relationship we had at the time when I was her back-up vocalist. She was no longer Celine Dion the big star, but Celine, my sister, who I could talk to about my joy and my pain. We see each other less now since she has undertaken an international career, but despite this, we've stayed very close.'

Ghislaine was not the only troubled family member. Her brother Clement once had an addiction problem, but he recalls how supportive Celine was of him: 'My cherished memory is that Celine played a pivotal role in my life, on a very personal level. In 1991, when she phoned me from Paris to congratulate me on having successfully completed my course of treatment for detoxification and therapy, it was the most beautiful gift in the world in my eyes. She was the first to encourage me.'

But this bond with her family was something that Celine needed just as much as they did. 'Despite her extremely busy professional schedule, Celine does everything to keep close ties with members of the family and never forgets us . . . even when she's far away. She's down to earth, affectionate and generous,' says Clement.

Concealing her love for René troubled Celine greatly. She had given countless interviews, tears welling up in her eyes as she trembled with emotion, promising that she would soon reveal the identity of the man she loved. 'I am a girl who is strong on stage, but once the curtain closes I feel like a little girl who is very weak and feeble. I don't believe I can ever unwind anywhere else like I can on stage.'

It was a strange coincidence that Celine, who often felt despair at her lack of private life, and her feelings of loneliness, should meet the person who has since come to symbolize so many of these emotions – Princess Diana.

Celine and Diana had a lot in common, both having had the years sweep by without having a chance to live them, always going from commitment to commitment and often feeling sad, lonely and insecure.

Celine and Princess Diana met on 29 October, 1991 at the home of

Canada's former Prime Minister, Brian Mulroney and his wife Mila, after a concert performed in honour of Prince Charles and Princess Diana at the National Arts Centre in Ottawa, Canada's capital. Celine was one of the invited performers, and sang five songs, including 'Where Does My Heart Beat Now', a song Diana adored. Celine also sang in French.

The then Prime Minister's wife had suggested that Celine should appear at the concert. Canada's first lady was a big fan of Celine's. The two had met many times and Mila really loved Celine's talent . . . and her heart.

Celine and Mila Mulroney also had much in common. Both adopted the cause of the Cystic Fibrosis Foundation. Celine played the role of the Patron Celebrity of the Quebec Association at the time and Mila Mulroney was, in 1991, the Patron Celebrity for the Canadian Foundation, a role that Celine would take over several years later.

After the concert, a vehicle waited at the door of the Arts Centre to take them to the prestigious dinner for the 'guests of honour' Princess Diana and Prince Charles. It was held at the Prime Minister's residence, the famous 24 Sussex Drive.

It was a wonderful experience for Celine. In her black evening gown, with her long dark hair cascading down in ringlets, she was as elegant as a princess herself, as she conversed with the woman who was the embodiment of natural charm and the epitome of fashion.

That evening, Princess Diana was also radiant in a black V-neck dress with a stunning black choker necklace.

Suddenly, Celine had the surprise of her life! At the dinner table, they had reserved a place for her to the immediate right of Princess Diana. Completely taken aback, Celine tried to compose herself but her heart was pounding.

The dinner started promptly at 9.15. Celine sat down nervously beside the Princess and was still in such shock that she didn't utter a word for fifteen minutes. Then Diana broke the ice, turning to Celine and remarking that she had heard that she had a big family. Talking about her family was something Celine loved to do and she immediately started to relax. As they continued to talk, Celine gained more and more confidence and realized that the Princess, despite her rank, was a very genuine and likeable woman. Celine's worries had been unfounded.

Princess Diana, in turn, spoke of how much she loved Celine's 'extraordinary' voice.

'In the beginning, I wondered how everything would go,' Celine confessed, 'but the Princess put me quickly at ease.' Their conversation together continued throughout the dinner and Celine hardly noticed the dozen or so servers fluttering around the tables. Celine spent the entire evening beside the woman whose life had become public knowledge throughout the world since her marriage to Prince Charles.

It was just after eleven o'clock when the dinner drew to a close. Diana said that she hoped to see Celine in England one day and the two women, who had formed an immediate bond with each other, wished each other good luck. Then Princess Diana and Prince Charles said a final goodbye and left for the airport.

Celine found Diana incredibly warm and caring. 'She was very kind and down to earth,' remarked Celine. 'Shy, funny and very beautiful. She had a good word to say to everyone and a smile that was genuine.'

This was one of the most memorable events in Celine's life – forming a friendship with the magnificent Princess, a woman who personified natural radiance, even though it camouflaged her deep pain and unhappiness. Princess Diana's sadness and despair were revealed to the public the following year but, even as she tried to regain a 'normal' life after her divorce from Prince Charles in 1993, she continued to be the most photographed woman in the world right up until the day of her death six years after Celine had met her. Princess Diana's tragic death on 30 August 1997, in a high-speed getaway from the paparazzi, brought an outpouring of sorrow throughout the world, the like of which had never been seen before.

A package arrived for Celine from Buckingham Palace, several months after their encounter in 1991. It was just in time for Christmas: two photos of Celine and Princess Diana and Prince Charles from the office of Princess Diana. Celine would cherish this gift for the rest of her life.

After Celine met Diana, she had kept in contact with the Princess, and her death hurt her deeply. 'Princess Diana had told me that she would like to work on a project together for cystic fibrosis.' She suddenly looked very sad at the recollection . . . but Celine was no stranger to sadness.

On stage Celine was getting ovations that lasted almost as long as her songs. Off stage, her insecurity reared its head. 'I still feel small,' she had confessed. 'When I sing, I take myself seriously. I am like an actress and I have confidence in myself. But when I leave the stage, I become the fourteenth child of a big family.'

If she was sure of herself on stage – elsewhere in her life she was sure of nothing. It seemed that Celine was at an emotional crossroads. 'Deep inside I have dreams that don't go with me. I come from a very modest family and I have extravagant desires. I want to be rich and famous, possess lots of houses but I dream also of ironing the shirts of my husband and playing in a sandbox with my children.'

By now, Celine's reputation as Quebec's biggest star and her dream of reaching 'always higher' had seen her expand her market to English Canada, the United States and Europe. But her strongest emotional tie was always the one she had with her parents. 'There has never been anything more important in my life than my parents. I have sworn to myself that I will take advantage of every moment that I can spend in my life with my parents.' But those moments were getting fewer and farther between. Maman confessed sadly: 'She misses me enormously. She is almost never home any more.'

Celine admitted, 'Sometimes I feel lonely and I think it would be good to have a family member with me. But I couldn't accept the strain of someone trying to follow my work rhythm. I think about my family often.' Since the age of twelve she had given everything to her career, putting boyfriends and adolescent friendships aside and seeing less and less of her family in order to keep on progressing.

Even family members noticed the strain she was under. 'No one is sheltered from difficult times or depression,' said her sister Pauline. Celine missed her family desperately and didn't have a lot in common with friends. What would she talk about anyway? Another story about her career?

Her strict regime set her apart from others. As she said, 'It's not always fun – to always be disciplined like an athlete, to try and eat well, wake up early, follow singing lessons, dance lessons, and to not talk during the day so that my voice is at its maximum in performances.'

Her hit single, the powerful and emotional ballad 'Where Does My Heart Beat Now' (a song that talked about lonely hearts), seemed to sum up Celine's own feelings. 'I find it hard,' she revealed, 'and the better it goes, the harder I find it.'

A lot of this pressure was due to the fact that Celine was a perfectionist. She was constantly striving to do better than her last performance. So she worked incessantly, without leaving space for other things in her life. 'I always give the best of myself and this is sometimes tiring.'

There was no denying that the price she had paid for stardom was enormous. But even the pressure, stress and absence of a social life were not as hard for Celine as the invasion of her privacy. For this reason, she had an ever-present bodyguard, Eric Burrows, a massive, muscular ex-college football player who swept Celine by the crowds. You never knew when a 'fanatic', rather than a 'fan', could pose a threat. Even though Celine was open and trusting by nature, she always had to be on her guard. Now that she was in the public eye, even her smallest gesture would be spied upon. She was often surrounded by an army of photographers even at the most discreet of restaurants.

Fans knocked on her door endlessly. 'I feel I give them everything on stage, I would like to have a private life as well,' she pleaded.

Yet loneliness was something that constantly plagued Celine. Although she was surrounded by an entourage that adored her and fans that worshipped her, Celine was often in turmoil. 'If you only knew what passes in my head when I'm alone in my room!' she has said. 'I think I lead an intense life, like I wanted, but sometimes the price to pay is heavy and imposes great sacrifices.' She found it hard to talk to her parents or brothers or sisters about her career because they had already read about it in newspapers or seen her on stage.

Feeling alone so often, Celine described having long monologues with herself in front of the mirror, which became her closest confidant. 'I even invented characters, situations and scenarios, to have the feeling of sharing something with someone,' she confessed in an interview in 1991.

She also confessed in the same interview that, to help combat her loneliness, she had kept a daily diary for many years. However, this became a problem too, because when she had to write about some unhappy experience she had a habit of embellishing the actual event to make it correspond with how she wanted it to have been. She did this so often that eventually she had to stop keeping a diary because it no longer reflected her actual life. In ceasing to write her diary, Celine lost a valuable outlet, and found herself feeling alone once again.

Celine confessed that, 'There are also moments where, sitting on the edge of my bed, I start crying without reason. Tears roll down my face without me really knowing why. It's ridiculous, but it's like this.'

'I am not unhappy about what has happened to me,' she has said, 'because it's the life I wanted, but sometimes I can't help noticing that my dreams have happened in my life even before I had the chance to dream them.'

Celine is essentially a down-to-earth person. She has always been extremely generous, and very attentive to her entourage. She wants people to appreciate these traits in her personality. It means more to her to have people say what a nice person she is than to be told how beautiful her songs are.

'Deep down inside, what Celine wants is to be loved,' explains Maman. 'Since she was young we surrounded her and cherished her.' It was what Celine still needed.

Sometimes it appeared that there were two Celines: the meeker Celine with big dark-rimmed glasses and little make-up, and the Celine on the stage. The superstar.

And when she cried, she didn't always cry because she was sad or vulnerable, or depressed. Sometimes she cried just because she was so happy, and touched by the emotion she evoked in her audience.

This aspect didn't go unnoticed, as television interviewers remarked that Celine often cried when she sang. 'When I started to realize my dream, being a singer and being on stage to see people singing the words of my songs and looking at me . . . it touched me,' said Celine. 'I used to cry much more when I was younger because I couldn't control my emotions.'

Now she was trying to get a stronger grip – trying to be more composed and in control.

As Celine's career reached greater and greater heights, her life went at an increasingly fast pace. It was an exciting time but Celine was the first person to recognize the price she had paid for her success. 'I do all the things. I'm on a TV show . . . I'm on tour . . . I'm in a recording studio . . . I'm on a photo shoot . . .'

Events . . . people . . . places . . . rushing past her as if she were watching from a train window. 'It's like it goes so fast and I come home and I didn't have time to *live* it. I just did it.'

CHAPTER 10

The Fairytale Begins

'Being part of a classic might happen to you once in your life –
maybe never. For me, at twenty-four, it happened.'

– CELINE DION

When Celine was younger, she often pictured herself in a fairytale. Little did she know then that she would one day actually be living one, with the world's greatest fairytale creators: Disney. Singing a song on the *Beauty and the Beast* movie soundtrack was a brilliant career move for Celine. But, before her Disney fairytale begins, there is another tale to tell.

Once upon a time, Celine was supposed to sing the finale song 'Dreams to Dream' for Steven Spielberg's movie *An American Tail: Fievel Goes West*. Earlier, in July 1991, she was thrilled to have been chosen to sing the theme song for his animated film.

The previous theme song 'Somewhere Out There', from Spielberg's 1986 animated release *An American Tail*, was sung by Linda Ronstadt and James Ingram and won the Grammy Award for Best Film Song. James Horner had composed this song as well. And the producers predicted the same success for Celine – maybe even an Academy Award.

By the beginning of August, everything was on track. Celine was supposed to record the music video on 23 August, the record would be launched to the public in October, and Celine would participate in the promotional events leading up to the release. It was wonderful for Celine and she absolutely loved the song. She sang it everywhere, and couldn't get it out of her head. It was 'her' song.

But, for Celine, this was where her Spielberg fairytale ended. Suddenly Linda Ronstadt, who originally had not been interested in singing the song, said that she had changed her mind. The impossible happened. Steven Spielberg told the songwriter and producer to let Linda Ronstadt try the song. Celine's career was only just starting to flourish in the United States, so the director decided to play it safe and go with Ronstadt. The most painful moment came when René found out about it. It was a disaster. Celine would be broken-hearted. But there was hope for a while – songwriter James Horner did not like Linda Ronstadt's version of the song. Celine's version still had a chance. Yet, once again, fate was not on Celine's side. Ronstadt re-recorded the song and, this time, it was accepted. As James Horner puts it, 'Greater minds than myself felt she hadn't arrived.' It was over – a very unhappy ending for Celine.

But all was not lost. There must have been a fairy godmother looking out for Celine because she was about to enter the magical world of Disney.

The Disney Corporation announced that they wanted Celine to sing the theme song for their 1991 animated release of *Beauty and the Beast*. This was Disney's thirtieth animated feature. Set in France, the story revolved around the beautiful heroine Belle and her love for the hideous beast who had once been a prince. It was classic Disney.

When Celine was chosen to sing the duet with Peabo Bryson for the film's theme song 'Beauty and the Beast' it was the start of another fairytale – for the poor French Canadian girl from a family of fourteen children who aspired to win over the world through the magic of music.

Alan Menken's score and the lyrics by Howard Ashman were both whimsical and heart-warming, and the music for the film was a wonderful follow-up to that of Disney's highly acclaimed *Little Mermaid*, first released in 1989. Celine and Peabo Bryson's voices were in perfect harmony with each other as they recorded at the Walt Disney Music Company studios.

'I can say, without hesitation, having been chosen to sing the song for *Beauty and the Beast*, rather than *An American Tale II: Fievel Goes West*, like it was planned in the beginning, was a change in decision that literally permitted Celine's career to take on a whole other dimension,' says René, recalling the events that led up to the recording of 'Beauty and the Beast'. 'It's really this song that gave the precious momentum to Celine's career.' And the adventure had only just begun.

In autumn 1991, Disney offered the New York Film Festival a chance to see an unfinished print of *Beauty and the Beast* as a 'work in progress'. The *New York Times* theatre critic Frank Rich called it 'the best musical comedy score of 1991'.

The song was beautiful; the movie, a huge success. For Celine, it was a dream. Now it was as if she too had been sprinkled with some of that magic fairy dust. On 18 December, 1991, Celine signed a massive contract with Sony Music International – a 10 million dollar deal for five albums within ten years – the biggest recording contract in history for a Canadian artist. It was a huge triumph. But there was more – the 'Beauty and the Beast' theme song had been nominated for an Oscar at the Sixty-fourth Academy Awards. The biggest career event in Celine's life was to take place on 30 March, 1992, Celine's twenty-fourth birthday.

'The Oscars were a pretty big thing for me,' says Celine emotionally. 'I remember when I was very, very little, I watched all these big shows. I told everybody, "One day I would like to sing on that stage." I wanted to be a part of this. I kept dreaming about it and it happened.'

The Academy asked her to sing that night. Her performance would put her in the spotlight and make Celine Dion a household name. As Oscar night approached, the 16 March edition of the *Wall Street Journal* wrote that Celine Dion had 'a once-in-a-generation voice'.

Thus Celine found herself in Hollywood, on the day of her twenty-fourth birthday, surrounded by the biggest stars in the world. 'I was in the hotel in Los Angeles preparing myself and I was really nervous,' she remembers. . 'I thought to myself that it was truly wonderful that I was at the Oscars for my birthday. What a wonderful gift. But at the same time, the real gift for me is to be with my family and my parents.' She was suddenly filled with sadness. It was too bad that her parents weren't there. How she wished that they had been able to come . . . Her thoughts were interrupted by a knock at the door.

It was René. 'I have a gift for you for your birthday,' he said. Celine opened the door and her parents walked in. 'It's impossible,' Celine shrieked. 'They took the plane, travelled to Los Angeles, showed their passports – how could they do that alone without speaking English? I just couldn't imagine. My dad is my biggest fan. Every time he comes and sees me performing he gives me a standing ovation. My mom is very emotional inside . . . I love them so much.'

Celine was thrilled. But it was time to finish getting ready. Celine had joined the fashion big league, wearing a dress by New York designer Pamela Dennis, whose star-studded celebrity client list included Elizabeth Taylor, Whitney Houston, Cindy Crawford, Madonna and Michelle Pfeiffer. This was what fairytales were made of. International designers Chanel and Armani had offered her a dress for the gala as well, but there was always next time. For tonight, Celine had chosen a black close-fitting, low-cut dress with spaghetti straps in a silhouette that accentuated her slim 5 foot, 7 inch figure.

The Academy Awards took place at the Dorothy Chandler Pavilion and *Beauty and the Beast* had been nominated for six of the awards, including Best Picture (a first for an animated film). The film was also nominated for Best Original Musical Soundtrack as well as Best Original Song. Out of the five songs nominated, an unprecedented three Oscar-nominated songs were from Disney's *Beauty and the Beast* film, including the theme song, 'Beauty and the Beast', as well as 'Be Our Guest' and 'Belle', all composed by Alan Menken with lyrics by Howard Ashman.

This night was a dream for Celine. Soon she would be on stage, singing in front of an estimated two billion television viewers across the world, from forty-seven countries. As ecstatic as she was, Celine points out that 'Singing the song from *Beauty and the Beast* at the Oscars was hard.' She was in awe of the stars – mesmerized by Tom Cruise and Michael Douglas . . . 'They are even more beautiful in person,' said an enamoured Celine. 'The one who made the biggest impression on me was Paul Newman. He has those eyes. When I came across Elizabeth Taylor in the elevator, I was flabbergasted. She is very small and beautiful beyond belief. All that I could see was her eyes. And you should have seen the security guards around her! My parents and I, we couldn't believe it!'

There was no denying how nervous she suddenly felt. While they were putting the final touches to Celine's make-up, René found himself in another room, equally overwhelmed by the big stars. 'I felt like a real groupie,' he explained. 'I told myself that Celine had to see this. I didn't even consider the fact that she might be having stage fright and I went to get her to come and take a look at all the stars.'

Just before Celine was about to sing, she became terrified. 'I was backstage and I couldn't breathe. My hands were so cold and I was sweating and freezing! I could my knees go "clack, clack, clack", banging together. I heard the man saying 'Beauty and the Beast' – please welcome Celine Dion and Peabo Bryson to sing the song!'

'I took a big breath and I went on stage. I could barely walk. My dress was *sooooo* tight,' recalls Celine.

'I was scared, but I went and started to sing.' Angela Lansbury joined in at the beginning of the song and then stood off to the side. 'Then I opened my eyes and I was in front of the stage and I just couldn't believe it. Barbra Streisand was just there!' (Her idol, right in front of her in the audience!) 'Then I started to sing, and I wanted to do something but I was on camera.' Celine described feeling an overwhelming urge to say something to Barbra, during her song, like 'Hi, I love your music.' But she sang on. Celine stood tall and sang dramatically, her long dark wavy hair cascading down over her shoulders, her hands moving in emotional gestures. If she was nervous, no one would have known it. All that emotion blended perfectly with Peabo Bryson's rich baritone voice.

When the song was finished, Celine, Peabo and Angela smiled on as they drew thunderous applause from the audience.

The award for Best Original Song came just after midnight. Its presenters were Liza Minelli and Shirley Maclaine. For Celine, the night was magical. The Oscar went to 'Beauty and the Beast'.

The team of Alan Menken and Howard Ashman earned the Academy Award for the title song 'Beauty and the Beast'. Lyricist Howard Ashman had died of the AIDS virus shortly before the film's release and was awarded an Academy Award posthumously.

Afterwards, Celine's performance was noted by other film producers. 'We received at least fifteen offers for Celine to sing film theme songs,' commented René.

Celine summed up the whole experience this way: 'Some people have said, that 'Beauty and the Beast' will be with me for the rest of my life. I'm proud. I hope it's going to be with me for the rest of my life. It's a classic and being part of a classic might happen to you once in your life, maybe never. For me (at twenty-four) it happened!'

Disney continued to produce many more blockbuster animated movies, like *The Lion King*, *Pocahontas*, *Toy Story*, *Hunchback of Notre Dame* and *Hercules*, starting in that very year, 1992, with the magic carpet ride of *Aladdin*, whose music would win two Academy Awards as well.

Meanwhile, Celine was on a magic carpet ride of her own.

CHAPTER 11

Love Can Move Mountains

'Remember the name because you will never forget the voice.
One of the strongest ballad singers in pop music today.'

– JAY LENO

T he fairytale was just beginning. Basking in the glory of an Oscar-winning song the day after the Academy Awards was the perfect time for Celine to launch her second English album – right on the set of *The Tonight Show*. It was her fifth appearance on the most celebrated of American talk shows.

It was 31 March 1992 and Jay Leno was the guest host that night.

'The first time I went on the show I was very nervous,' recalls Celine. 'The second time I had started to get friendly with *The Tonight Show* staff. By the fifth time I was part of the family!'

Celine's new album – her eleventh in ten years – was simply called *Celine Dion* and was launched with the slogan: 'Remember the name because you will never forget the voice.'

The Tonight Show marked the launch of this new album to the American market. The album had already been introduced in Canada, and in a couple of weeks, on 15 April, it would be distributed worldwide.

The album was a masterpiece, including Celine's first rhythm and blues number, 'Love Can Move Mountains', which soon became the inspirational song of the year. Celine became the darling of the talk-show circuit and was asked to sing the song over and over again.

'Beauty and the Beast', which was on Celine's album, was already a huge hit as well as the film's soundtrack. The *Celine Dion* album was recorded in New York, San Francisco and Quebec, over a four-month period of painstaking work. The powerhouse producers who worked on it included Walter Afanasieff, who had worked with Mariah Carey and Whitney Houston, and Ric Wake who had produced for Natalie Cole, as well as Guy Roche and Humberto Gatica.

Great collaboration included a ballad called 'With This Tear', written for Celine by Prince, before he was known as 'The Artist Formally Known as Prince' and well before he called himself simply 'The Artist'. Celine recalls that when she first spoke to him on the phone, 'The fan came out of me. He talked little, and I felt obliged to fill in the silence and I talked and talked. When the conversation ended I was convinced that I made a fool of myself.' Celine was very sensitive and still had a tendency to hero-worship other stars.

Also on the album was 'If You Asked Me' by Diane Warren (originally sung by Patty LaBelle) as well as 'Water From the Moon', 'Nothing Broken But My Heart', and Kenny G. on saxophone in the song 'Halfway to Heaven'.

An exhausted but exhilarated Celine arrived back in Montreal the day after appearing on *The Tonight Show*. She was greeted by throngs of fans and deafening cheers, and all the press people awaiting her at Montreal's Dorval airport took her by surprise. But it wasn't an April Fool's joke. Celine *was* a superstar – even if she didn't feel like one yet. Wearing large black-framed glasses (Celine is short-sighted), she posed for photographers and met fans who showered her with flowers and had prepared a moving plaque in her honour. Celine reminisced about the greatest night of her life at the Academy Awards. 'You can't even dream about what has happened to me.'

'The timing had been perfect,' added René. 'The Oscars one night and then the launch of her record to the American market on *The Tonight Show*. The appearance of Celine at the Academy Awards represents, for me, the number one point of her international career. You've seen nothing yet,' beamed a confident manager.

Sony Music presented their protégé with an immense birthday cake in honour of her twenty-fourth birthday, also announcing that 350,000 copies of the new *Celine Dion* album had already been sold – and it had only just been released!

Even the album cover was different from any of her previous ones: a beautiful sunlit photo of Celine in a dreamy pose. Recalls Celine, 'The photo was completely improvised and what we see is my reflection in the mirror of an apartment while I was waiting for my hairdresser.' She happened to be sitting close to an open doorway so the sun was shining directly down on her bare legs – one of her best features.

In April, Celine was back in the United States, for a massive marketing push that would take her to many cities. In New York alone, she was working nineteen hours a day promoting the new album, and staying in lavish hotel suites. Celine was now the epitome of glamour – a pale yellow Chanel jacket and black pleated skirt for daytime interviews, and elaborate eveningwear from the cream of Paris *haute-couture* designers. With her tall, slender frame, she wore clothes well. And on her high heels, she often appeared to stand a regal 6 feet tall.

Being 'Queen Celine', as she was crowned by Canada's *Maclean* magazine, meant getting up at five o'clock in the morning, doing her beauty routine of setting her hair in red Velcro rollers, and her own, painstakingly perfect make-up. Radio show appearances, interviews with music critics . . . radio stations . . . telephone interviews, dinner parties . . . Celine took it all in her stride.

Always at her side was René, who she describes as almost never without his cellular phone, talking, dealing, arranging and reading *Billboard* magazine. The single 'If You Asked Me To' was already in the Top Twenty and climbing. All the talk shows wanted her – *Good*

Morning America, Entertainment Tonight . . .

'It's starting,' nodded René, as if clairvoyant, seeing the months to come . . . when *Arsenio* and *Live with Regis and Kathie Lee* would all clamour for Celine.

'Celine was a public relations dream,' says Terry Cone, of Epic Records in New York, Sony's label in the United States. She answered every question and often gave almost twice the time allotted for the interview, unless, of course, it was after a performance and she was not talking any more. When Celine decided to go mute to protect her voice, that was it. Then she would use a type of sign language or scrawl her answers, but she would not say a word.

One night in New York heads turned as Celine walked into a lavish dinner party on the Upper East Side, wearing a skin-tight black jumpsuit with rhinestones. Radio executives and magazine editors were invited and they found her charming. Celine 'had arrived'.

Big news. Michael Bolton wanted Celine to tour with him for a month, as the opening act for his *Time, Love & Tenderness* 25-city American tour that summer. It was a great opportunity. She agreed.

Celine and René continued travelling from city to city during the promotional campaign, and it was hectic and stressful for both of them. René was always planning, orchestrating and – very often – over-indulging in rich food.

They were in Santa Monica, California, on 29 April. 'We were all packed and ready to leave the hotel but we still had time so we went to the pool. Naturally René was on the phone, busy talking and planning,' Celine explains. René told her that he felt pain in his back. She rubbed his back for him, thinking that he was just overworked or had strained some muscles.

René went up to his hotel room to rest. Celine recalls it vividly. 'He said he was too hot. I was still at the pool, sipping my iced tea, but I felt something was wrong. I went up to the room. He was on the bed and he couldn't breathe . . . his face was so white! I called the hotel operator and said . . . "He's having a heart attack! Send an ambulance!" They said the Mount Sinai Hospital was only a block away so I brought him down in the elevator and took him there by taxi.'

'I was strong for him. I looked at him and said, "You're going to be okay." But once we were at the hospital emergency I screamed, "He's having a heart attack!" Everybody looked at me. I was still in my bathing suit. I had been strong until they told me to just wait outside the room. There was nothing I could do. Then I started shaking like a leaf. I wasn't cold. I was so scared. After, René called all his kids to tell them he loved them. René was going to be okay but I had to leave for New York right away to do a series of talk shows. It was the hardest time in my life,' says Celine.

The degree of Celine's reliance on René was evident later on in New York, when she discovered in the hotel lobby that she had neither the number nor the key to her suite. 'I have never checked into a room myself. I don't even know how to order room service,' Celine agonized. Before, René had always been with her. He woke her up, ordered her breakfast, took care of the luggage, tips and registering in hotels. 'I did absolutely nothing,' she lamented. 'I only had to think of singing, without worrying about all this.' Now Celine had to take charge. For the first time, at twenty-four, she had to deal with her own career and all the harsh realities of life.

While René recuperated with drugs and a new diet, he travelled less and less with her for a while. Celine didn't want him to over-exert himself after his heart problems. 'I knew that if I wanted to keep René for a long time, I had to accept to have him less often at my side on trips. We travel a lot and this represents a stress.' Celine revealed her greatest fear when she said: 'I'm afraid of losing those close to me. I hope René lives for 150 years! It was when he had his heart attack that I really knew how precious he was for me. I had already appreciated what he did but I really became aware of all his value and his importance. It has also made me take on more responsibilities.'

But, for Celine, this was still very difficult. On 14 May 1992, Celine received her first World Music Award in Monte Carlo, as the Best-Selling Female Canadian Artist. By June 1992, René was still at home recuperating in Montreal and Celine had to continue on a promotional tour in Europe. Although her mother had accompanied her on the trip, Celine was interviewed in Paris as saying, 'René is the engine of my life, and, without him, there are things I simply can't figure out.'

Celine's career was thriving and her songs were playing everywhere – yet she felt sadder than ever. 'Celine Finds Fame Difficult to Deal With' was one newspaper headline. It seemed that she had everything going for her. Except happiness.

Celine was constantly between flights, often suffering from jet lag, stress, pressure, fatigue and tonsillitis. 'I've never had as much need for "air" and I've never had so little of it,' she said. All this made her vulnerable, yet she drove herself harder than anyone else could: 'It's hard but I don't live in the past. I don't have the intention of resting on my performance at the Academy Awards on March 30th, 1992, and on five appearances on *The Johnny Carson Show*. I don't want my life to end there. I don't want to reach thirty years old and still live with the memory of the Oscars. Today, it's this . . . But tomorrow, I want there to be something more. I want to go farther.'

CHAPTER 12

French . . . The Language of Love?

'I am not political. I am music.'

– CELINE DION

F rench – the language rolls off the tongue like poetry. The deep French cultural roots in Quebec go back over three hundred years and Celine has always said that her French heritage occupies the deepest place in her heart. Maintaining a passionate fan base amongst French Canadians, while, at the same time, building a reputation as the world's hottest female vocalist in English has not been easy. Not only has Celine had the challenge of coming out with hits in both languages, but she has been faced with an even greater predicament – politics. Quebec's 'highly charged' political situation has been in the world spotlight many times over the years. Its 7.5 million population is approximately 80 per cent French-speaking (or Francophone), with English (or Anglophone) as the minority. The province's largest city, Montreal (with a population of 3.3 million), is the largest French-speaking city in the world, after Paris. In Montreal, there is a real polarization of views between the French (the majority) and the English citizens.

During the first hundred years of Canada's confederation, up until 1967, English was accepted as the primary language throughout

Montreal, Quebec and Canada. But by the seventies many French Canadians were starting to voice the belief that Quebec should be a separate, French-speaking state., independent of the rest of Canada. After all, the President of France, Charles De Gaulle, visiting Quebec in the sixties, had declared: 'Long live a free Quebec.' It appeared that France supported the idea of Quebec separating from the rest of Canada, but to others this was unthinkable.

The tension came to a head in the 'October Crisis' in 1970, when members of the Quebec Liberation Front, trying to gain attention for the separatist movement, set off letter bombs and kidnapped two government officials, British Trade Commissioner, James R. Cross, and Quebec Labor Minister Pierre Laporte. The murder of Laporte sparked fear and panic among both the English and French-speaking populations. The Prime Minister at the time, Pierre Elliot Trudeau, sent Federal troops into Montreal and declared Martial Law during the month of October.

The province's separatist Part Québécois (PQ) party came into power in 1976 with Premier René Lévesque (who, in 1980, called the first 'yes' or 'no' vote for the province's separation from the rest of Canada). The answer was 'Non!' – the people of Quebec wanted to stay part of Canada. But tensions remained high, with new institutions such as the French language office (nicknamed by the English population 'the French language police'), who saw to it that all official correspondence, shop signs, street names and so on, would be in French.

The referendum would come up again years later, when Parti Québécois premier Jacques Parizeau was in power, again reaching a 'No' vote for separation, although this time the vote was a close one. It would remain a highly contentious issue in 1995 when Lucien Bouchard took over as leader of the PQ.

Yet it was not always a case of French versus English. Many French-speaking citizens did not agree that Quebec should separate from the rest of Canada. Opinions were split down the middle. This controversy touched the lives and emotions of each and every person living in Quebec.

And Celine was no exception. All she wanted to do was sing and be loved. 'I am not political. I am music,' she said. However in 1992 Celine was in the public eye in Quebec – not for her singing but rather for her apparent support of a united Canada. To commemorate Canada's 125th birthday, on 1 July 1992, Celine joined the massive celebration which was being held on Parliament Hill in Ottawa, the capital of Canada, before Queen Elizabeth herself.

Celine was not actually there in person. She was away at the 1992 Universal Exposition in Seville, Spain, but she joined the celebration direct via satellite transmission.

An uproar ensued because, on that particular Canada Day, Celine sang the Canadian national anthem 'Oh Canada' and declared that Quebec's political separation from Canada would be 'terrible'. She openly expressed her own desire for a united Canada, one in which both English and French cultures could live together, side by side. And she cited the example of Switzerland, where three cultures live together in peace and harmony.

Celine's comments caused a furore in the media. Article after article either criticized her or sided with her. Even her mother, who had raised fourteen children, scolded her and reminded her that: 'When you have fourteen around the table, there could be fourteen different opinions. Not talking politics is the best way to avoid arguments. To each his own I always say, but never discuss politics.'

Over a month later, Celine was still the subject of controversy. She tried to put it behind her, saying 'What counts for me is love and music.' But, without wishing to offend anybody, Celine still wanted to explain her declaration. 'My position has never changed. I am against separation but I will stay *Québécoise* to the end. What I want is respect for the two cultures in a united Canada, that we continue to speak French and that Quebec attains its due.'

This was a time that caused Celine a great deal of pain. 'I find it hard,' she confessed afterwards to a Quebec journalist, tears forming in her eyes. 'I have never found it as difficult as today. I feel like a little girl and yet, I realize very well that I can no longer make mistakes. I must always be *good*.'

Celine was back in Quebec in August 1992, but the controversy took a long time to go away. Being a politician did not suit her. The Canada Day incident was not a mistake; it was a lesson. Now she knew that talking politics was not desirable for her career. At twenty-five, Celine reflected on what had happened: 'The incident in Seville took on immeasurable proportions, I didn't want to implicate myself politically, I only wanted to express myself but I didn't know the consequences of gestures like this one. Now I know. I have learned to be careful. I no longer talk of politics.'

Celine had a new doctrine: 'I talk music, not politics.' And she made a firm distinction between the two. 'Music is a means of international communication.' Celine had no intention of being mixed up in a political debate that had nothing to do with music and her career. But the whole experience still had a deep impact on her.

'I find it difficult not to have the right to make a mistake. It's hard, the life I live presently,' said a tearful Celine. 'Sometimes, I have the impression of rambling on like an old person. People always ask me to recount what I've experienced up to now, while, for me, what has passed, has passed. I live for tomorrow, not for yesterday.'

Celine's 'tomorrows' had included her dream of success in the United States. She had set her career off in a new direction by recording in English and appealing to the American market. The *Celine Dion* album received a massive push from Sony to capitalize on Dion's higher-than-ever profile in the United States. And part of that push meant dropping the usual French accent on the 'e' in Celine's name. Written in French as Céline, the accent on the 'e' gives the letter an 'aye' sound, which means that her name is actually pronounced 'Saylin'. Now, on all her English material, she would use simply 'Celine'.

Even this change led to tongues wagging in Quebec, and debate over whether or not Celine was becoming 'too English'. It seemed that even taking off the accent in her name could lead to controversy. Yet Celine took it all in her stride: 'What's the difference . . . it's *my* name.'

She had gone to great lengths to learn the English language. According to René, 'If you are going to sing in English then you have to understand it.' As a result, she had a surprisingly perfect English accent when she sang. However, when she recorded her first English album, she admits that her command of spoken English was shaky. And, by her second album in 1992, Celine was still having some difficulty with English-speaking interviewers and members of the music industry. 'When people make jokes in English, I laugh because I want to be nice. But sometimes I don't understand everything or else I really want to say something but it doesn't come out as well as I want.'

In French, Celine was known for her passion, wit and great sense of humour. She was completely at ease with the audience. Her French material was passionate and provocative, as in the *Dion chante Plamondon* album (Dion Sings Plamondon), 1991, later released in France under the title *Des mots qui sonnent* (Words That Ring). The album featured the complex, pop-rock rhythms of Quebec composer Luc Plamondon with such hit singles as *'Ziggy'* and *'Je danse dans ma tête'*.

Celine's English songs were often romantic ballads and musically they were sensational. But, in concert, she was less at ease when it came to conversing with the audience in English. It would take years to perfect her style. In the meantime, it was a tough challenge. 'I have to pretend I am a strong person. But really I am afraid of making a mistake,' she admitted.

Celine was always proud of her heritage as a French Quebecer and saw nothing wrong with pursuing her dream of a career in the United States. She kept up a balance of English and French album releases, to appeal to both language groups. But when she first embarked on her English singing career, there was a price to pay.

The incident occurred after the release of her first English album, *Unison*, in 1990. Celine had already won Quebec music awards for her work in French almost every single year. But then, at the Twelfth annual ADISQ awards gala, she was presented with the award for Anglophone Artist of the Year. Celine refused the award and it was the beginning of her first politically charged scandal.

Celine had been put in an impossible position, because of the importance of her French language and heritage and also because of the rising political tensions in Quebec. While she had expanded her horizons to include the English market, she felt she had to refuse the award because it was unfair to be labelled as an English performer.

This scandal had far-reaching effects. 'I didn't even want to touch the trophy,' said Celine, even though her sister Claudette had been on stage to present the award to her. In declining the trophy, Celine emphasized, 'It's not a politically motivated gesture.' But politics was politics, and English Canadians felt insulted over her refusal of the trophy.

René's colleague, Ben Kaye, who often spoke to the English media about Celine's career at the time, tried to ease the situation, but René was angry with the show organisers. 'It was a poisonous trophy. Celine had recorded only one album in English at the time. She is not an Anglophone artist because of this.'

As René recalls, 'They wanted to teach us a lesson because Celine sang in English. I was furious. Celine was furious. We refused the trophy. You can never convince me that a true artist only wants to succeed in Quebec. Those that say the contrary are jealous.' Afterwards, once they had explained that the wording of the award had put them in a no win situation, their message came across loud and clear.

The next year, Celine attended the Quebec awards gala and shocked the audience, appearing in an androgynous 'Victor Victoria' outfit. Her hair was slicked back in a 1920s style, that gave it an almost black lacquered look. She wore a man's suit, shirt and tie, and dramatic eye make-up and lipstick, as she sang her number, *'Les Blues du Businessman'* (The Businessman Blues).

That evening, Celine won another award that she did accept, but the wording of the award had been carefully changed to read, 'The Quebec Artist who has been the Most Successful in a Language Other than French.' Celine declared: 'I hope you will always be proud of the way I represent you outside Quebec.' She had had enough of politics.

CHAPTER 13

The Sky is the Limit

*'There could never be a movie about Celine's life. Nobody would
believe it.'*

— RENE ANGELIL

Despite her physical and emotional fatigue, Celine was preparing to appear as the opening act for Michael Bolton's Time,
Love & Tenderness Tour, while promoting her new *Celine Dion*
album. She confessed, 'I could use a week of vacation, but not now . . .
not yet.' For now, she had to work.

Celine opened for the Michael Bolton tour in sixteen cities — it was
her first tour in the United States. Beginning in mid-July 1992, there
were twenty-five concerts and Celine sang 'Beauty and the Beast' as well
as 'Where Does My Heart Beat Now'. 'For them, I am a newcomer.
They were surprised that my show was so professional. They didn't
even know that I had been on stage for eleven years,' she said from her
hotel room in Indianapolis on 11 August 1992. Celine opened in
Toronto for 30,000 people on 25 August. It was a great experience for
her and Michael Bolton was a hot topic.

'He's gorgeous . . . I love him,' gushed Celine. 'The last show that I
did, I was about to sing my last song and the music wasn't starting and I
was worried a little bit. And then I looked at the audience and nobody
was looking at me anymore. So I looked. Michael Bolton came on stage

with this *beautiful* suit, no shirt under, with twenty-four red roses and he gave those flowers to me. I didn't smell the flowers. I smelled him!'

Meanwhile, the *Celine Dion* album was climbing higher and higher. It was already gold, selling more than 500,000 copies in the United States, and it appeared on *Billboard* charts for eighteen weeks in a row.

Already top music stores in the United States, such as Sam Goody's in New York, had life-size displays of Celine's photo. She was heavily involved in promoting the album and would be performing on 15 August 1992 in Montreal. Later that autumn, and after shows in Quebec and Ottawa, Celine was on her way to Australia, Japan, and Switzerland (where Sony was holding their big International Convention that year).

Whereas most singers have one show, Celine actually had to create three separate shows, depending on her audience (a mostly English performance for the United States, a primarily French show for many parts of Quebec as well as France, and a show for other countries which combined English and French songs).

It wasn't easy and the pressure on her was tremendous. But her career was on a roll and the Celine machine had to stay in motion, with René orchestrating every move. Amid all the excitement, Celine confessed to experiencing bouts of depression. 'It's hard the life I lead,' she often said. 'You have to be made for this type of life. I think you have to have it in your blood.'

Yet, despite constant fatigue and frequent episodes of acute laryngitis, Celine was not one to complain. 'I am perfectly happy in what I do. I work hard, it's true, by my situation is far from being as alarming as some people may believe.'

Celine was humorous on talk shows – they brought out the natural clown in her. She even made fun of the way people always mispronounced her name, calling her 'Celinnnnne Diiooooonnnnnne'. 'It's incredible. Sometimes I feel like I'm 'Salon Selective,' she joked. Like Whoopi Goldberg once, she was reading the cue card and said, 'Please welcome Sealon Dealon'. 'I have a French name and people have trouble pronouncing it.' (Actually, her name is pronounced 'Cell-in Dee-on' with the 'on' very soft, and the 'n' hardly pronounced.)

The three topics the talk shows were really interested in were her family, her English and her love life. Just before Christmas 1992, Celine was a guest on *Live with Regis and Kathie Lee*. When they asked about her love life, Celine confessed, for the first time on national television, that she had had a boyfriend for six years.

'Six years!' exclaimed Regis.

Suddenly Celine looked uncomfortable. 'I mean . . . we don't . . . sometimes he comes on tour with me. Sometimes not. We don't see each other every day, that's for sure. Maybe that is the reason why we are so close and we love each other so much. Because we miss each other, and that's great.'

'She's a passionate French Canadian!' affirmed Regis.

'Yes,' agreed Celine. It was getting harder and harder to conceal her love, because she *wanted* to tell the world. But it was not the time. Instead, she focused on a career that kept reaching new heights of technical and musical virtuosity. She was shifting away from the image of the over-protected child star. Her clothes were different and her style was different. Now she grasped the microphone in her left hand and gestured expressively with her right. Large, dramatic movements were slowly becoming her trademark.

On the set of *The Tonight Show* on 8 December 1992, Jay Leno introduced her as 'One of the strongest ballad singers in pop music today'.

Celine took control of the microphone as if it belonged to her. There was no question about it – she connected with the audience in a big way. 'I want to touch everybody . . . to be loved by everybody,' Celine had once said . . . 'I need to connect. It's what music is all about for me.' Millions of viewers all felt the same thing – Celine had *emotion*.

Celine felt that she was just beginning to know herself. She was no longer playing the role of a great star. She *was* the star.

In 1992 Celine received a gold record for the *Celine Dion* album in the

US to mark sales of 500,000. This was her second gold record in the United States and the soundtrack of *Beauty and the Beast* was now a platinum record.

It was almost time for a break, something that Celine looked forward to tremendously. After her appearance on *Good Morning America* on 21 December 1992, she was back home for Christmas. By now Celine had almost thirty nieces and nephews and there was a huge celebration. 'It's the best day,' she explained. 'Everyone's excited because it's the only day during the year that everybody in the family can be all together.' Dion-style that is. 'We are about sixty people, all family, and my mom cooks for everyone. We eat in shifts, and at two in the morning some people are still eating turkey and meat pie! It's a wonderful time. My father plays the accordion and everybody dances.' These were moments that Celine truly cherished.

It was the start of a new year. If 1992 had been the year of the talk-show circuit for Celine, 1993 would be the year when she truly seemed to be moving mountains, not only in her career, but in her personal life as well.

If there was ever a symbol of Celine's having realized her American dream, her invitation to participate in one of two galas celebrating the inauguration of William Jefferson Clinton to the Presidency of the United States had to be it. The events leading up to the day he took that oath would be watched all over the world. Celine found out in mid-December and, according to her wonderful 'behind-the-scenes-man' Ben Kaye, who is involved in public relations, publishing and just about every other aspect of her career, 'When the White House gets down to the list of artists that the future President likes, it's a big honour.' Celine was thrilled.

She was to perform on 19 January 1993, a historic day at the 'celebration of youth' investiture gala, featuring young talent at the Kennedy Center in Washington.

For the gala event, Celine sang 'Love Can Move Mountains' which was expected to top worldwide sales of two million by January. Her performance was outstanding and she was personally congratulated by First Lady Hillary Clinton. The event would also be shown on the Disney channel. 'It was a thrill,' remarked Celine. 'But especially, if someone asks you to sing and you are not from the United States, and they ask you to come and join the family of the United States, the American people, to share a very important moment, it's special. It's a big honour.'

Now the world was an open book for Celine and the pages unfolded to tell a story of success. Love had truly moved mountains for this simple girl from a small rural community but many once-in-a-lifetime experiences still lay ahead for Celine.

On 25 January 1993 Celine participated in The *American Music Awards*, televised on ABC, as an award presenter and entertainer. Celine and Peabo performed the theme song from *Beauty and the Beast* in a venue that offered a professional, high-energy show with great music and spectacular sets.

Celine, dressed in white, made a huge impact with the Disney song. Before coming on stage she was a little nervous but when she appeared she was feeling very proud to be the first Quebecer to sing at the prestigious American Music Awards.

After the show, an article in the *Los Angeles Times* said that Whitney Houston's most serious rival wasn't Natalie Cole, who did well at the American Music Awards, but . . . 'that French girl from Canada'. For Whitney, there was no doubt that Celine (whose popularity was growing every day) would be the singer to watch during the next year – she believed the producers of *Beauty and the Beast* had had good reason to choose Celine to sing the theme song.

'I would like to be loved by everybody in the world, singing everywhere, and getting married and having children,' said Celine. This was her dream.

'A singer wants to sing the best way she can. Conflicts, competition, all the stories, it's the press that makes this up,' said René Angelil. It seemed that Celine was really only in competition with herself, always trying to better her last performance.

But, despite all her success, Celine could never have expected the phone call she got while she was vacationing in Aruba. She was in her hotel room when she found out that she had been nominated for *three* Grammy Awards.

The trophies were already lining up. Now it was the Grammys. The next few weeks went by in a blur, and, before Celine knew it, the annual gala of music and song had arrived. The Thirty-fifth Grammy Awards were held at the Shrine Auditorium in Los Angeles in February. As one of the most prestigious galas in the world (along with the Academy Awards), the Grammys, presented by The National Academy of Recording Artists and Sciences was the most visible symbol of achievement in music. For days before, she had had butterflies in her stomach.

Celine was nominated for: Best Female Vocalist, Category Pop; Best Album for *Celine Dion*; and Best Duo Recording, with Peabo Bryson for 'Beauty and the Beast'. The musical score soundtrack of the movie was also nominated in four other award categories.

Celine was ranged against k.d. lang, Annie Lennox, Mariah Carey and Vanessa Williams for Best Female Vocalist of the Year. Even though the award went to k.d. lang, Celine was happy just to be in their league.

Numerous awards had been given out off-air before the Grammy Awards were televised. 'I was in the audience at the pre-show,' said Celine, 'and I decided to sit down quite far in the audience, because I said, "I'm going to let all the artists who are pretty sure to win (sit closer)." ' Although elated, Celine was sure at the time that she wouldn't be one of the winners, 'I sat far away . . . I just wanted to be a part of it. When they say the "nominees are" it's going to be nice to hear my name,' she thought.

So, when they announced that Celine Dion and Peabo Bryson had won the Grammy for Best Pop Performance by a Duo or a Group, it came as a total surprise to Celine. 'When they called out my name, I stood up and then I was so far in the audience it took so long to come in with the dress and everything.' Her dress was so tight that she could hardly walk. 'The announcer said "She's not here."' But, as Celine recalls, 'I said, shouting loudly and waving my arms, "I'm coming . . . I'm coming!"' That night Celine performed 'Beauty and the Beast' with Peabo Bryson.

After the Awards, Disney went all-out with a big party for *Beauty and the Beast*. And Celine was finally able to relax. 'I'm very happy this show is over,' she said, describing how her heart was still pounding from the excitement. 'I'm going to dream good dreams tonight.'

And the dreams continued. On 20 March 1993, Celine received the *Billboard International Creative Achievement Award*, to mark her achievement around the world.

The following day, at the Canadian equivalent of the Grammy, the Juno Awards, Celine won four Juno Trophies and she was the host of the twenty-second gala held on 21 March 1993 in Toronto. This was the first time she had hosted a show.

Explains René, 'Those around strongly advised me not to accept the proposition. There was a risk. Celine had never hosted a show in English. But I thought, if it works we will win over her career in Canada.' Celine triumphed. But then, just as her career was starting to soar, tragedy struck.

CHAPTER 14

Come Fly With Me

'One day, I had her in my arms, and I started to sing softly in her ear and out of nowhere her eyes closed. I recall looking over at Maman and saying, "It's happening." One tear came down Karine's cheek . . . and then she went.'

– CELINE DION

Perhaps no other event in Celine's life would tug at her heart like her niece Karine's battle with cystic fibrosis. Karine was only sixteen when she died in Celine's arms, on 2 May 1993 – the memory still brings tears to Celine's eyes today.

Only a month before she died, Karine insisted on watching Celine perform in Montreal. Although she had to be accompanied by nurses, Karine had somehow found the strength to go to the concert. In the weeks leading up to her death, Karine was confined to bed, in critical condition, barely able to swallow.

At the time, Celine was touring out of the country, but when Karine took a turn for the worst, and had to be hospitalized, she cancelled her performances to be with her. It was as if Karine had waited for Celine. 'I had her in my arms,' says Celine. 'And I started to sing softly in her ear and out of nowhere her eyes closed. I recall looking over at Maman and saying "It's happening." One tear came down Karine's cheek . . . and then she went.'

Celine believed in reincarnation, and this belief helped her cope with the loss. After Karine's death, one of Celine's songwriters, Jean-Jacques Goldman, presented her with a French song, called *'Vole'* which was later recorded in English as the song 'Fly'. It was dedicated to her niece Karine. The song had a lot to do with the spirit flying free, and Celine, who believed in the after-life, believed that Karine was now finally happy.

'Today she breathes,' says Celine. 'All she wanted was a normal life.' For Celine, the shock of first finding out about Karine's illness had happened so many years ago. But the pain was as real as if it was just yesterday.

It had been a happy occasion when Karine was born, on 28 February 1977. Celine was approaching her ninth birthday and she adored her beautiful new niece. Celine *loved* babies. But only two months later, in April, Liette came to the house, worried about her daughter. Karine had been sick with what the doctor had said was simply gastric flu. But Liette sensed that something was terribly wrong with her. On her way to the clinic, Liette stopped by the house. After all, no one knew more than Maman when it came to babies. Maman went outside and bent over the pram to hug Karine. Suddenly she recoiled in shock. 'Quickly!' she begged. 'Go quickly to the clinic . . . there is not one minute to lose!' Maman was terrified at how sickly the baby looked. She could tell in her heart that she was dying.

Liette and Karine arrived at the nearby clinic within minutes. The doctor took one look at the baby and called an ambulance. They were all rushed to the hospital.

It wasn't until later that night that Liette returned to the house, distraught. It hurt Celine to see her sister in so much pain. At first Liette was barely able to utter a word. But Maman took her aside and Celine and Papa waited breathlessly in the kitchen. When Maman finally came out to them, her eyes were red and swollen with tears. Celine was devastated. 'I was incapable of seeing my mother cry. I started crying as well,' Celine painfully recalls.

Finally Liette told them: 'Karine has cystic fibrosis.' Maman was still in shock. Even though she had worked as a nurse's aid before she was married, Therese had never heard of this disease.

Liette explained that it was an extremely rare hereditary illness that could be passed on by two people carrying the gene for cystic fibrosis, a fatal disorder which primarily attacks the respiratory and digestive systems.

Then Liette said something that Celine would never forget. 'It's terrible, the doctors don't even know how much time she has left to live,' she sobbed. Celine was horrified.

Day after day, Liette and her husband Ronald returned to the hospital. They were told that the baby only had a few weeks left to live, so they decided to baptize Karine at the hospital. They kept a vigil, still clinging onto hope.

Miraculously, one day the doctors said that Karine was strong enough to go home. 'We never thought that she would come out of the hospital,' recalls Celine. The Dion family started reading up on the illness. The more they read, the more they understood. Maman found out, to her amazement, that one of her cousins who lived in the United States, had two of seven children afflicted with cystic fibrosis. Now, many of the Dion children wondered if they might also one day have a child afflicted with the disease. It was a terrible time for them. Life became extremely difficult. Most of all, Karine suffered a great deal.

At every meal, she had to have as many as eighteen pills. This was because she had to consume a large number of artificial enzymes to help her absorb sufficient nutrition. She also had to undergo a daily routine of physical therapy designed to keep her lungs free of congestion and infection. They had to put a mask on her in the evening to unblock her lungs or else she would choke.

It was a devastating time, that caused them all pain. But they dealt with it as a family, and always stood united. And what Karine lacked physically, she gained emotionally from the love this massive family showered on her. Especially her young Aunt Celine, who said, 'She is the child I love most in the world because she has this terrible illness. This incurable illness.' From the age of fourteen, Celine gave special fund-raising performances to help finance the search for a cure – something she would continue to do throughout her career.

Celine spent as much time with Karine as possible and did whatever she could to make her happy, like taking her to shopping malls – oxygen tank and all – and buying her anything she wanted. Celine cherished this loving child. 'Karine made me discover something marvellous, and indefinable,' she explains. 'Something between love and hope.'

Celine was particularly close to her sister Liette, who explains that, 'Even though we are physically separated because of her career, we have always had deep feelings for each other.'

'When my daughter Karine was sick with cystic fibrosis, even though Celine was so busy with her rising career, she was always close to my little one. We had always kept this close emotional bond that was so precious to us. In my heart, what she did for my daughter, she did for me.'

One incredible memory for Liette was when Celine performed at Montreal's Place des Arts Theatre for the first time in May 1983. 'Celine dedicated a song to me,' recalls Liette. 'She sang, *'Tellement j'ai d'amour pour toi'* ["I Have So Much Love for You"]. Before singing that song, she told me on the microphone: "Liette, imagine that it's your own daughter who is singing to you. This evening, I dedicate this to you only." ' And, from all the wonderful memories of their childhood and teenage years, this was the most beautiful moment of all.

Celine had been involved as a provincial spokesperson for the Cystic Fibrosis Association for over ten years by the time Karine died. In August 1993, Celine became the national Celebrity Patron of the Cystic Fibrosis Foundation Association, and her support and benefit concerts raised millions of dollars. She desperately wanted to help find a cure for the disease which affects over 3,000 Canadians (one-third of them in Quebec), 30,000 Americans, and thousands of children across the world.

Posters, information kits and her participation in fund-raising events have all demanded a great deal of Celine's time and energy. On awareness campaigns, Celine's photo appears with a sick child, and the words: 'To a child with cystic fibrosis, your help is a special miracle. Cystic fibrosis chooses children. It destroys their lungs so they can't breathe, and leaves them gasping for air.'

'The pain of CF has touched my family too, as it's touched the lives of so many for so long. CF has stolen the future from so many children. But special miracles are showing us every day that all things are possible.'

In all Celine's album booklets she included the message, 'Celine supports the Cystic Fibrosis Foundation', as well as special tributes, such as 'Karine . . . I'm with you today, as always'.

The research has helped tremendously. In 1960 when the association was founded, the life expectancy of a child with CF was only four years. Decades of research have raised this threshold to early thirties or higher, with the possibility of a lung transplant, sometimes the last hope. Celine continues to be dedicated to finding a cure – a cure that did not come in time for Karine.

'But she breathes today,' Celine recalled, on the *Oprah Winfrey* show, many years after Karine's death. 'All she wanted to do was live a normal life. Every breath was an effort. It was not taken for granted. We are healthy. You wake up in the morning and don't even think of health.'

Celine's appearance on the show was an emotional roller-coaster for the audience, as well as for Celine's family, who were also there. As Celine sang the song 'Fly' she looked directly at her sister Liette, with tears in her eyes. Liette wept almost the whole time, and when the song ended Oprah wiped the stream of tears from her cheeks. 'That song wiped us all out,' said Oprah afterwards.

'It is a hard song to sing,' explains Celine. 'But when Jean-Jacques Goldman wrote the French album for me, he gave me that song and he said: "Don't look at it. It is a gift I give you." I recorded a whole album –

except for this song – and after the end of this album I looked at it. And of course I cried a lot. I wanted to sing it. This is something I wanted to say to her. This is something that I wanted to give her. That gift. I started to sing this song many times but I was crying too much. It was too hard for me. Then I changed my mind, came back to the studio and did it live with a piano. I'm glad I did.'

There would be nothing as heart-wrenching that would draw attention to the pain and suffering caused by cystic fibrosis than the television episode Celine would star in years later. The special 100th episode of *Touched By An Angel* was so moving, it 'touched' everyone in North America.

In the episode, Celine played herself, and the central character was a young boy who was dying of cystic fibrosis. His mother was played by Wynonna Judd. They boy's best friend was a young girl, also named Celine, who idolized Celine Dion, and dreamed of seeing her. The boy, named Petey, had a wish list before he died and one of the wishes was to fulfil the dream of his best friend – to one day meet Celine Dion in person. With the help of an 'angel cast', the children met Celine in her dressing room. As she spoke to the dying boy, the pain of losing Karine flooded her memory. The words came straight from her heart: 'Sometimes you come through the darkness and back into the sunlight.'

CHAPTER 15

The Colour of Her Love

'You know people, lately, they change relationships and partners so easily, like they change TV channels. And I don't believe in that. I believe in love. I would do anything to keep this love alive. Anything.'

– CELINE DION

C eline's second movie theme song was for the Tristar Motion picture *Sleepless in Seattle*. For this film, she sang the song 'When I Fall in Love', a remake of the 1950s Nat King Cole classic, in duet with newcomer Clive Griffin.

The film was released on 24 June 1993. And the story revolved around widowed architect Sam Baldwin (played by Tom Hanks) who relocates to Seattle with his young son Jonah and on Christmas Eve finally finds love with Annie Reed (played by Meg Ryan).

'Singing a Nat King Cole song was a great experience. I loved it,' said Celine. The only problem was that, after Celine shot the video for the song, she suddenly decided to cut off her long hair. It always bothered her when she performed. So she had it cut short by New York hairstylist-to-the-stars, Frederic Fekkai. Celine loved it!

René was concerned. 'Celine was having great success in the United States with her song "When I Fall in Love", her seventh song to be on the *Billboard* magazine Top 10. In the video clip of "When I Fall in Love" she had long hair and, as she was invited on *The Tonight Show*, it would have been bizarre that she suddenly appeared with short hair. So we had the idea that she wear a wig.'

'It was so hot under that wig,' cried Celine. But she had to endure wearing a wig, for two long months, until the day a press conference officially launched her new look, with short hair. Everything in Celine's life that could have a negative effect on her career had to be analysed and planned.

Sleepless in Seattle earned over 100 million dollars at the box office. It seemed that Celine's movie songs were always destined for success.

Meanwhile, the course of Celine's own love affair was as captivating as any movie script.

Love could not be denied – Celine could not keep her love a secret any more. Terrified, of public opinion, of the age difference between them, of what people would think of the manager/protégé relationship that had turned into love and passion, afraid of anything that might put the smallest blemish on her career, she had kept silent. But the pressure had become unbearable.

Frustrated by the years of secrecy, she thought of how best to tell the world how much she loved this grey-haired, pony-tailed 'magic genie' of her career . . . Through song. Celine was about to launch her third English album in November 1993. The album was called *The Colour of My Love* and it was, according to Celine, 'My way to tell the world how much I loved this man.' Her public testimony of her love for him.

'Yes, it's René that I love,' Celine finally proclaimed – during a press conference for the album launch. Celine was frank and honest about how happy she was to finally tell the world. And she confessed her love in a tribute to René, which appeared in the sleeve notes of her album:

'René, for so many years I've kept our special dream locked away inside my heart . . . But now it's getting too powerful to keep inside me . . .'

The words said it all. And the title song, 'The Colour of My Love', was also dedicated to René.

The couple said later that they actually became engaged on 30 March 1993, Celine's twenty-fifth birthday, but they did not mention it until eight months later, at the time of the album launch. 'I've had enough of hiding this beautiful thing,' said Celine passionately. 'Once the record is out, I will feel a little more solid. It's true, I love René and he loves me and I hope to marry in one year from now.'

It was such a weight off her shoulders. 'I was incapable of keeping the secret,' continued Celine. 'I knew it would come out one day. I have said this for a long time to René, but he hesitated.'

Said Quebec journalist Suzanne Gauthier, 'I remember one evening I had surprised the singer and her manager alone together in a restaurant in Los Angeles. I was, in the space of a few minutes, convinced that what was going on was a romantic dinner. As soon as they realized we were there, the manager became the "manager" and Celine the "singer".'

'I am anxious that the world knows it,' said Celine. 'I am anxious to be able to take the hand of my love in public. I am fed up with hiding. I am twenty-five years old and I think I've merited this marvellous gift that makes my life. I am not giving into pressure, but more, I had decided that it was the moment. Before, I felt that I was too young. I was, perhaps, insecure. There were a lot of other things happening in my life. Everything in its time,' she said, with a wisdom beyond her years.

It was actually René who had suggested they keep their love a secret. 'I was afraid of what her parents would say,' he explains. He was right to be afraid. Maman Dion was completely against it at first. Maman made it clear to Celine that she thought René was wrong for her and that the right guy – someone her own age – would come along.

Celine recalls what Maman said to René, ' "This is my princess and you are twenty-six years older!" Maman was hopping mad.' But in time, Maman grew to accept René in his dual role of manager and lover of her daughter. After all, he was Celine's magic genie – a man who seemed to make miracles happen.

René Angelil was a no-holds-barred type of man – a gambler who went for the ultimate win. A brilliant career strategist. Yet René – as his name Angelil implies – was also her 'Angel'.

He was there, by Celine's side, almost everywhere she went. And he has been called one of the greatest career architects of all time. A pensive, analytical man who never gave up, René didn't have words like 'can't' or 'impossible' in his vocabulary. When he dreamed, he dreamed big. He was born a dreamer.

René Angelil was born on 16 January 1942 of Syrian descent, to parents Joseph and Alice Angelil. He was extremely close to his mother, who called him a son of 'gold'. Joseph had been born in Damas and came to Montreal when he was thirty-seven to marry Alice Sara, a Catholic girl of twenty-one, who was also of Syrian descent. She was the youngest of four children and her marriage to Joseph Angelil was a union that had been 'arranged' by their families. 'This didn't stop them from living perfectly happily together for thirty years,' as René later commented.

During his childhood in Montreal, René was a 'boy wonder' – an achiever who was always at the top of his class.

His brother André was born on 4 May 1945 and always looked up to René. 'Since I can remember,' he says, 'René was an example of success and a model of tenacity.'

René's love of song began when he was an eight-year-old choir boy. By the time he was fifteen, he cut a dashing figure in full uniform as a member of his high school marching band. In sports, he excelled in basketball. He was also brilliant at public speaking. But at nineteen, he left school to start a musical career with *Les Baronets*. His parents were not happy with his decision. He had worked in a bank for a while and Alice had thought that he would become a businessman.

But René was determined. And, as a young man, the world of showbusiness was a fascinating one – he set out to be a star in his own right. He was strikingly handsome, 6 feet tall, with penetrating dark brown eyes and natural charm. One thing was certain – René Angelil had style.

In 1961, he created his group with two other musicians, Pierre Labelle and Jean Beaulne. They became a hot band in the sixties with a look that resembled the Beatles – a group that René idolized. The dark-haired trio wore identical suits and thin ties. And they were managed by Ben Kaye, a showbusiness wizard, who would later play a pivotal role in René and Celine's life.

During the sixties, *Les Baronets* were at the top of the charts, doing cabaret and recording French versions of Beatles songs. Their first song 'C'est fou mais c'est tout', released in 1964, was the French version of 'Hold Me Tight' by the Beatles. At the time the trio of twenty-two-year-olds were living high, and earning 1000 dollars a week. 'We partied all the time,' recalls René. He bought a magnificent red Thunderbird with a sun roof. Nine days after buying it, his beautiful car was written off in an accident on the highway. But nothing fazed René.

He had a big fan base, who were attracted not only to his music but to his deep brown eyes, dark hair, full lips, and mischievous smile. When a policeman stopped him for running a red light, instead of writing him a ticket – he asked René for an autograph for his daughter!

René spent days at his mother's house, compiling statistics with the intention of winning in Las Vegas. He finally came up with a formula which he called 'The System' that he hoped would win him millions at the roulette tables. He persuaded three friends, including Pierre Labelle, his fellow musician, to each invest 1000 dollars. René asked his brother if he wanted to be part of the mission but, warned by his mother that René had 'gone mad', André declined the offer.

In a Las Vegas casino, René won 700 dollars in less than half an hour. His 'System' was working! Or so it seemed . . . An hour later, he lost everything. 'My mother was right,' joked René. 'I had gone mad.'

There are a lot of stories about René's gambling adventures. He was up and down all the time. When he juggles numbers Angelil is a serious man. But he also loves hoaxes and practical jokes. For instance, according to fellow *Baronet* Pierre Labelle, he made out that he had 'bought' Radio City Music Hall in New York, in order to pass for a wealthy European. Recalls Pierre, 'He's an extraordinary prankster.'

Another friend adds, 'I remember all his stories about the practical jokes. He once dressed up in full garb as a wealthy Arab sheik – with a turban and robes – and went from casino to casino in Las Vegas, posing as a man of great wealth.'

'Rich one day . . . poor the next. I even declared bankruptcy once,' admits René.

But *Les Baronets* were no gamble. They were a solid group that continued to record and appear on TV shows in Quebec. Amidst all this, René's father, Joseph, died of a massive heart attack in March 1966.

René married Denyse Duquette in December 1966 and they had a son two years later, named Patrick. The group continued to grow in popularity, touring in Atlantic City and elsewhere in the US. René not only sang; in 1971 he also acted in the movie *Après Ski*, a rather saucy, romantic comedy set in the Laurentian mountains.

However *Les Baronets* broke up in 1972, after recording twelve albums, and so did René's marriage to Denyse. By 1973, it was over. The cause of the divorce was adultery. Twelve days later, René married Anne-Renée Kirouac, a pretty blonde singer who was sixteen years younger than him. She had been a successful singing star in Quebec and frequently appeared on a Quebec television show. They had two children, Jean-Pierre and Anne-Marie.

Afterwards, René continued in showbusiness, teaming up for a while with a fellow Quebec impresario, Guy Cloutier. They began managing other artists, most notably René Simard, the Quebec child star. Then René began managing the talented ballad singer Ginette Reno. He was a man who loved music and knew by heart almost the entire repertoire of the Beatles, Michael Jackson, Elvis Presley and Edith Piaf. He also liked good food and wine and gambling. When things did not go according to his well laid out plans, René found solutions and got rid of obstacles. He was a skilful and crafty negotiator.

An unhappy end to his management of Ginette Reno's career left him very disillusioned with showbusiness. When he heard Celine's demo tape back in 1981, it changed his life. Later, he said, 'I always believed in Celine, but never as much as she believed in herself. From the beginning, Celine said that she saw herself there, at Michael Jackson's side at the American Music Awards. I said, "Yes, yes." But deep inside myself I asked myself, "How will we do it?" ' When he met this skinny young girl on the verge of adolescence he had his doubts. But 'when she sang in front of me her eyes . . . it was her eyes. And that voice that comes from here,' René says as he points to his heart. 'She did make me cry actually.'

'From my first meetings with Celine in 1981, I knew that she had the potential to become a very great artist,' he explains. 'Since then, I have always treated her like we treat the great singing stars. That means surrounding her with the best team possible and refusing to compromise on the quality of her albums. I don't believe that Celine would be where she is today if I had.'

Like a good genie, he set out to make all the dreams of his young protégé come true, one by one. 'The first rule of success is patience,' René maintains. He weighed every decision, and he followed through on his ideas systematically. His passion for gambling now led him to take his biggest gamble of all – on the career of a young, impressionable adolescent.

René's wife Anne-Renée had stopped singing and was now René's associate in their company Les Productions TBS Inc. Both René and his wife were totally focused on Celine's career, and she travelled with them everywhere in the early years. Anne-Renée helped Celine a great deal and, as a teen, Celine referred to her as, 'The woman that I adore. I consider her like a sister.'

One morning, the young thirteen-year-old Celine heard René and Anne-Renée arguing – it was only over what she would wear on a talk show in Paris that day. But things were not going well in the marriage and it finally fell apart in 1985. The divorce, due to 'mental cruelty', became official in 1986.

In court documents, Anne-Renée alleged that one night René woke her in a violent manner, and wouldn't allow her to go back to bed. She called the police. After the police left the house, Anne-Renée alleged that René continued to harass her and, fearing for herself and the two children, she called the police again, this time leaving with them to seek refuge at her mother's house. She claimed to have been intimidated and harassed by him, yet his children painted a picture of him as the soul of kindness and generosity.

Things may not have been working out well for René as far as marriage was concerned. But other aspects of his life tell a different story. He was known to be extremely generous, always quick to help out a friend. He was adored by his children and his friends, and highly respected in the music industry. René was smart, worldly-wise and a straight talker. 'I don't bullshit,' was René's way of putting it. When he said something, he meant it.

As Celine's career began to soar, René received the Quebec music award for Manager of the Year, an award he would be honoured with time and time again.

In talking about his career, René also spoke candidly about show-business, 'You can't do this profession for the money. If we play our cards well, money will follow. I tried to make all the decisions concerning Celine by asking myself, "Would I accept this offer or contract if I had a million dollars in my pocket?" If I answered no, then I refused it, even if I had empty pockets.'

As one tour promoter noted: 'René's astounding ability to manage Celine's career was recognized by just about everyone. He's never made a mistake in terms of management. He is a very smart man, a former singer, who knows the important deals to make to build a career structure. She follows the advice. She doesn't play manager. She stays the artist.'

As René puts it: 'An artist is precious and I try as much as possible to free Celine from all problems so that she can concentrate all her energies on her profession.' Over evening meals, René would often sit perusing American hit chart lists in *R & R* and *Billboard*. He was euphoric when he first started seeing Celine's name among talent like Bette Midler, Elton John and Phil Collins.

'At the start,' he recalls, 'it was easy because, as a beginner, everyone wants to help you and see you succeed. When you reach a certain level that's when problems start. Our challenge is to stay where we are. And that's the hardest thing.'

As René and Celine fell in love, the years of secrecy were mostly his idea, as he would not do anything to hurt her parents, or harm Celine's career – or Celine herself.

'I am aware that she possesses one of the most beautiful voices in the world, but her biggest, greatest strength, is her personality,' explains René. 'She has charm. She is a young woman of disarming simplicity. She doesn't have an ounce of malice. Celine has showed us, up to now, half of what she can do,' he says. 'She has talents many don't even know about, such as songwriting. A lot of people don't know that she is a very good pianist and she composes superb melodies. But, in the meantime, as she is very critical of her work, she doesn't play piano in public.'

René Angelil had a formula for success on the international scene. 'I can say that 25 per cent of the success of an artist is attributed to talent; 50 per sent to a sense of discipline and 25 per cent to the team that surrounds the artist. Not all artists are ready to multiply the sacrifices like Celine has had to. Personally I must admit that she amazes me day after day.'

An elegant man with almond-shaped eyes, René usually wore his grey hair in a ponytail or braid. With his well-coiffed beard, he was the picture of class – a man that you noticed in silk shirts, his large hands adorned with bracelets. He had bought a big house in Rosemere, Quebec, and two of his three children lived with him. He was 'the man'. And, with his raspy, quiet, deliberate voice, and his worldly demeanour, there was a certain quality about him. Something authoritative.

Yet it's hard to imagine two people more different. René weighs over

200 pounds, and has a voracious appetite; Celine eats small portions and is extremely thin. He sleeps only a few hours at night, moves slowly and weighs up every word he says. Celine needed twelve hours of sleep in the early years of her career, but now manages to get by on eight or ten hours. She talks quickly and spills out long anecdotes that go from the comical to the emotional. As Celine talks she is like an open book, her face and voice revealing all her thoughts and feelings. René has a way of keeping his outer shell intact. René is calm and reflective, while Celine is emotional and impulsive. So different, yet they complement each other perfectly.

But, by 1993, Celine and René's relationship had sparked gossip. There were rumours everywhere. On 1 April 1993, the Quebec French daily *Le Journal de Montreal* reported that the couple had married in Los Angeles. René didn't appreciate this April Fool's joke. 'I found this cheap,' he commented.

'Our kind of love – you see that in the movies and you think it's not true. It won't happen. It happened. We used to kiss on the cheek,' René said, referring to the French tradition of kissing on both cheeks. 'Well, the cheeks just got smaller.' So Celine and René met somewhere in the middle. And finally the kiss was not a secret any more.

After the album was launched, Celine and René were photographed embracing warmly, and Celine went on a lot of shows to talk about their relationship. It was even a topic years later on *The Rosie O'Donnell Show*, when Celine recounted the story of her engagement – Rosie went ga-ga over her huge diamond ring. 'On my birthday . . . we got engaged. It was so funny. Because when he asked me to marry him, we were casual, in bathrobes . . . relaxed. And then he said, "I want to aaah . . ." and then he started to cry and I said, "Oh, honey, what's going on? Are you okay?" And then he takes the little box . . . and, instead of giving me the ring, he kept the ring, he looked at it and started to cry.'

'He was thinking about the bill!' joked Rosie.

Celine and René had already been sharing a house together in

Rosemere, Quebec, that they had bought from the General Director of the Colorado Avalanche NHL hockey team. All in all, Celine was happy with herself and at twenty-five she said, 'You see before you a young woman who "feels really good in her skin".' This was an expression Celine often used. 'Maybe this is my charm. To be at peace and in harmony with myself.'

She had worked tirelessly while recording *The Colour of My Love* album, collaborating with six producers. The album included her hit song 'When I Fall in Love' from the *Sleepless in Seattle* movie, and eventually sold 15 million copies across the world. It was a blockbuster album and there was no greater comment on her love, and her life, than the first track, the number that will always be remembered as one of her greatest songs – 'The Power of Love'.

This was a new Celine. The song's music video was one of her most sensuous yet, with bedroom scenes that suggested warm, tender love, and lovers sleeping, held tight in each other's arms. 'The Power of Love' soon became one of Celine's most celebrated songs, stirring over-whelming emotion in everyone who heard it. It was the song people wanted for their first dance at weddings, and fans openly told Celine that the song helped them in their personal lives.

The album's title track 'The Colour of My Love' was a romantic ballad, and, according to Celine, 'It's a song that was written by David Foster especially for his wedding with Linda Thompson. Everyone had wanted to sing that song: Whitney Houston, Barbra Streisand, Natalie Cole, Julio Iglesias . . . David played the song to René and me, and we both cried so much. René said, "David, come on, you have to give Celine this song," and he did. I said it deserved the title of the album. I call it my forever song.'

'The voice that seduced the world,' said the commercial promoting the album. Celine had crossed into international stardom. Every 'Power of Love' performance elicited chills. Every rendition of 'Think Twice' was a moving journey into heartbreak, 'Misled' was a sultry song of deception, 'When I Fall in Love' a time for tears, and 'The Colour of My

Love' Celine's own tribute to René, her mentor, manager.

By now, Celine had short wavy hair, in a sophisticated style, and often appeared in a black jacket and pants with a ruffled, retro shirt. She sang 'The Power of Love' on *Arsenio Hall*, and other talk shows clamoured for her. But, again, the relentless pace took its toll and even unveiling the secret of her love for René could not lessen the enormous pressure Celine was under.

'With more and more success though, does it get harder? Does life get harder? Easier or harder?' coaxed Joan Lunden, on a 15 November 1993 appearance on *Good Morning America*.

'Harder,' replied Celine. 'Because there's more pressure . . . I can realize my dream because I wished to be a singer for the rest of my life. But, it's hard. Nothing is easy I guess,' she said.

Celine's entourage always tried to relieve her of any pressures that did not directly relate to singing. 'I know nothing about managing money,' Celine had often said. 'On the business side I have a wonderful team that I've been working with for many, many years and this team is getting stronger and stronger. I have a wonderful manager. I've been working with him for thirteen years, since the beginning. My work is to be able to sing my songs the best that I can. To put in as much emotion as I can. But this is the best part. This is, I would say, the easiest part when I sing. But there's work, just before that. There's work between all the stage performances.'

At Sony, Celine was now what they called a 'priority artist', with the release of her third album in English. Being a 'priority artist' was a great coup for Celine – she shared this honour with Michael Jackson and Mariah Carey, Bruce Springsteen, Barbra Streisand, Pearl Jam and Michael Bolton. It went without saying that Celine could utilize all the massive technical expertise and human resources at Sony. They put their private Sony jet at her disposal, and they would do just about anything to make her happy – except give her a lengthy vacation.

Celine's career was on an upward spiral and she was constantly in demand. The pace was hectic and the media spotlight growing.

Celine wearing a studded black leather motorcycle jacket and faded blue jeans . . . Celine wearing a white tank top . . . Celine wearing a black evening gown . . . She was on magazine covers all over the world. The look was never the same for long.

Now Celine starred in a Disney special called *The Colour of My Love* which aired in Canada on 5 December 1993 and in the United States in February 1994. But her life was not always as much of a fairytale as people thought. One of the headlines read, 'Tired Celine Urgently Comes Back From Europe to Rest!' There was no doubt about it – Celine was exhausted and her world tours were taking a huge toll. She came back prematurely, on 28 January 1994, on the last leg of a promotional tour in France and England that was supposed to have continued to Germany until 1 February. She was also expected at Cannes at the MIDEM, the annual celebration of European song. But Celine wasn't going anywhere except home. She needed a break and she wanted to be well rested for the start of her new American tour.

On 12 February 1994, Celine achieved the greatest success ever by a Canadian artist when 'The Power of Love' stayed at Number 1 on the prestigious *Billboard* Hot 100 Singles (all categories) for four weeks.

The Colour of My Love tour saw shows that were sold out the first day tickets went on sale. Celine began her first major American solo tour in San Francisco, on 11 February 1994. Here is her exhausting itinerary for the month of February alone: Los Angeles, Atlanta, Miami, Chicago, Cleveland, Washington, Boston, ending in New York on 28 February.

In between it all, Celine, who was riding high on the charts with the song 'The Power of Love', had to make time for the special invitation she received from Michael Jackson to sing the hit single on a two-hour television special on the Jackson family. The show called *The Jackson Family Honors*, was recorded on 22 February 1994 in Las Vegas at the MGM Grand Hotel, and broadcast on the NBC network, simultaneously, in thirty countries around the world. More than 13,000 people attended the show, with tickets ranging from 500 dollars to 1000 dollars. US profits went to Los Angeles earthquake victims.

In September 1994, during a series of sold-out shows at the Olympia in Paris, Celine recorded another live album, called *Celine à l'Olympia* (Celine at the Olympia). This sixteenth album featured many of Celine's English and French hit songs.

For the Christmas season, Celine had recorded 'Little Father Christmas' on the album *A Very Merry Chipmunk*, with Alvin and the Chipmunks.

On 24 November 1994, Celine received a diamond album to celebrate over one million copies sold of *The Colour of My Love* album in Canada. The album had also gone multi-platinum in the United States. Sales were starting to skyrocket – but Celine did not seem to care about the charts. She cared about René. And she would do anything for him. It was almost like the story of one of her love ballads, 'You know people, lately, they change relationships and partners so easily, like they change TV channels. And I don't believe in that. I believe in love. I would do anything to keep this love alive. Anything,' said Celine.

'He's my everything. I don't care what people say. Even if it's like, "She loves him too much, or she's dependent on him too much." I wouldn't want him to be twenty years younger,' she added. 'I don't think he would be the same.'

Celine might have felt that their love blended them seamlessly together, and that the age difference no longer mattered. But in spring 1994, Celine and René found that they could not escape the glaring accusations of tabloids that caused a great deal of pain for them.

The cover headline read: *'Celine Dion's Bizarre Love Life'*. Inside, the cover story was alarming: 'Globe blows the lid off singing sensation's bizarre love life' in white text over a red highlight bar. The photo on the cover was none other than a grinning René Angelil, with Celine resting her head and arms on his left shoulder. Inside, the story was scandalous, alleging that they had become romantically involved when Celine was just fifteen. The story goes on to allege that their relationship developed into a sexual one when she was eighteen (the age of consent in Canada).

This story in the *Globe* was just the beginning of troubles for Celine and René. An even greater scandal was caused when an edition of the Montreal-based French-language tabloid, *Photo Police* featured a shocking cover headline beside a brooding photo of René that read: 'Punishable by two years in prison.' The *Photo Police* story speculated about what the legal consequences might be *if* their relationship was sexual when Celine was under-age, and René was found guilty of having sex with a minor. To make matters worse, the story said that her mother had given full blessing to the relationship. René, Celine, and her mother sued *Photo Police*, claiming damages for defamation of character as well as asking for a retraction to be published. Finally, in August 1997, *Photo Police* settled the claim, agreeing to donate an undisclosed amount to the Cystic Fibrosis Association of Quebec, and agreeing to print a front cover retraction of the allegations.

Despite all the speculation from the *Globe, Photo Police* or otherwise, the end to all this mess was actually a new beginning, where Celine and René could now openly embrace in public, where the weight of their secret love was finally lifted, and where the well-publicized engagement was about to see fruition in the wedding of the century.

CHAPTER 16

A Storybook Wedding

'Five hundred guests . . . just an intimate crowd.'
— CELINE DION

A fairytale wedding. It wasn't just a cliché. In Celine's case all the elements were there. It was just as she had pictured it years before. No expense would be spared in creating the perfect backdrop for a Princess and her Prince Charming. On Saturday 17 December 1994, all eyes would be focused on what would be described as 'Canada's Royal Wedding'.

Even the design of the invitation was wondrous to behold, with an elaborate lace closure and gold lamé thread. The initials of the bride and groom graphically symbolized the union of two very different personalities: an elaborate scripted 'C' for Celine, joined with a strong and solid typeface 'R'. This monogram would not only decorate the invitation, but also the wedding souvenir album, and many elements of the décor at both the ceremony and the reception. Also inserted in the envelope was the address of the Quebec Cystic Fibrosis Association, and, in lieu of gifts, guests were encouraged to contribute to the charity.

Celine's last pre-wedding appearance was a benefit on Wednesday 14 December 1994, in Montreal, which raised 200,000 dollars to fight cystic fibrosis. Later that evening René and Celine were shown handing out a giant cheque for 85,600 dollars, made out to the Cystic Fibrosis Association.

Celine was absolutely radiant. Her silk wedding dress was stunning, decorated with French lace and pearl-beaded embroidery. It captured her sweet sophistication and innocence and yet it was low-cut to reveal her cleavage, reflecting the more sensuous side of Celine Dion. Her veil was heavily beaded and her hair pulled back in a classic braided style. Her beautifully manicured fingers were accentuated with long flared sleeves, ultimately drawing attention to her magnificent diamond eternity wedding band.

The spectacular train was over 20 feet long – long enough to be held by Celine's twenty-seven nieces and nephews! Her fairytale dress had been one of the fashion world's best-kept secrets. Designers Mirella and Steve Gentile, owners of Bella di Sera, a Quebec boutique specializing in bridal gowns and evening wear, ultimately came up with a dress that was said to have cost 100,000 dollars.

'Our first call was on Sunday, from Florida,' recalls Steve Gentile. 'It was from René. At first, I thought it was a joke. He said "Celine wants a fairytale wedding. Do what it takes to make her happy." ' Celine wanted a 'princess dress' with a romantic, full skirt. With her thin waist and tall, model's physique, it was going to look spectacular. Mirella would see to it. The vivacious redhead was an expert at elaborate gowns and, by the time she had finished, Celine really would look as if she had stepped out of a fairytale. Celine even named the dress 'Age of Innocence'.

'I want to be the most beautiful on this day,' said Celine. 'And I hope to marry only once . . . I'm a traditionalist. I can tell you – I'll have the dress of my dreams.'

They started with sketches and then came the endless fittings. Tight bodice, small waist, big sleeves, low cleavage and a train that went on and on. Not just one train, but two were created, one of which was detachable.

'Every time we had a fitting, Celine would ask for more skirt,' says Mirella. 'She kept saying "MORE! MORE!" and we kept adding petticoats and crinolines.' The silhouette of the dress made Celine's 23-inch waist look even more minuscule. And it was getting thinner by the hour. The hotel concierge recalls that Celine even brought her tread-mill with her to the bridal suite!

For over one thousand hours, a team of over a dozen seamstresses worked their magic – sewing, hand-beading, pearling. The spectacular silk gown gradually came to life a vision of lace and lustre.

The last fitting was on Thursday and, with only two days to go, there was no sleep for the skilled seamstresses! They worked feverishly day and night . . . until *voilà!* The dress was ready. It was 1.30 a.m. Mirella called Celine, who wasn't sleeping anyway. 'Your dress is ready!' Despite the time, Celine asked Mirella to come straight over to her bridal suite at the luxurious Westin Mount Royal Hotel. The dress was everything she had dreamed of. 'I hope he will find me beautiful,' said Celine.

It was almost time. All the arrangements had been made and nothing was left to chance. Celine and René had booked 150 rooms at the Westin Hotel. Early on the morning of the wedding, all the guests were invited to come down to collect a pass to enter the historic Nôtre-Dame Basilica for the ceremony, as well as the reception at the hotel. After all – Celine Dion was getting married and the event had to be perfectly orchestrated. Just like a concert.

The Westin Mount Royal Hotel was the most elegant of venues. All other wedding contracts for that night were re-routed to other hotels. This wedding had to be one of a kind. The event had been planned to the last detail, at an estimated cost of over 600,000 dollars. It was to be the ultimate wedding: sophisticated yet sensational, an event as glitter-ing as Celine's wedding gown.

Outside the church, before dawn, a huge team put up barricades, cleared away snow and installed broadcast equipment. Inside, another crew prepared for hours. As one of her guests, show promoter Donald Tarlton (of Donald K. Donald, who had been involved in booking her tours for years) observed, 'It's the show of the decade, and it's sold out.'

The photographers at Celine and René's wedding worked for a

Quebec French-language magazine, 7 *Jours*, that paid 200,000 dollars for exclusive rights to photograph the ceremony for a special wedding album edition. This had sparked some controversy. Other newspapers wanted to enter the church as well. But finally, only six hours before the wedding, a judge upheld the couple's right to keep uninvited reporters and photographers from entering the church.

With only hours to go now, the 26 year-old bride and 52-year-old groom waited anxiously. All the years of secrecy were about to end at a wedding ceremony that would follow the most solemn of Catholic traditions.

According to Montreal's English-language daily, *The Gazette*, one of the few aspects of the wedding that was not publicized was how René managed to convince the Catholic Church to forget about his two previous marriages and have a priest perform the ceremony in the Nôtre-Dame Basilica. Prior to wedding Celine, René had taken steps to have his first marriage annulled and a religious counsel had approved his petition. His second occurred outside a church so, as far as the Vatican was concerned, it didn't count. What did matter was that this should be the wedding of Celine's dreams. All the years that she had sacrificed a social life, all the time away from her family, the loneliness and tears, were suddenly forgotten. Now it was a time for celebration.

Only minutes remained before Celine would leave her sumptuous bridal room at the Westin Hotel. She was nervous. A team of five experienced professionals all had their roles to play. Everything had to be perfect. Right down to her diamond necklace. Like in a fairytale.

Every princess needs her crown. For Celine, it was a bridal head-dress of 2,000 Austrian crystals, over a wooden frame that weighed more than 15 pounds! Her long-time hairstylist Louis Hechter and a team of hairdressers had the challenging job of making sure that the magnificent tiara would stay on Celine's head all day, and all night. She had chosen a bridal hairpiece from Paris, an imported, Evita Peron style braid.

Celine told them to do whatever it took to ensure that the massive head-dress stayed on. 'This thing has to hold! I don't mind what you have to do. I don't care.' She imagined the horror of what would happen if the huge head-dress fell off. 'This cannot happen!' said a desperate Celine. 'So there was only one solution,' according to Celine. 'They really sewed it to my hair.'

Before the ceremony, Celine did most of her own make-up, but a professional make-up artist completed her look. Deep pink lipstick gave a fuller definition to her lips; and her eyes were accentuated with liner and mascara, with a combination of dark and light eyeshadows enhancing her large, warm, chestnut-coloured eyes.

As Celine was ready to leave for the church, she was greeted by her father. At seventy-one, he was about to give his last daughter away. She had accomplished so much through the years and Papa recalled with a sentimental smile how determined Celine had always been. Wherever her dreams took her, 'One thing. She always kept her two feet on the ground,' he reminisced, a picture of sophistication and charm in his top hat and grey gloves.

Papa took one look at Celine and couldn't help being overcome with emotion. As the tears rolled down his cheeks, Celine cradled his face in her hands. These moments between Celine and her father needed no words. Celine embraced him, kissing him on the lips. Papa had always called himself Celine's greatest fan and she agreed. 'I just love him,' Celine had said on so many occasions. Now, he was giving her away. His youngest, his brightest star.

Maman was soon by her side. At sixty-seven years old, she was not just a mother, but a best friend. Maman had given everything she had to Celine's career when she had shown the desire to be a star. 'Since she was small we found her to be full of qualities. That's why she is where she is today,' Maman beamed proudly. Maman carefully checked to see that everything was perfect. It was. Maman looked beautiful in an off-white suit with gold embroidery, wearing a string of pearls and large teardrop-shaped earrings. Her pride and joy at seeing Celine happy on this joyous day was almost too much for words. One look said it all.

Meanwhile, René was in his dressing room. He wore a three-quarter length tuxedo jacket that suited his large 6-foot frame. Underneath, a white embroidered vest and white wing-collar shirt. No white handkerchief in the pocket for him . . . instead, a black handkerchief and a long white ascot in lieu of a bow tie. The final touch was his tightly braided ponytail. He was ready. It was time to leave for the church.

Snow cascaded down outside. It was a world of white that greeted Celine as the Rolls Royce drove her to the church. A warm blanket of snow covered the whole of Montreal that afternoon and added a magical touch to the day, as if it had been orchestrated by Celine and René themselves. It was pure fantasy.

Celine stepped out of the Rolls and made her way up the steps of the ancient Nôtre-Dame Basilica. She was a magnificent confection of white. In years to come, Celine's bridal gown photo would adorn fashion magazines and tabloids, under headlines such as 'Fabulous Brides and Their Fabulous Gowns' and 'Singer Celine Knocks 'Em Dead in This Sexy Beaded Gown'.

A 10,000 dollar white mink jacket styled by Montreal furrier, Zuki, kept her warm. A white silk organza wrap covered her bouquet of winter flowers.

The Nôtre-Dame Basilica in Old Montreal was a magnificent backdrop. Outside, the crowds lined up, waiting as long as six hours to catch just a glimpse of the star.

Finally, a seventeen-car motorcade of stretch limousines brought guests and other family members to the church. In addition, a fleet of buses were on hand for the guests. By now the onlookers almost outnumbered the 500 guests!

Celine's eight sisters – Ghislaine, Louise, Pauline, Linda, Manon, Liette, Denise and Claudette – were her bridesmaids, all dressed in identical cream-coloured gowns with matching hooded capes.

Her five brothers, Clement, Jacques, Michel, Daniel and Paul looked very dashing in black tuxedos. The ushers were Vito Luprano, from Sony Music; André Angelil, René's brother; Paul Sara, René's cousin;

and friends and associates Jacques Desmarais, Pierre Lacroix, Guy Cloutier, Marc Verreault and Ben Kaye. Celine's nephew Jimmy, her brother Jacques' son, was the ring-bearer, and the flower girl was Audrey, her sister Ghislaine's daughter.

Celine was fashionably late for her own wedding, though René's Rolls Royce got him to the church on time. The three o'clock ceremony was delayed, but she was worth waiting for. Twenty-eight minutes later, Celine walked down the aisle, to the strains of 'Here Comes the Bride', walking regally, holding the arm of her father Adhemar Dion, trailing her 20-foot train and veil. She walked slowly and carefully to meet her long-time manager and soon-to-be-husband.

Each pew was adorned in gathered tulle fabric to look like a giant rose, with a yellow flower in the middle. The centre aisle was carpeted in blue, with the couple's cipher, 'CR', discreetly embroidered in gold at one end of it. In the first row sat Maman, Papa Dion, Celine's sister Claudette, her brother Clement, her nephew Jimmy, the ring bearer, and Audrey, the flower girl. On another aisle, sat four people close to René's heart. His mother Alice adored Celine. Alice, who was dressed in an elegant off-white ensemble, looked on with love and pride at what her son and Celine had built together. René's stunning daughter Anne-Marie wore a revealing and sensuous black gown, that showed most of her bare midriff. His sons Jean-Pierre and Patrick watched every moment, both in black tuxedo jackets, grey and black striped ascots, and grey trousers, vests, gloves and top hats.

Celine and René knelt before the altar while they exchanged their wedding vows and held hands during most of the ceremony. Many times Celine closed her eyes in intense emotion. René had his head slightly bowed, but still eyed the priest intently. He was a man who liked to go into things with his eyes open.

Once again, just before they became man and wife, Celine closed her eyes and bowed her head, with tightly clasped hands, as if making a special prayer that her marriage should be blessed. Tears came to her eyes.

During the hour-long Roman Catholic mass, six invited photographers constantly bounded over the communion rail and scrambled around, finding the best angle to shoot the service from. In keeping with their lives, the couple exchanged vows beneath the massive, high altar, amidst the flashes of cameras.

The music was traditional: Franz Schubert's 'Ave Maria' as well as the familiar march from Mendelssohn's 'Midsummer Night's Dream'.

Celine chose various readings from the Bible and a passage about the power of God's love from the Gospel of St John. And then both Celine and René received communion.

Magistrate Ivanhoe Poirier celebrated the marriage of Celine and René, in the purest tradition. He invited Celine to drink the holy wine from the gold cup. She raised the cup to her lips and then it was René's turn to drink the blessed wine as a sacred symbol of the marriage.

René appeared calm and serene during the ceremony but if one looked closely his eyes were red with emotion. As for Celine – her tears couldn't be held back. She wiped her eyes but more tears streamed down her cheek. Overcome, she tried to fight back her feelings and raised a trembling hand to her lips.

Her nephew Jimmy was all smiles as he carried the embroidered cushion that held the wedding rings. Celine slid the ring on to the finger of the man who was now to be her husband. It was the moment she had been waiting for and her look was solemn and intense while he beamed. Celine was elated. As she had said before, on so many occasions, 'When I get married, it will be for life.'

Their kiss was tender and passionate, and the guests reacted with a standing ovation. René put his hand around her waist and they signed the register. Celine's mother gave her a loving kiss on both cheeks, and Celine, always using expressive gestures when she was overcome with emotion, cradled her mother's face with her hand.

Now it was official. They had done it! Suddenly, the roaring voices of the Montreal Jubilation Gospel Choir broke into a medley of spirited gospel favourites, in their red and gold robes. Celine and René did some dance steps and everyone was clapping their hands to the music. René was beaming and Celine, radiant, gave a thumbs up sign.

The newlyweds made their way towards the exit, the bridal train so long that, as she approached the first pew, her train extended all the way back to the altar.

There would be plenty of time to celebrate! Now it was time to give the media a chance. They had called a press conference at the Westin Hotel. Both Celine and René wanted to let the throng of reporters know, first-hand, how everything had gone.

'It was the ceremony of my dreams,' announced Celine to the roomful of journalists. 'It was what I had always hoped for. It was magic . . .'

'I wanted the dress of a princess, like the one we dream of in our dreams, but I'm paying the price for it today because it's not easy to get around in this. It's very heavy!' she joked. 'But I'm very happy to do it, especially for you René, because I love you so much,' she added, turning to him. With the photographers snapping furiously, Celine gave René three kisses and pretended to faint – perhaps from the 'power of her love' for him.

It was time for the reception! The décor had been recreated from Tchaikovsky's *Nutcracker*. White and red rose petals adorned the stairways. The guests walked under a magnificent arc of branches at the entrance and two life-size toy soldiers stood by an enormous Christmas tree. The whole ambiance was one of musical fantasy. Even a large cage with four white doves was a wonderful reminder of the 'dove' song Celine had sung for the Pope when she was sixteen.

It was as glamorous as a Hollywood production. Thousands of tiny lights suspended from long branches culminated in a bouquet of pale yellow, pink and white roses that, on cue, descended to just above the centre of the table.

There were trees and glittering lights everywhere. Roses upon roses. It was a room transformed. The 500 guests were serenaded by twenty-one violins and the irresistible music of Montreal's ten-piece Perry Carmen Orchestra.

The food was an enchanting gastronomic experience: thin slices of smoked salmon in a five pepper sauce with a tartare of salmon and caviar quenelle (a dumpling); heart-shaped minced duck ravioli in a creamed sorrel sauce; crêpes and golden sautéed breast of chicken, with potato patties and a bouquet of vegetables; warm goat's cheese seasoned with thyme; tarts flavoured with anise; and a spectacular tulip-shaped trio of sherbet, with fresh raspberries, raspberry *coulis* (sauce) and chocolate. Not to mention the over 750 bottles of wine that were served that night.

Celine was an incurable romantic. The head table was decorated with roses, Celine's favourite flower. And the massive backdrop had bunches of floral clusters in tulle fabric with roses at the centre. Her father was to her right and René to her left. Every so often, Celine and René would kiss passionately, in the transparent cocoon of her veil. Her arms embraced his neck. René gave a moving speech and Celine had a red nose from all her crying.

The opening song for their first dance was, 'The First Time Ever I Saw Your Face', by Roberta Flack. For Celine, it was one of the most beautiful songs in the world. Celine and René danced the traditional first dance. Her arms were wrapped around him, her eyes tightly closed, the veil around them both.

There was also a moving moment when Celine danced with her father. It hadn't been easy for him, seeing so little of Celine these past years, and this was something that touched each and every one of the Dion family – most of all, Celine.

'She misses us terribly,' said Maman, while an emotional Claudette told Celine, 'My heart is always open for you.' Even her brothers were deeply moved. 'I don't always get the chance to say I love you, but this is the perfect occasion,' said Michel.

The guest list included more than a hundred family members with all the children and relatives. There were many, many people from the music industry, as well as Celine and René's 'Sony family'. The guest list also included former Canadian Prime Minister Brian Mulroney and his wife Mila, songwriter-producer David Foster, and songwriters Diane Warren, Jean-Jacques Goldman and Luc Plamondon. Hockey great Patrick Roy was there, as was talk-show host and close friend Sonia Benezra. Even Celine's trusted ear, nose and throat doctor Gwen Korovin was there. Naturally, her musicians were there, including Claude 'Mego' Lemay, her band leader.

Given René's passion for gambling, another theme of the evening had to be the casino. Tables were set up and, at the entrance to the theme casino area, guests were given a deck of monogrammed playing cards. There were blackjack tables and craps tables and Adhemar had a great time pulling '21'.

The *pièce de résistance* was the 7-foot-high wedding cake – a magnificent *croquembouche*, a crunchy sweet delicacy prepared by the celebrated Maison Lenotre in Montreal. It looked like a Christmas tree, with over thirty delicious tiered layers rising to a point, crowned with white roses. According to the hotel concierge, 'It was so high that we had trouble getting it in the door! We had to take it apart and bring it into the banquet hall in three sections, where it was then reassembled.'

As the wedding unfolded, it was everything Celine had imagined it would be. Years before, she had fantasized about her wedding. 'When I get married, I want to live the experience to the maximum. I feel it's a beautiful gesture of love. One thing is for certain, when I get married it won't go unnoticed. There may be those who find the event exaggerated but I have no intention of doing things halfway. It will be unbelievable!' Her wedding day had more than lived up to those dreams.

It was now four o'clock in the morning. Celine and everyone sat around the piano singing Frank Sinatra's 'My Way'. But it had been *her* way – all the way. Celine had had the fairytale wedding she had always longed for, and she wouldn't have changed a thing.

Now, as Celine recalls, 'The time was five o'clock in the morning and

I wanted to go to bed, so they took the tiara out.' The heavy bridal head-dress, which had been sewn to her hair, had pierced through her hairline, gouging her scalp. 'I was bleeding! But I didn't care. I loved him that much!'

Celine and René left for their honeymoon the day after the wedding. They would be spending it at their winter home, in West Palm Beach, Florida. It was more than a honeymoon – it was an anticipated work-free month. Just weeks before the wedding, Celine had performed in Osaka, Nagoya and Tokyo.

Now she could revel in doing the 'normal' things, like cooking and relaxing, even going to a movie. But in the third week the honeymoon was cut short so that Celine could appear on the television show *Top of the Pops* in London. Celine's 'Think Twice' was a huge hit single in Britain, with sales of over a million. The girl from Quebec was topping the charts and it was time to get back to work.

Only months after the wedding, Celine had been introduced as the 'definition of world music', by Olivia Newton-John at the World Music Awards, and had swept through an endless sea of performances and paparazzi in France and Italy. In England, Celine was now treated like royalty. Her hit single, 'Think Twice', had been named there as one of the twenty most beautiful songs of all time. It was the song Celine sang at the royal gala benefit called *Prince's Trust: Live for Peace* under the chairmanship of Prince Charles. There, Prince Charles greeted Celine personally, and she took her place among the highest echelons of British celebrities, including Michael Caine and David Frost.

'Today, crowned royalty wanted her, record sales accumulated and the public didn't cease asking for her,' René said exuberantly from his hotel suite. 'One night, we were at a restaurant, a place a friend had particularly recommended as being discreet and quiet. However, once the meal was finished, and we walked out of the door, there seemed to be a real fireworks display of camera flashes going off and camera floodlights shining brightly on Celine at the same time. We had to drive with a lot of caution to avoid crushing the crowd of people who were running around the car.'

Celine appeared again on the British show *Top of the Pops*, and presented her second single, 'Only One Road'. Record sales were climbing, especially in Europe. *The Colour of My Love* album had been number one in Belgium, Denmark, Portugal and Switzerland. She was loved in Australia, on the hit charts in Russia, and had invitations to sing in China, Japan, Korea, Thailand and New Zealand.

Celine had performed six sold-out concerts in the United Kingdom, and received the 'royal star treatment'. The concerts were spectacular, and no sooner had they finished, then Celine was off to Holland and Spain. Meanwhile, in France, the French daily newspaper *Liberation* had written that 'Celine could sing a telephone book and it would sell records anyway!' The languages, the picturesque scenery, the country-side – it was all a blur to Celine. Her tours went by so fast that she often had to 'think twice' before talking to the audience, just to be sure what city she was in. But she rarely complained. Her mother explained, 'What do you want? It's the price of glory.'

Whether it was *amour* or love that Celine sang about, the world listened. By December 1995, Celine even had huge sales in Japan, with *The Colour of My Love*. This album release included the beautiful ballad 'To Love You More' which had been used as the theme song for a popular television drama in Japan called *Koibito Yo* (My Dear Lover). *The Colour of My Love*, had sold more than 12 million copies worldwide, including a million in Canada and a million in Japan.

Her success was based on a foundation of song that knew no language barrier, the essence of emotion that was understood across the globe.

But even a year later, as Celine and René approached their first wedding anniversary, the world remained fascinated by their wedding. Talk show after talk show referred to it and highlighted some of the most spectacular moments.

'The wedding was huge!' said Jay Leno to Celine, after seeing glimpses of the event on *Entertainment Tonight.*

'It was a big wedding. Very intimate,' added Celine. 'With 500 people!'

'That's just your brothers and sisters,' he joked.

Even Oprah described the wedding as something straight out of a fairytale. 'Most unbelievable thing you've ever seen,' she said. 'Canada's Royal Wedding.'

'Why such an elaborate wedding?' asked Oprah, seemingly awe-struck, while looking at some wedding footage.

Celine responded: 'You know I love him big time and it's that simple. I'm a big dreamer and I dream about showbusiness, big time. I dream about big families, big time, and I just wanted to have this beautiful big dress.' It was quintessential Celine – totally honest and open.

'Was that big wedding your idea or his?' asked Bryant Gumbel in a CBS television interview years later. 'The big one,' Celine answered, pointing to herself. He laughed.

'It was like a fairytale,' said Bryant.

'It was and it still is,' she answered.

CHAPTER 17

As Luck Would Have It

There are many good luck rituals and it would take two hours to talk about them. The one that is the most important is when I touch the thumbs of all my musicians to transfer the energy.'

– CELINE DION

'I am the luckiest one,' said Celine Dion to an inquisitive Kathie Lee Gifford. The co-host of the *Live with Regis and Kathie Lee* television show had just asked her if she was the most talented member of her family – a difficult question for someone who has thirteen brothers and sisters and two parents who are all musicians and singers. It was a good answer.

Celine explained that she was the luckiest not only because of the way her career had gone, but also because her very existence was due to a twist of fate. 'I'm the youngest and they call me "the accident" because I wasn't supposed to be here. I'm happy to be here and I'm the luckiest one because I wanted to be a singer and everyone was pushing and supporting me.'

Celine feels that she was born under a lucky star. Her success has, she believes, a great deal to do with luck, destiny and a whole series of superstitions and rituals.

It all started when Maman put that red ribbon around twelve-year-old Celine's first cassette for good luck. Seeing where her career has taken her so far, there's a lot to be said for good luck charms and Celine believes in her luck as much as she believes in her talent. Her good luck charms and good luck rituals are sacred. And it's more than just simply a case of touching wood and crossing fingers (which Celine does too). 'I'm a *sorcerer* in the nicest sense of the word,' confides Celine.

Her lucky charms have brought her success as far back as Celine can remember. At thirteen, when she competed in the Yamaha World Popular Song Festival in Tokyo, she won the gold medal as contestant number five. And five has remained her lucky number ever since. 'My lucky number is five. I used to always find nickels on the ground,' explains Celine. One day, many years ago, Celine picked up a nickel she found that was minted in 1968, the year she was born. She picked it up, put it in a small plastic bag and has since kept it with her in her purse, everywhere she goes. She even has a large collection of nickels that she keeps in a jar at home.

Anything to do with the number five seemed to bring Celine success. So, when she invested in a chain of restaurants in Quebec, with business partners René, his cousin Paul Sara, and Peter and Lawrence Mamas, Celine called it – what else – but Nickels, after her good luck charm. The restaurants offer a retro, *Happy Days* or *American Graffiti* diner-style atmosphere, with fifties décor, chrome fittings, black-and-white check borders, red vinyl seats, some framed gold record albums of Celine's and a whole host of memorabilia on the walls. Celine made frequent appearances at the restaurant in the beginning, appearing in ads and posters which were hung throughout the dining area.

Maman soon became involved, owning two of the restaurants. Celine's brother Paul also joined the business, as did Claudette who later acquired a Nickels restaurant. Other than the locations that are owned or managed by family members, the rest were franchised and became a huge success. Now there are over thirty Nickels restaurants throughout Canada as well as Florida.

Celine's fixation on the number five has given rise to a great many superstitious rituals. Before each flight, Celine does something that she believes brings her good luck. As her brother Michel explains, 'I was surprised to see that before getting on an airplane Celine must absolutely press five fingers of one hand firmly on the cabin.'

When Celine signs her name, she always signs the same way, using only her first name and writing it in precisely the same way: 'Celine x x . . .' There are no exceptions. After signing her name, Celine adds 'x x' (the symbol for two kisses) followed by three dots, to make a total of five. She believes that it brings her good luck. In fact, even when a fan asked her to only write 'Celine' on the back of his shirt, without the 'x x . . .' she said that she could not, answering, 'This is the way I've been signing my name for sixteen years and I cannot change it.'

In honour of Celine's fascination with five, when the Molson Center, a massive entertainment and sports complex in Montreal, was created, the star dressing room first had a number '1' on the door. Then, realizing Celine's passion for five, the managers had the room number changed to a '5' (as it has remained permanently).

Celine also has a superstition about the number three. For example, when she drops something, she doesn't just pick it up. She drops it two more times (to make a total of three) according to her superstition that goes 'never two without three' or 'three times the charm'.

In her professional life, Celine's good luck charms and rituals are almost as sacred as her singing. For instance, in her dressing room, Celine has lots of stuffed animal plush frogs in all shapes and sizes. 'Many fans leave me frogs,' she says. 'Frogs have been the mascot of my tours for years.' A favourite of hers is a medium-sized frog with a yellow belly and yellow spots on its back that a fan gave her at the beginning of her career. Eventually, Celine even created her own souvenir plush frog (wearing a Celine T-shirt) that fans could purchase at concerts.

There are numerous other 'scared rituals' that Celine compulsively carries out before each show. When a fan once asked Celine to describe them, she replied, 'There are many rituals and it would take two hours to talk about them: I have to eat salted soda biscuits, because salt promotes saliva. I find it necessary to touch the thumbs of each musician for energy. I do a special dance with my band leader. Before a show I put on my deodorant, left arm first, then right and then left again. The one that is the most important is when I touch the thumbs of all my musicians to transfer the energy.'

Before each show, Celine carries out a ritual that never changes. She gives a kiss on each cheek to René who waits backstage. She always kisses him on the left cheek first, followed by the right cheek. Then René puts his hands on her shoulders, looks her in the eyes and gives her a gently push, saying, 'There we are. You are ready.'

These are only a few of her performance preparations. Before a full concert when Celine is with all her musicians, she carries out a ritual that she finds deeply comforting. As the audience take their seats, little do they know that, behind the scenes, Celine is doing her pre-show ritual. No audience member will ever see it, but without it Celine could never go on.

Backstage, Celine does a childlike pantomime with her musicians. She enters the shadowed area of the stage, feeling her way as she walks, and finds her stage manager, who holds out the microphone to her. Before Celine takes it, she squeezes the stage manager's bare arm three times. Celine then turns towards René, who gives her their ritual kiss. Then she does a little dance with Claude 'Mego' Lemay, her band leader of almost ten years, and accompanies him to his keyboard. She pretends to press a button that controls the lights and the raising of the curtain. Mego acts as if he is shocked by her actions – and he pretends to hit her! The last part of the pantomime is when Celine walks around the stage and touches her right thumb on the right thumb of every one of her musicians and back-up vocalists in a special handshake, to 'transfer the energy', as she puts it.

Finally, Celine merges on stage, an embodiment of strength. The child-like game is over. She is now 'Celine the Star'.

Celine believes in astrology. She's an Aries, Ascendant Lion, the Monkey in the Chinese horoscope, and has all the characteristics of these signs. According to Celine, 'I am an Aries and I have a hard head.

When I want something – it could take years, but I will take all the means to achieve it.'

Some say that there is also a link with numerology in a lot of Celine's successes. For instance, it was an amazing coincidence that Celine's first Academy Awards show, which saw her song 'Beauty and the Beast' win an Oscar, fell on her birthday, 30 March 1992.

'I like magic, mysteries . . . the things that cannot be explained,' says Celine, who also believes in reincarnation. 'I have already lived in another time and another place and I was certainly a singer.'

CHAPTER 18

Falling Into Success

'Music has no barriers. No matter what language you talk, if people say something to me . . . even if I don't understand the language, through their eyes I see the sincerity and the love and it touches me. And when I am on stage and you talk to me in a foreign language, I feel you. I don't know what you said to me, but I felt it. That's why I love music so much because we can travel through music and there are no barriers.'

– CELINE DION

Luck was with Celine. 'In Europe alone, she had sold over 10 million records in 1995 . . . the biggest-selling artist in Europe,' according to Richard Ogden, vice-president of marketing for Sony Music Europe.

In early 1996, Celine was named 'the best ambassador of the French language' and she was made a Knight of the Order of Arts and Letters by the Minister of Culture in France. Soon after, Celine was honoured with a trophy at France's annual music gala festival (the MIDEM). The following month, in Paris, she won two more trophies, called the *Victoires*, and France's *Gala* magazine named her Woman of the Year, as voted by its readers.

Celine's latest French Album – was the biggest success story of her French-singing career. The album (her fourteenth in French) was called

D'eux. The punning title meant 'Of Them' and also 'Two' (*deux*), as in two people in love. The entire album was made up of romantic melodies about love and hope, written by the wonderfully talented Parisian songwriter/musician Jean-Jacques Goldman. The intensely emotional ballads were instant hits throughout France and Quebec. In the United States, the *D'eux* album had been released under the title *The French Album*.

Meanwhile, in Quebec, Celine was being held up as an embodiment of old and new Quebec values in a two-part analysis in the Montreal *La Presse* newspaper's opinion pages. 'All Francophone Quebecers identify with Dion,' wrote Christian Dufour. 'She has become a "superstar on a planetary scale" all the while remaining authentically Québécoise,' he continued. 'She combines a "modern synthesis" between old French Canada and modern Quebec, a combination that never succeeded in politics.' Celine was about the only personality to win unanimous support from the Atlantic to the Pacific.

Her brilliant strategy, of alternating English and French albums, kept her magic alive and well throughout the two cultures.

In Brussels, Berlin, Amsterdam, Paris, London and New York the screams were the same: 'Celine, we love you!' In any language, it was understood. Celine's success had surpassed Sony's wildest dreams. The music industry had been in a slump and Celine was their dream girl. She was often compared to Barbra Streisand for her vocal depth and five-octave range, and to the legendary great lady of French *chanson*, Edith Piaf, for her soulful ballads.

Wrote one Canadian music critic, 'her emotional reserves are as deep as Babs'. She glides from a whisper to a full-throated cry with more power and grace than any woman working the circuit. She believes in what she's singing, of that there is no doubt.'

The world was in love with Celine. But it hadn't happened overnight. 'Maybe there are people who think that her success fell out of the sky. But I know all the efforts and sacrifices that she made to arrive where she is today,' says her sister Claudette.

Nevertheless 'today' the world was at her feet. In February 1996, Celine and René were invited to Donald Trump's home in West Palm Beach, where there was a private concert at his exclusive Mar-a-Lago resort. Later that night, microphone in hand, the tuxedo-clad Donald Trump called Celine 'one of the really great talents in our country today. She's really fantastic. I think her career is about as big as you can get anyway. I don't know if it can get any bigger. She's doing really well – I'm not sure she can do better.' But Celine could and did.

'After all,' Celine was now in the habit of saying, 'the sky is the limit.'

Just weeks before her twenty-eighth birthday, in 1996, Celine launched the *Falling Into You* album. Although it looked as if her success had fallen out of the skies, it was really the culmination of fifteen years' work. This album was the greatest success of her career thus far, reaching new heights that led her to perform over a hundred concerts across the world in 1996 alone. On 12 March 1996 Celine released *Falling Into You* to the world and the first 3 million copies of the album were sold in record time. Reaching international sales of 26 million, *Falling Into You* became one of the best-selling albums of all time. The album would change Celine's life forever, catapulting her into a new level of stardom.

The *Falling Into You* album was a spectacular combination of fifteen songs of passionate musical intensity. The most celebrated one was 'Because You Loved Me', the theme song written by Diane Warren, and produced by David Foster, for the Touchstone Pictures movie *Up Close and Personal*, starring Robert Redford and Michel Pfeiffer.

The movie was a huge success, based on an inspirational romance between an awkward but talented would-be reporter and the seasoned veteran who takes her under his wing. Sound familiar? No wonder 'Because You Loved Me' was René's favourite song.

The *Falling Into You* album produced a host of hits. Executive producers Vito Luprano and John Doelp, and producers David Foster, Jim Steinman and Humberto Gatica put together an album that was musically astonishing.

Originally, reclusive pop genius Phil Spector was supposed to produce the album. But the collaboration ended, and control of the record changed hands. It was a bitter moment, but the sweet victory of the album's success made it easier to swallow. Ironically, though, Celine did end up recording one of Phil Spector's big hits when she did her rendition of Tina Turner's 'River Deep, Mountain High', produced this time by Jim Steinman.

Celine sang her heart out. She had always been a powerhouse singer but, with this album, she seemed to pour her very soul into the songs. Her flair for drama and her emotional presence were as moving as the songs themselves. She was the quintessential entertainer, the essence of intensity.

It was all raw emotion, vocal power, and a synergy of musical styles – from the Olympian climax in 'All By Myself' to the soulful 'River Deep Mountain High'; from the reggae 'Make You Happy', the sultry 'Seduces Me', the ballad 'It's All Coming Back to Me' (Celine's favourite) and the melodic 'Falling Into You' title track, to the emotional song 'Fly', dedicated to the memory of Celine's niece Karine.

In a rather lack-lustre year for record sales, anxious retailers desperately needed a hit. They breathed easier once *Falling Into You* was released. 'In only one store, the CD sold 400 copies in two hours on the first day it went on sale,' said Rob Mitchell, national director of press and publicity for Sony Music Canada. Sony shipped a staggering number of copies and was already taking repeat orders just two days after the album's release.

The new album showed off Celine's incredible vocal range and power, as in 'All By Myself', which featured frequent key changes and also required her to hold a note for over ten seconds for an 'Olympian vocal climax' as one critic called it. The remake from a 1975 original version was not only musically sensational but also especially poignant because it spoke of the deep loneliness that Celine herself felt at times.

Despite the fame and the glory, she still had her fears and clung desperately to her family and René. She partly attributed her fear of being left alone to being so much younger than her siblings. In 1996 Celine was twenty-eight years old, but eight of her brothers and sisters were well into their forties and fifties. Even though they had always been bound together by music, they were generations apart and – in terms of life experience – worlds apart. Her mother was almost seventy now, and her father was already seventy-four.

Celine was still concerned about René's health since his heart attack in 1992, and René was now fifty-four. Celine did not want to end up all by herself. 'What counts the most for us today is to give life to a child,' she said. 'This will be the most beautiful news of our life.'

Even before the 12 March album release, Celine was already making waves on the talk-show circuit. She sang 'Because You Loved Me' for Jay Leno on *The Tonight Show*, where he introduced her as one of the most beautiful voices in pop music. Wherever Celine performed the song – and she seemed to perform it *everywhere* – it captivated audiences. 'Because You Loved Me' soon became the emotional ballad of the year. It was the song to which people said their marriage vows. Couples and families across the world made it 'their song'. It became the biggest adult contemporary music hit of all time, propelling Celine's *Falling Into You* album into the *Billboard* Top Ten for fifty-two consecutive weeks.

She was still Celine – gentle, kind and simple, yet she had risen to the highest echelons of fame as the best-selling pop vocalist in the world. When the media started calling her 'the hottest singer on the planet' it was clear that she had captured the hearts of people everywhere.

Everyday René pored over the steady stream of hit chart magazines and reviews. Seeing her climb the charts was his greatest thrill.

'Because You Loved Me' reached the number one spot on *Billboard's* Hot 100 Singles, by only its third week and stayed number one for six weeks. 'Because You Loved Me' spent sixteen weeks in the Top Five. Most important of all, it became the biggest adult contemporary hit of all, staying on top for nineteen weeks! Over-riding the previous record of thirteen weeks (belonging to Mariah Carey and Boyz II Men for their song 'One Sweet Day'), 'Because You Loved Me' was the most-played song in the US, number one in the airplay chart for fourteen weeks!

The *Falling Into You Around the World* tour was Celine's most ambitious concert series to date. Her performances were sensational, bringing in the classics as well as new numbers, often starting with the song that had rocked the hit charts, 'The Power of Love', and somewhere along the way her once-upon-a-time hit 'Beauty and the Beast'.

On stage Celine is completely at ease. The stage is where she comes alive, where she is whole. Celine talks about her fans as if they were her reason for existing: 'You are my life but, in a way, the only way I can touch and reach you and see you, is when I am on stage so I share a stage. I think it's the gift of showbusiness.'

Celine has always talked about her need to connect with the audience and her need to be on stage. For it is only there that she is in total control. 'When I go out there nobody can come on stage and tell me what to do or what to say. "Celine be careful . . . don't do that . . . don't be too funny . . . don't be this . . . and that . . . and don't forget to mention . . ." I can just go on stage like an animal out of a cage.'

Falling Into You took her to more places in the world than she had ever been before and, for Celine, language was no barrier. 'When I see the fans sing with me and I see their eyes . . . they give me back so much and I need to give them back something. The best time of my life is when I'm on stage.'

One of the main ingredients of her show was her personal chats with the audience in between songs – funny anecdotes about her life, with a warm, humorous quality that was uniquely Celine. 'I stood on the kitchen table when I was five years old and they gave me a pencil to use as a microphone. But I knew that it was not a real microphone. I knew that it was only a pencil,' she would tell her audience, who were as easily moved to laughter by her stories as they were moved to tears by her songs.

She had a worldwide fan base and she was adored everywhere even if she didn't always understand the language. 'It is nerve-racking, a little bit, to go on stage and say "Hello everyone" and they respond to you in another language. Sometimes it's funny, sometimes it's touching, sometimes it's embarrassing, but it's still wonderful.'

She had a great relationship with her fans but it could be overwhelming at times. Her massive bodyguard Eric Burrows explains: 'It all depends on how Celine perceives the situation. She's very good with fans. If she gets a good vibe from the fan she'll talk to them. If there's a bad vibe then I'll just handle it my way and that's that.' And 'his way' is to sometimes pick up a fan and just move them to the side. For fans like Stéphane Soucy, who have followed Celine's career since she was a teen, 'Celine is always friendly, always nice. She is the kindest person and always gives everything she has on and off the stage.'

Her shows now included everything from passionate love songs to pop rock, where she stood centre stage, showing off her long legs, swaying to the beat, even thrusting her hips out Elvis-fashion.

Celine grasped the microphone in her left hand as her right hand danced through a million and one gestures, clenched in emotion, raised for impact, held out in front of her for drama. Her face contorted. And her tears flowed, especially if, she talked about her family or anything moving. The comic in her came out in a diverse array of facial movements. Celine winked her right eye at the audience and sometimes even crossed her eyes – whatever it took to illustrate her anecdotes. She arched her back until her head almost touched the floor. And Celine's rendition of a sax or electric guitar was not to be believed when she introduced the band members by vocally imitating all their instruments. She mimicked André Coutu on guitar, Marc Langis on bass, Yves Frulla on keyboards, Dominic Messier on drums, Paul Picard on percussion, the sweet soulful voices of back-up singers Terry Bradford, Elise Duquay and Julie LeBlanc, and – last but not least – Claude 'Mego' Lemay, her orchestra leader on piano.

For Celine, an audience of 10 or 10,000 was all the same. Except that now it was more like 20,000, 50,000 or 70,000. No matter. She was still connecting one to one. And the reviews were almost unanimous: 'Dion sells without selling out', 'Seamless effort soars above', 'Dion comes from a place many of her peers will never reach.'

Celine, who had performed in Marseilles, Lyon and Bercy in France and Brussels in Belgium earlier in 1996, was on a new concert tour for *Falling Into You* that would see her spiral to the top across the world. From 18 March to 1 April, Celine gave nine concerts in Australia and New Zealand for the debut of her *Falling Into You* tour.

Celine was even on tour on her birthday. When the clock struck midnight, on the day of her twenty-eighth birthday, she was in front of a huge audience in Australia. Celine 'wowed' the crowd and was then 'wowed' in return, as the entire audience (who had found out that 30 March was her birthday) broke into a cheery rendition of 'Happy Birthday' when the clock struck midnight. Moved by their affection, Celine sang on and on . . . extending her performance for the crowd of well-wishers.

What a birthday present! *Falling Into You* entered the French Top Fifty in second place, as the first place was still occupied by *D'eux*. (That album had outsold Michael Jackson's legendary *Thriller* album in France, which had held the previous record of 2.5 million copies sold in France. *D'eux* had sold more than 4 million and established another record.) Between 1 April 1995 and 1 April 1996, over a fifty-two week period, *D'eux* was in the number one spot for forty-four weeks. Ironically, it was only the *Falling Into You* album that nudged *D'eux* off the top!

Despite her global success, home is still where the heart is and Celine came back to Montreal on 10 April 1996 to cut the ribbon at Montreal's new concert hall and sports complex, the Molson Center. It was a magnificent venue for her concert series. Celine commanded the room and looked every bit the vision of success, dressed in a sophisticated white suit and with a lighter, layered hairdo. Her songs sent an emotional shiver through the crowd, her voice was 'a diamond with no audible flaw', according to one reviewer.

Her voice quivered with vibrato as she brought in the muscle of her past hit 'The Power of Love', then rocked the house with her hips swaying to the beat. She captivated the crowd when she arched her back and almost touched the floor behind her in her soulful rendition of Tina Turner's 'River Deep, Mountain High'. The band was in perfect sync with her . . . and the beat was hot . . . until Celine changed pace, as three video screens showed scenes from the movie *Up Close and Personal*, and she sang her latest theme song 'Because You Loved Me'. She was not only centre stage, she found herself sharing the screen with Robert Redford and Michelle Pfeiffer.

Her songs were played on the radio all the time, although Celine confessed that she did not listen to her own songs on the airwaves. 'When I hear my songs, I change the channel,' she said. But millions of others were happy to tune in to Celine whenever they could.

Meanwhile, with all the excitement of the new album, there was still more to come. Celine had been chosen to sing at the opening ceremony for the Olympic Games in Atlanta. She would perform 'The Power of the Dream', a song written for the event by David Foster, his wife Linda Thompson, and Babyface. David Foster had also produced Celine's hits 'The Power of Love' and 'Because You Loved Me'.

It seemed that Celine had been chosen over American singer Gloria Estefan. Estefan, who had prepared a song written specifically for the occasion, had apparently been relegated to the closing ceremony instead.

During the months leading up to the Olympics Celine kept up her strict regime of rest, vocal exercises, and total silence for long periods to keep her voice in top shape, even though she did take time out to accept a World Music Award in Monaco, in May.

The world was at her feet, and when it was time for the Olympics there was never an athlete as toned and prepared as Celine. Then the moment arrived. Celine would reach the biggest audience of her life and become a true world-class athlete of song.

On 19 July 1996, Celine counted the hours until the evening, when she sang at the opening ceremony of the Twenty-sixth Olympic Games and took her place on that pedestal. Celine sang 'The Power of the Dream' as only she could, in front of 100,000 live audience members and 3.5 billion television viewers. From her first song, 'It Was Only a Dream', at the age of twelve, to 'The Power of the Dream', at this very moment, it was as if her life had come full circle.

Celine later said that this performance was the highlight of her career so far. 'You know, I was so honoured to be part of the Olympics. I have to tell you, it was definitely the biggest moment of my career when they asked me to sing the song that was written especially for the athletes.' Celine donated the money she received for the occasion, plus a contribution of her own, to the Canadian team to support Canadian athletes. 'It was really an honour for me to be here tonight,' said Celine. 'Nothing is more grandiose than this.' ' The Power of the Dream' was also released on the B side of the single, 'It's All Coming Back to Me Now'.

It had been an incredible experience for Celine, but she would need every ounce of her athletic stamina for another series of concerts that she was due to start throughout North America. The five-week tour began on 23 July 1996 and included an exhausting twenty-five concerts in nineteen states. These sold-out concerts were a marathon for Celine who only faltered near the finish line as she doubled over in pain with stomach problems that forced her to cancel her last two concerts, scheduled for Portland on 31 August and Seattle on 1 September.

Celine's appearance on the *Rosie O'Donnell* show came right at the time of her stomach problems and her two concert cancellations. 'You know what,' Rosie told her audience, 'Celine Dion actually had to cancel two concerts because she is not feeling well. And, in fact, she's going to go to the doctor right after this. But she's still here. Isn't she a trooper?'

When Celine came out on stage, Rosie's audience went wild. Celine stood, taking it all in, with her new, softer-styled, shoulder-length, auburn-streaked hair, her slim figure accentuated by a black mini skirt and a black short-sleeved, tight-fitting blouse. Backed by a choir of seven, Celine sang 'It's All Coming Back to Me Now'. When the performance was finished, Rosie couldn't stop hugging her.

'Look it,' she said to Celine, motioning to the audience. 'That's our first standing ovation, you know.'

'I'm telling you, you have a heck of a crowd,' said Celine.

'I'm telling you . . . you have a heck of a voice,' replied Rosie.

If Celine's songs were a hot topic, her family provoked even greater fascination.

'You're one of thirteen kids?' remarked Rosie.

'I'm the fourteenth. Some people know that i'm the youngest of a big family. But you know what, here is something you don't know. What you don't know is when my parents got married, my dad didn't want to have any children. And nobody believes him. But it's the truth. He didn't want to have any children,' admitted Celine.

'Really?' asked Rosie in amazement.

'Poor dad, eh?' answered Celine.

'Obviously! Who was the boss in that family?' Rosie asked.

'Who was wearing the pants?' repeated Celine. 'I don't know.'

'Nobody,' answered Rosie without skipping a beat. Celine and Rosie burst out laughing as they high-fived each other in the air.

But some sexual innuendoes were no laughing matter for Celine.

From time to time, less pleasant surprises had been in store. For example, in September 1996 the French magazine *Psychologies* ran an article by Isabelle Taubes that stunned many readers by comparing Celine's voice to a phallic symbol. Later, Taubes explained that she had only meant this in psychoanalytic terms!

When Celine appeared on the cover of the international edition of Time magazine on 12 August 1996, the publicity was much more welcome. The issue came out while Celine was hard at work on her

American tour. The cover was spectacular, with a headline that read: 'The Divas of Pop'. The smaller headline read: 'Olympic songbird Celine Dion leads a chorus of women heard around the world'. Inside the issue, the article, called 'Tuned in Everywhere', read: 'It takes more than awesome talent to make Celine Dion a global superstar'.

Although this issue was not distributed to all countries (*Time* magazine has several different cover versions throughout the world) the article definitely put Celine at the forefront. 'The power behind the song . . . is her bring-the-house down voice . . . a soaring pop aria. The voice that glides effortlessly from deep whispers to dead-on high notes . . . a sweet siren combines force and grace,' wrote *Time* magazines' Charles P. Alexander. Though the article talked about the domination of pop by many divas – like Houston, Carey, Estefan and Lennox – it mainly focused on Celine. She was climbing higher and higher with every passing month. 'I'm so lucky to have a career like this,' she said. 'But I need momentum. In showbusiness, timing is very important, and right now it's happening.'

This was only the beginning of a whole new avalanche of magazine articles and talk-show appearances that year, including *The Late Show with David Letterman*, *The Oprah Winfrey Show*, and *Live with Regis and Kathie Lee*. The crew from *Good Morning America* on the ABC network even came to Quebec City to do a special segment on Celine with just the right 'French' ambiance.

On 23 and 24 August, Celine gave her first concerts at the legendary Caesar's Palace in Las Vegas. Another dream of Celine's had become a reality. René, with his passion for gambling, was no stranger to Caesar's Palace. In fact he stays there with Celine in their own penthouse suite on a regular basis. But this time it was different . . . It was not only the gambling machines that glittered. The giant billboard outside the hotel, that read simply 'Celine' also lit up the town.

As a performer at Caesar's Palace, Celine had all the right moves, as she enthralled the audience in her shiny wet-look black leather top and pants. Her sister Manon was there too. She had started accompanying

Celine on her tours and it was great to have a sister around. In addition to doing Celine's hair and helping her with her wardrobe, it was reported that Manon could also read Celine's lips when she put herself in a self-imposed mute state before and after performances.

CHAPTER 19

Barely Time to Breathe

'Sometimes, I don't even remember what city I'm in. I always double check before going on.'

– CELINE DION

C eline lived from performance to performance and from plane ride to plane ride, seeing the world through the windows of her privately owned jet. She was constantly soaring through time and space. Where was she this morning? Paris, Amsterdam . . . ? The skies had become her home.

Her European tour saw her performing in forty-four concerts from 29 September to 29 November 1996, as she sang her way through France, Belgium, Germany, Denmark, Sweden, Norway, Italy, Switzerland and the United Kingdom. Always in touch with her fans, Celine even ran contests where they could win an all-expenses paid trip to any one of her European concerts. Her talent knew no limits, but her career was moving at a dizzying pace. 'Sometimes, I don't even remember what city I'm in and I always double check before going on,' she revealed.

As Celine travelled the world, it was not so much what she saw of the world, but rather, what the world saw of her. For the most part, Celine never had time to look at the scenery. The exhaustion and stress had caught up with her several times already, but now, as she prepared to embark on a world tour, it was her marriage that she reflected on.

It was now nearly two years since her fairytale wedding and Celine was finding that marriage took a lot of work and compromise. It wasn't easy for any couple, but she and René had the added pressure and stress of all the touring. 'I don't talk to anybody about it,' said Celine. 'We're two adults. We can fix our own problems. When we fight, he has a hard head, and so do I,' she admitted. How easy was it to be married to someone who also managed your career? How easy was it to be the husband of the star?

There were anecdotes that Celine would tell from time to time. 'We had one memorable fight concerning René's telephone attachment. It made me crazy,' she confessed in an interview with the Canadian magazine *Chatelaine*. 'He's talking *about* me, but I'd rather he talk *to* me.' Celine made her point. 'When I toured in Australia this spring I left him for almost a month, and he missed me so much, he made a promise. He said, "When you come home it'll be just the two of us. No phones." '

But Celine was also quick to point out how difficult she could sometimes be. 'I take out my frustrations on René. It's true.' Being in the limelight wasn't easy. Pressure, pressure, pressure. But at least they were both driven by one vision.

'She wanted to be a star . . . I wanted her to be a star,' says René.

'We both have the same dreams,' adds Celine.

René is always nearby. Whether he is beside Celine in an interview, behind the scenes (his favourite place), or observing from the audience, Celine often looks to him for answers when asked certain questions. You don't always see him, and you don't always hear his voice, but you feel his presence wherever Celine is.

During one particular television interview on the Canadian information show *W5*, interviewer Sandie Rinaldo put René in the hot seat. 'There are people who say that you totally control and totally dominate the relationship, professionally and personally. Do you agree with that?'

'Na,' answered René. He was wearing all black and spoke with his characteristic rasping voice, deliberately, slowly, measuring every word.

'I'll tell you, people that know us, that are around us, they know exactly what's happening.'

'You're not a control freak?' she asked pointedly.

'I'm not a control freak,' he replied expressionlessly.

Sandie Rinaldo stared at him, ready to ask him her most searching question yet. 'Are you a Svengali?' she asked.

He sighed in disgust. 'Puuuh,' he mumbled. 'Look, I love what I do. When she was twelve, or thirteen, fourteen . . . With the experience that I had in this business, she counted on that.'

Sandie had her own views on René's role in her career. 'It was Angelil who convinced her to learn English and orchestrated her move to the world market. He also transformed her from an awkward adolescent to a sexy songstress.'

Celine was loved throughout North America and in just about every corner of the world. Some fans even followed her from concert to concert, according to her bodyguard Eric Burrows. She was 'Queen Celine' wherever she went – Europe, Africa, South America, Asia, over-riding even the popularity of the Beatles, the Rolling Stones and Michael Jackson.

Even on the Internet, Celine was one of the 'best connected' stars in the world, with close to 5,000 websites, in a variety of languages, including English, French, Afrikaans, Chinese, Dutch, German, Italian, Portuguese, Spanish, Swedish, Danish and Greek.

Celine had her own official website and a variety of others set up by dedicated fans who had vast numbers of Internet subscribers glued to the screen, anxious for the latest news, or the lyrics of a new song. There was even a 'chat line', enabling fans across the world to discuss their fascination with Celine.

One couple fell in love while conversing on the Internet. She was from Montreal. He lived in Copenhagen. When they finally met, after years of talking on the net . . . it was love at first sight. They recently married and went back to Denmark to live – that's the power of love!

Celine continued to travel the world . . . although her life was ever more exhausting, she never complained, according to Maman Dion. Agrees her close pal, Montreal talk-show host Sonia Benezra: 'She *detests* when people say, "Poor little one . . . you must be *so* exhausted . . ." She knows that she is lucky to live in extravagance and luxury. She doesn't complain. On the other hand, she doesn't have the time to savour life.'

Celine saw less and less of her parents, but still tried to keep in contact with her mother as often as possible. 'I call my mum every single day,' she said. 'I could be in Australia . . . in Japan . . . in Toronto . . . wherever I am, no matter the hour or the time change, I call my mum. I don't talk long, I just say, "Hi. How are you? I know you're sleeping right now. I just want you to know that I'm fine. I ate today. And everything is okay. I love you." '

Late in September there was another important development in Celine's career. *Falling Into You* had reached the number one spot on the *Billboard* Top 200 chart for the year. It was in first position for a total of three weeks in 1996. This was the first time an album of Celine's had reached the top of *Billboard*.

Celine now had a truly international audience. She had even recorded the song 'Solo Otra Vez' (the Spanish version of 'All By Myself').

These days, Celine spent more time abroad than at home. In a magnificent castle in Prague, she recorded the video for 'It's All Coming Back to Me Now', and at the magnificent Zenith Concert Hall in Paris, Celine recorded another album, *Live à Paris* (Live in Paris).

Live à Paris featured songs from the *D'eux* album, the best-selling French-language album of all time, plus other French hits of hers and successes in English, such as 'The Power of Love' and 'River Deep, Mountain High'. But the gem was 'To Love You More', with sensational lyrics written by David Foster and Edgar Bronfman Jr., and a wonderful violin accompaniment by Taro Hakase.

On 1 November 1996, Celine wrote a new page in the record book of the French music industry. She became the first artist to have three of her albums in France's Top Twenty – all at the same time! That week,

Live à Paris entered the charts in the top position, her third number one album in France. (*Falling Into You* and the *D'eux* album were in the Top Twenty as well.)

Celine's 1996 European tour ended on 29 November at Wembley stadium in England, but it was not the end of her travels. She also participated in the Billboard Music Award show in Los Angeles, in early December and a few days later, on 5 December, she appeared on *The Tonight Show* – again.

It had been an incredible year for Celine – a truly record-breaking one. In fact the *Guinness Book of Records* for 1996 included Celine (in good company, with Steven Spielberg for highest box office sales of 868 million dollars for *Jurassic Park*, and supermodel Claudia Shiffer for 600 magazine covers in a year). Celine had the record for the song '*Pour que tu m'aimes encore*' ('For You to Still Love Me') from her *D'eux* album. The song had achieved the world's longest reign on top of the hit charts, staying at number one for sixteen consecutive weeks.

During that single year, Celine had given 116 concerts, in front of nearly a million and a half people. She was topping the charts everywhere – it was the best career year of her life so far.

It was finally time to come back to Montreal. Celine could not hide her inner loneliness as she travelled across the world. It was the bittersweet price of stardom. 'I love coming home,' she confessed. 'It is secure and I need the security of home. Two days every six months to come home is very, very hard. I miss my origins. I miss my family.'

Celine and René celebrated their second wedding anniversary in Montreal on 17 December, giving a press conference outlining all her achievements and future plans and kicking off a series of three concerts – the first one that very night.

Sony announced the worldwide sale of 18 million copies of *Falling Into You* by Christmas, including 8 million in the United States. And Celine received a diamond record for over 1 million copies sold in Canada, the first artist to get a diamond record for two consecutive (English), albums. All the top executives from Sony USA (550 Music) and Sony

International came to Montreal to present Celine with congratulations and plaques.

But, despite the accolades at the press conference, reporters had other questions in mind. The main topic of discussion was Celine's desire to have children. Celine seemed frustrated by the flood of questions about the couple's attempts at having a child. At the same press conference, she announced that she was still not pregnant, but remained intent on starting a family.

Over the years, Celine had been known for answering every question, from the sublime to the ridiculous. For example, even when the British magazine Q asked her whether she ever had sex to her music, she gamely replied, 'Wow, I've never thought about anyone making love to my music but I like the idea of sharing people's most intimate moments. I personally don't do it to music, but, mmmm, it sounds good.'

They also questioned her about whether she would ever have plastic surgery. 'Three or four years ago, I wouldn't have said no to it, but not now. A lot of people have suggested I change my chin but I'm a singer and it might change the way I sound. I'm not a model whose job it is to look beautiful. My work is to put as much feeling into my songs as I can.'

But today, the day of her second wedding anniversary, things had become a little too personal. 'Look,' she said angrily. 'I don't think it's news to say that we have been trying to have a child.' Then she composed herself, and succumbed.

'We're still trying,' she told the packed press conference at the Molson Center before her show at the arena that night. Even this was rare for Celine – to give a press conference and use her voice before a concert. As for the gossip, Celine only appeared nonplussed by it, though it clearly bothered René.

'I'm not affected by that,' she said. 'I know who I am. I just want to have, as much as possible, a normal life. I don't read newspapers, I don't listen to the radio, I don't want it to sound rude, but I don't care.'

One thing Celine admitted was that she was 'under stress' and said, 'Of course, I don't have to tell people what my schedule is like. If you're under stress, your body is working against it. I hope it'll happen as soon as possible and I think it'll happen when I take a break.'

A year before, she had looked forward to 1997 as a sabbatical year. But, at the press conference, René said it would have to be delayed to May.

'Oh, now it's May 5,' she quipped in mock exasperation.

Celine would have loved some time off. A year was what she had hoped for . . . especially as she felt that some time off would make it easier for her to get pregnant.

However Vito Luprano, who was now the vice-president of Sony Canada, said that Celine probably would not take a year off this year – only a few weeks now and then – because she was in such demand.

Celine was wanted just about everywhere.

CHAPTER 20

The Price of Glory

'There is a price to pay and the biggest price is to be away from the people who love you the most.'

– CELINE DION

I t was early one February morning in 1997 when René leaned over his dreaming wife. He had already been up for hours. 'You've been nominated for four Grammy awards,' René told her. Lying in bed, Celine smiled. 'Well,' she said, 'is it sunny outside?'

In her own way, she was trying to deal with her vast fame. Despite the special place her Oscar and Grammy for 'Beauty and the Beast' had in her heart, and the countless other awards she had won across the world, by early 1997 her main preoccupation was trying to cope with her success while keeping both feet on the ground.

As New York City's Madison Square Garden prepared for the 26 February show, Celine confessed, 'Prizes are no longer my top priority.' Having children was. She often mentioned how badly she wanted children, but the stress of life in the public eye, coupled with her history of an irregular cycle, had made starting a family tough. Meanwhile, life had to go on.

'If it happens, it happens,' she said. 'If it doesn't, it doesn't. In any case,' she added, with a grin, 'René and I are having a wonderful time trying.' On talk show after talk show she would say, 'The rehearsals are going great.' It was a joke that took the edge off the pain of the emotional roller coaster she was on.

Around 9,000 members of the National Academy of Recording Arts and Sciences had to vote for Grammy nominees and Celine was a top contender. When the day of the Grammy awards finally arrived, Celine won Album of the Year and Pop Album of the Year, both for the *Falling Into You* album. Diana Ross and Sting presented the award for Album of the Year. And when they called out her name as the winner she was visibly overcome and had to be helped out of her seat by René!

Celine walked up to the podium, wearing a taupe dress that clung to her slim body like a glove. But she had decided not to wear a slip with the dress. And, as she approached, the bright stage lights and the cameras started flashing, and the dress became transparent, revealing a perfect outline of her panties.

Of course Celine did not know she had just become a photographer's dream as she accepted the award for Best Album from presenters Diana Ross and Sting. The most transparent thing about Celine was her emotions and it was easy to read the joy in her heart as all her producers came on stage and surrounded her.

'This is incredible!' Celine said. 'Is anybody taking a picture right now!' Little did she know . . . It was only later that Celine found out about the *faux pas*. The 'slip-up' had tongues wagging the next day, when a photo of Celine's translucent Grammy attire appeared in newspapers and magazines everywhere – even *Playboy* magazine. Celine was mortified. 'You could see right through! I'm not an exhibitionist,' she explained. 'And I don't want to be perceived like Madonna.'

Later she confessed, 'I felt completely undressed,' although she said that she didn't lose any sleep over it. 'After all, I didn't pose nude. I was wearing a knit dress. Since I found it opaque enough, I decided to wear it without a slip. No one paid any attention to it until the moment I was in front of photographers who, with their flashes, saw through my dress.'

Falling Into You had already sold more than 21 million copies worldwide by February 1997, less than a year after its release. Celine clearly had a gift for deeply emotional songs of love and inspiration.

'Her emergence has come at a time when people are tired of hearing doom and gloom and "I hate myself," ' said Lee Chestnut, vice-president of programming for VH-1, the US video channel. 'Pop music has been positioned for a comeback for a while. Celine was in the right place at the right time and rode along the wave.'

On 9 March 1997, at the Twenty-sixth Annual Juno Awards in Canada, Celine won Female Vocalist of the Year, Best-Selling Album (foreign or domestic) for *Falling Into You*, Best-selling Francophone Album for *Live à Paris*, plus the International Achievement Award which she shared with fellow Canadians Shania Twain and Alanis Morissette. Newspapers called her 'Celine: the Queen of the Junos'.

Canadian artists had sold 65 million albums around the world in 1996. By 1997, Celine's own sales neared that number, with over 60 million albums sold. Always sentimental and patriotic, Celine told country star Shania Twain, that 'When I travel, I hear your music and it feels so good inside. I'm so proud.'

Celine's mantelpiece had to be a big one, with awards in the music industry that year in Greece, South Africa and Ireland as well. By March 1997, *Falling Into You* was number three on the *Billboard* hit charts. It had been on the Top Ten of *Billboard* for fifty-two weeks since the album's release a year before.

In the spotlight, Celine was the star guest of an entire *Oprah Winfrey Show* on 19 March 1997. Celine retold the story of her original song, the one her mother had written. 'It's about a little girl who had a dream and wanted to be a singer. Who wanted to be part of this magic world and who was watching from this big TV set so close that I was on stage with the artists, and I kept dreaming about it. I think dreams are very powerful.'

Then Oprah gave Celine the surprise of her life. She had the entire Dion family – her parents and thirteen brothers and sisters – behind the stage, and they started coming out, one by one, beginning with Maman.

'Surprise!' yelled Oprah.

'Oh, my God,' cried Celine, hugging and kissing everyone, including Oprah.

'This is, to me, this has got to be the most wonderful thing. I can be in showbusiness, and sing, and travel the world and meet some wonderful people, but at the same time there is a price to pay and that's very normal. I'm not complaining. I can just retire and stop right now if I'm not happy, but what I mean is, there is a price to pay and the biggest price is to be away from the people who love you the most, and for you to do this, I love you very much,' she told Oprah.

Oprah was equally moved. 'I know you were upset because you were going to be away during your mother's birthday and you weren't going to be able to see her, and now you can.' Maman was celebrating her seventieth birthday the next day.

Together, the entire family sang Celine's first song, *'Ce n'était qu'un rêve'* ('It Was Only a Dream') and Celine kneeled down on the floor, so as not to block anybody in her family from the audience's view. 'This is your moment,' she said.

But such reunions were rare, even though Celine would do just about anything for her family. For Christmas she had given 100,000 dollars to each and every one of them, including her thirteen siblings and her parents (making a total of a million and a half dollars).

Celine was soon off again, headlining on a major tour of Asia, including Japan, and then returning to North America for a US concert run, also hitting the cities missed on the previous year's road trip. When Celine went to Japan as part of the three-week Asian tour, she didn't relish the thought of going without René. Leaving him always made her sad. 'For starters, travelling to exotic places is no fun without René,' she said. 'It's weird, because I don't care about seeing the beauty of foreign countries if he's not there.'

Celine was then off to the palace of the Sultan of Brunei, off the coast of Borneo. The absolute monarch Hassanal Blokiah, said to be the richest man in the world, had requested her performance. Celine sang there in March 1997 (unaccompanied on this trip by René Angelil) and performed for the Sultan during a concert that lasted approximately one hour. She did not disclose exactly how much she received for this special performance . . . but it was astronomical. (Michael Jackson had received 10 million dollars for singing there in front of 5,000 guests.)

Celine's stay there was uneventful, and she had already left the palace before Miss USA 1992, Shannon Marketic, alleged that she had been pestered for sex by members of the royal household during a promotional visit organized by an LA agency. For Celine, all had gone well when she met the man whose fortune was at the time estimated at 50 billion dollars, including a palace of 1,778 rooms decorated in marble, gold, crystal and precious stones, and 500 cars (350 of them Rolls Royces), not to mention a slew of private jets.

The glitter of that performance was soon matched by Hollywood's splashiest event – the Sixty-ninth Academy Awards, which took place in March 1997. It was brilliantly hosted by Billy Crystal, with an opening overture that was an Academy award-winning performance in itself. It was the night of the underdog, as Geoffrey Rush won Best Actor for *Shine*, Frances McDormand won Best Actress for *Fargo*, and Cuba Gooding Jr. won Best Supporting Actor in *Jerry McGuire* ('Show me the money!'). Above all, it was the night of *The English Patient* which took home nine Oscars.

'Because You Loved Me' was nominated for Best Song, and Celine also performed the song that night. Barbra Streisand was at the gala with her beau James Brolin. Her song 'I Finally Found Someone', from *The Mirror Has Two Faces*, was also a nominee for Best Song. But Barbra would not be singing the song that night – Natalie Cole, daughter of legendary Nat King Cole, was supposed to perform the number.

As Celine sang 'Because You Loved Me' the audience was enthralled, not only by her talent – Celine also looked gorgeous in a spectacular silver Chanel gown, worn with a 658,000-dollar Chanel necklace that had four sweeping tiered swirls of diamonds cascading down her neck. There was a story behind the dress. When Celine had to choose an outfit for the Academy Awards, she had her sights set on a particular, low-cut, silver Chanel dress long before. 'I had a picture of a voluptuous model wearing the dress,' explains Celine. 'It was very low-cut and *very* revealing. I showed it to René and he said "Celine! Have you learned nothing about showbusiness. I promise you that if you wear this dress, your career in showbusiness will be finished!"'

But Celine was not about to give up – after all, she already had the dress in her closet! 'I went and tried it on, then stepped in front of René.'

'Wow, that is the most beautiful dress I've ever seen. You have to wear that to the Oscars,' he cried.

'But René,' I said, 'it is the same dress as in the picture – just the chest is different!'

As Celine finished singing 'Because You Loved Me', there was thunderous applause. However there was a surprise in store for her later that evening. Natalie Cole had come down with a throat infection and was forced to cancel. At the last minute, the producers of the show asked Celine to fill in. She accepted. This was the first time in the history of the Academy Awards that anyone had sung twice on a show.

Celine sat on a stool, with the words to 'I Finally Found Someone' on a music stand in front of her. Singing Barbra's song took a lot of courage. After all, Streisand was Celine's idol. But she gave a great rendition of the song, accompanied by Altoro Sandobal on trumpet and the wonderful Academy Award orchestra. The audience loved it.

But Barbra Streisand missed the whole thing! She had been out of the room at the time, in the bathroom. The next day the media interpreted this as some sort of slur against Celine, but this was far from the truth.

Neither Barbra's nor Celine's song had won the Oscar. (The prize went to 'You Must Love Me', sung by Madonna in the movie *Evita* and written by Andrew Lloyd Webber and Tim Rice.) But Celine triumphed that night in a more lasting way, singing with perfect pitch and passion

in front of the star-studded audience and more than a billion television
viewers.

'I really wish your song had won. You're a wonderful singer,' said
Barbra later on. With praise like this, from Barbra, Celine felt she had
already won.

Only weeks later, on 5 April, Celine made her Atlantic City debut,
appearing at Trump's Taj Mahal before a discerning crowd who knew
talent when they saw it. As ever, Celine was a huge hit. Donald Trump
watched the show from the front row, along with his daughter Ivanka.

Afterwards, Donald hosted a private party for Celine at the Villa
D'Este restaurant, and later that night, long after Celine had retired to
her room, René and many of the band members (including Celine's
bodyguard) were trying their luck at the casino. René loved the game
and had been known to wager on just about everything. After all, he
had wagered on Celine long ago and won. And, at twenty-nine, she had
already rewritten pop history.

After more tour dates, that would take her to Boston and the
Foxwoods Casino in Connecticut, Celine was off again – this time to
Monte Carlo.

A picturesque backdrop by day, a glittering casino haven by night,
Monte Carlo is the capital of Monaco, a land of intrigue and romance,
lying on the French Riviera, beside the Mediterranean. It was a perfect
setting for the annual World Music Awards, a renowned event held
under the patronage of His Serene Highness, Prince Albert of Monaco,
along with Princess Stephanie who hosted the evening, honouring
top-selling artists in the major record-buying countries around the
world. The 1997 awards took place on 17 April.

The World Music Awards gala is a milestone event for one of the
most celebrated families in Europe, who were brought to the socialite
forefront when the refined and classically beautiful actress Grace Kelly
(famous for her roles in films such as *High Noon* and *Dial M for Murder*)
married Prince Rainier III in 1956. Upon their marriage, when she was

twenty-seven, she was given the title of Princess.

Princess Grace was loved everywhere in the world, but sadly, in 1982, she suffered a similar fate to that of Princess Diana. Losing her life in a tragic car accident, she left behind three children, Princess Caroline, Princess Stephanie and Prince Albert – who is heir to the throne. Together, they continue the family tradition of devotion to the arts and charitable endeavours.

The World Music Awards was the one night of the year when premiere recording artists throughout the world gathered to give each other a bow. 'This year, the show is truly a family affair,' said Prince Albert, who commemorated the family's seven hundredth year in Monaco.

With tickets selling for 300 dollars each, the event raised a great deal of money for the Princess Grace Foundation and the Monaco Aide et Presence Foundation, two charities that help under-privileged children in under-developed nations of the world.

There was a showcase of stars, with Princess Stephanie hosting the gala, along with co-hosts actress Halle Berry and rock musician Jon Bon Jovi. In the audience, seated in the front row, right next to Prince Albert, was none other than Celine Dion in a beautiful gold-coloured gown that had classic elegance and just enough glitz. Celine looked like Cinderella in the fairytale, sitting between a real Prince on the right, and her Prince Charming, René Angelil, on her left.

As the first performer and first award-winner that evening, Celine was introduced as 'One of the world's most popular artists. An international superstar. The golden voice of Canada'. On cue, Celine appeared on stage in her spectacular gold Versace dress. What a fashion statement! The stunning embroidered dress had a very high slit that came up to just above her left thigh, and Celine wore the gown with an exquisite matching shawl. She was radiant, with her long, gold-highlighted hair brushed back, flowing down past her shoulders and slightly flipped at the ends.

Then Celine was presented with the award for Best-Selling Canadian

Artist. On accepting her trophy, she looked high into the balcony and said, 'I would like to thank all my fans all over the world,' which met with thunderous applause.

The show had a host of incredible artists performing on stage: the Fugees, Ace of Base, Roberta Flack, Lionel Richie, Kenny G., Julio Iglesias, and the Bee Gees. Princess Stephanie announced that Celine Dion had won the award for Best-Selling Pop Artist. But the biggest award was still to come, and it was once again for Celine Dion.

In presenting the award to her Tim Redwin, of the Academy of Arts and Sciences, said: 'Tonight I have the very great privilege of presenting the award to the World's Best-Selling Artist. This goes to someone who has an extraordinary talent. Her music has broken down language barriers, and her success, whether she's singing in English or French, has been sensational. Every country in the world has succumbed to her magic. Nowhere more so than here in Europe, where I'm delighted to say she has received multi-platinum awards for three of her recent albums. Last year alone, she sold more than 25 million albums globally.'

It was an emotionally charged moment. 'Because You Loved Me' was playing in the background as Celine stood up and kissed René on both cheeks and then on the lips. The audience gave her a standing ovation, a great tribute from all those other performing artists and music industry professionals.

Celine was suddenly overwhelmed, nervously tucking her hair behind her ears and staring down at the award. It was a beautiful statuette, holding a raised globe over its head, and Celine held it lovingly, close to her heart, with tears in her eyes.

'Most of all', she said, 'I would like to thank René, my husband, who is also my manager and always made sure I was surrounded with the right people.' René's gaze was solemn and intense, his eyes fixed on her from where he sat in the audience. Even at a distance, he stood out, his characteristic grey braid and beard a perfect contrast to his jet-black tuxedo which he wore with a fashionable banded-collar white shirt.

Celine wanted the world to know what René had done for her through the years. He had moved mountains for her and she for him. 'Let's say, from the day you mortgaged your house to do my first album, to tonight at the World Music Awards, it's been a dream come true with you . . . being married to you,' she emphasized, slowly and deliberately, staring straight at René as she spoke. The room grew silent. René gazed steadfastly at Celine as she spoke the adoring words, trying to keep his composure, but there was no mistaking the tear in his eye. 'I love you very much,' she said emotionally, and the room erupted into applause.

The show was capped off when the Bee Gees were presented with the award for Lifelong Contribution to Music (Outstanding Achievement for a Group) at the end of the show. The Bee Gees performed a medley of their greatest hits and Celine enthusiastically danced from her seat, then stood up clapping and swaying to the rhythm and having a great time. She loved their music. And it was in Monte Carlo that the idea of Celine one day doing a song with the Bee Gees was born.

Celine's dream that her career would take her 'always higher . . . and always farther' had come true. Despite all the money . . . and all the accolades, she remained humble. She awoke the next morning, reflecting on the new title of 'World's Best-Selling Artist' with which she had been crowned in Monaco. 'This makes me the artist that has sold the most records in the world? This is incredible. Nevertheless, I awoke this morning like all other mornings. Life, health, that's important. I have other priorities. Every evening I tell Maman that I love her. I love to make my husband happy.'

She was in the public eye wherever she went and her fan base was massive, extending from continent to continent. For the millions who had seen her perform through the years, she was an 'ambassador of song'.

'When I'm on stage and people show me notes in the audience, I try to read and understand them. They sing me welcome songs and I don't know what they are talking about but it is *so* sincere. That's what I love about music. Music has no barriers. No matter what language you talk, if people say something to me, even if I don't understand the language, through their eyes I see the sincerity and the love and it touches me. So when I am on stage and you talk to me in a foreign language – I feel you. I don't know what you said to me . . . but I felt it. That's why I love music so much because we can travel through music and there are no barriers.'

On 8 May 1997, Celine performed her first Internet broadcast live from her benefit concert at the T.J. Martell Foundation Gala in New York City. The 45-minute performance included her hits, 'Power of Love', 'River Deep, Mountain High', 'All By Myself', 'It's All Coming Back to Me Now', 'Love Can Move Mountains' and 'Because You Loved Me.' Over 8 million dollars was donated at this gala which is the leading charity of the music industry, raising money for research into leukaemia, cancer and AIDS.

Celine played a crucial role, as Celebrity Patron of the Cystic Fibrosis Foundation, in a variety of events, such as the Annual Ball to raise funds for research on Cystic Fibrosis which was held on 16 May 1997 at the chic Le Windsor Hotel in Montreal. More than 900 people attended the event, which raised 300,000 dollars.

Besides helping with publicity brochures and posters, the cause was always on her mind even when she was working and recording.

Not only was Celine involved in the Cystic Fibrosis Foundation, but she also tried to help other sick children. For example, one girl with terminal cancel had expressed a wish to go to a Celine Dion concert and Celine made it all possible. When they came to the dressing room before the show at Madison Square Garden, Celine fell to her knees near the girl's wheelchair and said: 'Here, this is like your place. My dressing room is your home. If you are too tired you can sleep on the sofa. You will hear the songs. Don't be scared.'

Celine was always concerned about everyone else's health. In the spring of 1997, both her mother and René's mother were at the Montreal Heart Institute.

Maman Dion made a full recovery. But, sadly, René's mother, Alice Sara Angelil, died on 27 May 1997 at the age of eighty-two. At her funeral service, there was an incredible level of emotion when Celine sang 'Vole' ('Fly').

René and his brother Andre wept openly and René's oldest son Patrick gave a touching tribute to his grandmother: 'You were love, and affection. We admired you. You were the true pillar of our family.'

René was very close to his mother and her passing left a huge void in his life. Celine was devastated and sobbed incessantly. But only a week later, she would have to be on the road again, living out of a suitcase. Still, she didn't complain: 'After all, I am doing what I love best in the whole world.'

Here is an example of the dizzying pace of Celine's world tour just in the month of June 1997: 12 June: Lansdowne Park, Dublin, Ireland . . . 14 and 15 June: Earl's Court, London, England . . . 18 June: Arena, Amsterdam, Holland . . . 20 June: Stade du Roi Baudoin, Brussels, Belgium . . . 22 June: Parken Stadium, Copenhagen, Denmark . . . 24 June: Walduham, Berlin, Germany . . . 26 June: Letzigund, Zurich, Switzerland.

Celine's music was technically impeccable, with big production numbers and arrangements from the best musicians in the world. She sang, she touched souls, but the music was so polished and sophisti-cated that some critics did not believe that such emotion could be for real. One Montreal music critic wrote: 'Whether you call it crying wolf or singing schmaltz, the big crooners sell soul and, in the process, sell their souls. Millions buy the fantasy.'

Picking up on the idea of schmaltz, Bryant Gumbel asked her in a television interview in 1997: 'One guy wrote that it's called calculated schmaltz.' Celine's command of the English language has come a long way but this Yiddish term seemed to really puzzle her. Her eyes were bewildered, searching for meaning. One side of her mouth curled up in confusion. 'What does that mean? Schma . . . schmaz?'

'You tell me,' retorted Bryant, without explaining the term. 'Another guy said that it was cold and mechanical. That the songs are formula. Does it bother you in the least?'

You could see the hurt in her eyes. 'No. I just came back from a wonderful tour in Europe. One place there were 75,000 people,' she said, referring to the massive inaugural outdoor concert she had played at Roi Baudoin, the gigantic new amphitheatre in Brussels. Her eyes start to fill as she responded to the remark. 'I would love this person to go on stage and tell them that exact phrase. If *they* think it's cold and mechanical. Are they all stupid? Seventy-five thousand people are all stupid?!!'

Celine had sacrificed a great deal to win the love of her fans, and the European tour had left her exhausted – both physically and emotionally. She was feeling ill and finally had to cancel her last concert performance of the tour, on 28 June 1997, at the Stade Couvert Ehrmann in Nice, France.

It wasn't easy. At the time, René was also looking forward to some time off with Celine. 'We'll stop for a year and then we're going to relax, to try to have a baby.' He paused, and then smiled. 'We're trying right now.'

'For two years we've been working on it,' added Celine.

In fact, when Celine cancelled her concert in Nice, there had been some rumours that it was due to pregnancy. These were untrue. But it *was* time for a break – she had earned it.

CHAPTER 21

A Question of Health

'Sincerely . . . I am not anorexic, that's for sure. That is a very grave illness, a grave problem, I couldn't hide that. I am not anorexic, I eat everything I want.'

– CELINE DION

Celine was exhausted. Her mother worried. Her sisters and brothers worried. Her fans worried. Was Celine okay? Not only had fatigue plagued her, but Celine's weight also became the subject of a great deal of public concern. Even in Celine's mid-twenties, when her career started to really take off in the United States, people had already speculated on her waif-like thinness. Why was she so thin? Was she eating? Did she have an eating disorder? Was she anorexic? Bulimic?

'I don't have an excess of weight, as they say,' answered Celine, making light of all the comments about how thin she had become. 'My waist used to be 23 inches or less, but I was too thin,' she admitted, explaining that she didn't watch what she ate, but just burned an enormous number of calories during shows. Over the course of a tour she could lose a lot of weight – when she toured with Michael Bolton, for example, she lost almost 8 pounds.

'I eat often throughout the day, but in small portions. I get my thin look from my father. He eats a lot! He could easily eat a dozen eggs and was far from big!' explained Celine. But Celine's mother had concerns. On one television appearance Celine admitted to having called her mother to reassure her that she had eaten. The talk-show host took one look at Celine and then said, 'I don't know, I think you're looking a little thin.'

Celine assured others that there was nothing to worry about. 'I eat. Some people think I'm sick . . . I don't eat – but I do eat. Don't worry.' She explained that her finicky eating started even as a child. 'When I was little, my mother had to have a lot of imagination for me to eat. I never had an appetite.'

At a press conference in Montreal in 1996, rumours continued to circulate. Celine carefully explained; 'People don't know, the public doesn't know, sometimes when they read in the newspapers or magazines, what is true and what isn't true. I am not anorexic, touch wood.' As she said this she touched the wooden table three times. 'Sincerely . . . I am not anorexic, that's for sure. That is a very grave illness, a grave problem, I couldn't hide that, I am not anorexic, I eat everything I want – especially bananas and cream.' She even confessed to a weakness for chips – at all hours of the night.

But, in years to come, the issue would come up again and again. Tabloids would speculate about her weight, and, on one particular cover of the *National Enquirer*, a photo of Celine was grouped together with those of starlets, such as *Ally McBeal's* Calista Flockhart, under the headline: 'Starving Stars: Diet Torture – Deadly Crisis Sweeps Hollywood'. Even though the article inside hardly mentioned Celine, the photo raised suspicions once again. 'It's absolutely false,' declared Celine. She ascribed her thinness to an active metabolism and pure 'nervous energy'.

But Celine did experience a host of other ailments, such as irregular periods and frequent stomachaches. She had suffered problems at the end of her five-week American concert tour, which began on 23 July 1996 and included an exhausting twenty-five concerts in nineteen states. At this time, Celine's stomach problems had forced her to cancel her last two concerts scheduled for Portland and Seattle. Her abdominal pains were said to have been caused by fatigue and stress. But, never wishing to disappoint the fans, Celine and René rescheduled the concerts for late March 1997.

Celine talked about these health problems when she had appeared on the *Rosie O'Donnell Show*: 'I want to thank you very much for saying to the people from Portland and Seattle that I couldn't be with them. I feel very bad but I want to make it up to them.'

'But you're feeling okay, right?' You're going to be okay?' asked Rosie, with genuine concern.

'I'll be okay,' she replied, looking pale and gaunt. 'I'm going to see the doctor tomorrow. It's just probably . . . I'm just very tired. I'm happy, but tired. My stomach . . .' Celine pointed to her abdomen with an expression of agony. 'I have fever and things like that so I'm going to check it out and I'll come back in top shape!' she added confidently.

Celine rested and tried to recuperate, but by September she had to begin a huge world tour for *Falling Into You*, and she forced herself to go on. She was to fly to Monaco to begin the 47-concert tour of twelve European countries. She had already sung her way through Australia, France and Canada, before stopping in London and doing a full quota of guest appearances on the talk-show circuit, plus recording sessions, and video shoots.

Celine did whatever it took, whatever her mentor told her to do. 'This is my whole life, and this is all I ever wanted to do,' she said. To bring her talent to its fullest potential, she worked harder than ever, with rigorous singing exercises and long periods without talking before and sometimes after performances, to save her voice. Celine constantly strengthened her voice, developed her own style, and polished her performance.

'It's showbusiness,' she said wearily, in an interview in *Time Magazine*, in August 1996. 'I'm not necessarily happy about doing it. But if I do a record I can't just sit down and tell somebody else to do the work.'

However, a week before the start of her European tour, Celine cancelled two performances in Monaco, due to chest and abdominal pains. These health problems also forced her to drop shows booked for 12 and 13 September 1996. They were the third and fourth concerts that she had cancelled in recent weeks. Even Sony Music had heard 'reports' that, at the time of Celine's concert cancellations, the 5 foot 7 inch tall singer weighed only 98 pounds! But a spokesperson for her record label vigorously denied that Celine was anorexic. Other reports said that Celine actually weighed closer to 112 pounds. But, with an average weight for someone of her height recommended to be close to 140 pounds, Celine *was* underweight.

While Celine rested at her home in Florida, the media speculated about her health. Not surprisingly, doctors who examined her for several days in a West Palm Beach hospital found she was suffering from extreme fatigue, as a result of a long and tiring tour.

'Rest, diet and medication have already resulted in significant improvement in Celine's symptoms,' said Dr Sidney Neimark, a specialist in gastroenteritis.

He said tests showed that Dion was suffering from gastroesophageal reflux disease. She had spasms in her oesophagus (the tube that propels food to the stomach from the throat). According to medical experts at the Johns Hopkins Medical Institution, reflux occurs when, for a variety of reasons, the lower oesophageal sphincter allows some acidic stomach contents to pass upward into the oesophagus. Severe, long-standing reflux can result in scarring, which can cause considerable difficulty. There was no question that Celine felt a lot of pain and discomfort because of this disorder.

The Monaco cancellations gave her a much needed three-week break between her US tour (which she had to end prematurely) and the new European tour. She arrived in Paris on Wednesday, two days before the first of five shows at the Bercy Sports Centre for the start of a 32-city concert tour of Europe that would take her to a different city every few days until 29 November 1996. Then, in 1997, Celine was on the road again, with another series of exhausting worldwide concerts. People were shocked when she cancelled her concert in Nice, France, because it was her last concert in Europe and the last leg of her tour. She was then supposed to take a well-deserved year off . . . but there were still big plans for her.

Over the years, Celine's health has constantly been an issue with fans and the media, even if they didn't know exactly what was wrong with her. Even Celine's family had concerns about her health.

'She is often very tired. She must take great care of herself,' said her sister Pauline.

Cancelling shows due to health reasons was not that unusual for Celine. She still had vivid memories of the many times, several years back, when she could not speak and was rendered mute for weeks, communicating to her entourage only through writing and signs. Even today, Celine often comes home exhausted and doesn't speak during the many days she is resting her voice. A strict code of discipline has always been at the heart of her success.

She often drew strength from her family. When she was away Celine spoke constantly to Maman, who passed on news about Celine to her many brothers and sisters. The family mostly filled in the gaps by reading about her progress in newspapers and following it on television.

As her brother Jacques recalls: 'When I have the opportunity to be with Celine, I avoid talking about her work. I want to know how she feels, if she's happy, if her health is all right. Sometimes she admits to being a little tired but she never complains. Like she says herself . . . she lives the life she had always dreamed of living . . . but Celine is as much a sister and a woman as she is a singer. She is very strong, sensitive and demanding towards herself. She gives a lot without waiting for anything in return.'

'I am a very nervous person,' Celine has confessed on many occasions. Her body language also tells one a great deal.

Celine's sister Linda, who is eleven years older than her, has always felt a special affinity with Celine. 'Between all of the sisters and brothers, I am probably the one who most resembles her. Celine and I are a lot alike. When we were young, we were amused to see that we had the same habits in common and also had the same nervous tics.'

Her sister Louise remembers this as well: 'Celine had a nervous tic as a child – I'm almost certain that she still has it today. She rubs her thumbs against her index fingers until she irritates the skin.'

Celine also has the habit of fixing her hair and tucking the left side of her hair behind her ear . . . over and over again. She could easily do this twenty or thirty times during an interview. When she was unhappy as a child, she had the habit of rubbing her nose, and talking about her nose. Celine has a very developed sense of smell. She smells everything before eating or touching it.

Despite the cancellations, Celine achieved great success with her *Falling Into You Around the World* tour. Even though she strongly believed in superstition and luck, the phenomenal success she was experiencing was by no means just due to luck. She worked at her profession . . . training as much as an athlete, and sacrificing much more; achieving her dreams through sheer hard work and self-discipline.

Celine demanded as much or more of herself than anyone else. Earlier in her career, she usually tried to get twelve hours of sleep each day so that she would have the energy to cope with her hectic schedule and performances. And years before, Celine embarked on a rigid personal programme of physical exercise and training. This included a great deal of warm-up, cardiovascular activity and weight-training. 'I could do it anywhere,' she said, 'even in my hotel room, and it's practical because I don't have time to go to a gym. If I don't have time to walk outside, I go up and down the stairs of the hotel.'

Celine often had trouble sleeping and she exercised at night – even after performances. 'The reason why I exercise in the evening is that in the morning I am too slow. It's important for me to do things at my own pace in the morning. I walk slowly, shower as soon as I get up, and I talk very low. I don't drink my fruit juice until it's at room temperature. I really function in slow motion . . .'

e was a smash hit at London's *Smash Hits* Awards. Celine considers her long legs
one of her best features

Celine and Rene walk hand in hand in Monaco

Celine and Rene at the 1996 Billboard Music Awards in Las Vegas

was a dream for Celine to record a song with Barbra Streisand. Their duet, 'Tell Him', s the first single released from Celine's *Let's Talk About Love* album

Grammy slip-up! Celine's dress turned sparent under the camera lights at the h Annual Grammy Awards

Celine turned heads as she, accompanied by Rene, arrived at the 1997 Academy Awards in this stunning Chanel gown and diamond Chanel necklace

Celine's self-confessed fetish for buying shoes means that she owns over 1000 pa

Celine doing her own hair before a performance

ne was thrilled with her People's
ice Award in 1999

A triumphant Celine drew regular standing
ovations at her performances at Madison
Square Garden in New York, September
1998

The Divas Live Concert, in April 1998, saw Celine team up with Aretha Franklin, Carole King and Shania Twain, as well as Gloria Estefan and Mariah Carey, to raise funds for music education in America's public schools

Stevie Wonder, Jon Bon Jovi, Celine Dion, and Spice Girls Mel B and Emma at the *Pavarotti and Friends* 'War Child' benefit concert in Modena, Italy

e Bee Gees sing 'Immortality' with Celine in 97, during the Bee Gees' first United States formance in five years, in the MGM Grand tel in Las Vegas

Celine wearing the *Titanic* necklace at the Academy Awards in 1998

an tenor Luciano Pavarotti kisses Celine's hands after their combined performance in *Pavarotti and Friends* concert

Celine launched her *Let's Talk About Love* tour at Boston's Fleet Center. She appeared with long hair extensions

Celine wearing her avant-garde backwards suit at the 1999 Academy Awards, held in Los Angeles. Celine was nominated for best song with 'The Prayer' from the movie *Quest for Came*

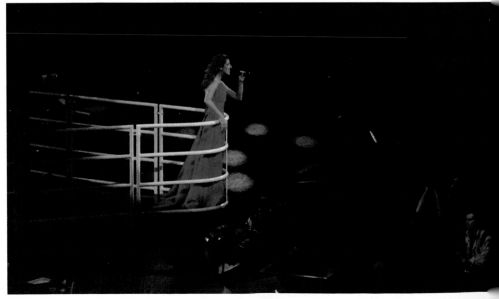

Celine performs 'My Heart Will Go On' during her *Let's Talk About Love* concert to

But nights were a whole different story! That was when Celine came alive – when she was vibrant, and full of energy, with a real 'rush' after a performance.

'After my shows, instead of walking around and chatting, and then later having difficulty sleeping because I am too full of adrenaline, I prefer to exercise. There is also the fact that a work-out puts me to sleep. For others, it stimulates them and gives them energy, but for me, it is not the case. It helps me sleep,' she has said.

For Celine – who took everything to the limit – her nightly exercise programme was not just a twenty-minute deal. 'This training takes two-and-a-half hours,' she says. Even after a concert!

'I do, notably, exercises to develop my cardiovascular system, thirty minutes on the exercise bike, twenty minutes of stretching, and I often lift weights. The stretching exercises are particularly important for me because I have the tendency to stand with my back curved forward. I have the same problem as my father in the way my shoulder blades are . . . My exercises help me to correct this problem . . . but it's up to me also to keep my back straight.'

Painful back problems have plagued her for many years. 'The problem is I have a deviation of the spinal column. I also have two vertebrae that are too close to each other and this sometimes causes inflammation. What is annoying is that this cannot be cured. I am supposed to go to three therapy sessions a week to do different stretching exercises. I try to go there as often as possible but my agenda makes it hard to respect this type of pace. I do everything I can to go to these sessions. When you have a back problem like mine, you don't fool around with it.' Eventually, Celine began travelling with a masseuse to ease her back pain during concert tours.

Celine also has a long-standing heart problem. She explains, 'It doesn't matter whether I am resting or doing any other activity, my heart . . . starts to race and beat very fast. It's really scary. My sister Linda suffers from the same problem. You feel your throat is tightening. You feel like you're choking . . . I could simply be watching television and suffer an attack . . . without warning. My heart starts beating like crazy, then everything goes back to normal.'

This is called tachycardia, – meaning an acceleration of rhythm and excessively rapid heartbeat or racing heart. 'It's a situation that I take seriously,' Celine says. 'That's why I consult my cardiologist regularly.'

However, she believes there is no reason for the public to worry about her health. 'Even if the events of my life take place at a crazy rhythm, I am conscious of what I'm doing and I know what I have invested in. I listen to my body, as they say, and I don't want to abuse my health. When I am tired, I know it, and I take the means necessary to remedy the situation,' she insists.

'I often push myself to the limit. I can explain this by being constantly overcome by a will to always do better . . . to always surpass my most recent performance. Professionally speaking, I'm not the type to let the wave of fame carry me along. I am more inclined to swim against the current, pushing the challenge even farther. But I don't go blindly to meet these challenges. I am aware of the efforts I deploy and the effects of these efforts on my health.'

Yet Celine is also the first to admit how hard she drives herself. 'I've been on stage sick – headaches, stomach pain, fever, even colds before a show when I can barely talk.' Yet, somehow, the 'adrenaline' almost always kicks in and gets her through it.

If Celine's physical health was an issue in 1997 – her mental health was just as important. The tours were physically draining and it was important for her to have as little stress as possible.

'The orders that are given to the members of Celine's entourage,' says her brother Michel, who works on her tours, 'is that she should not have any problems so that her concentration is not disturbed. She is therefore generally quiet in spirit, and, when she has to confide in someone, she can count on Maman or René.'

Over the years Celine has grown stronger and stronger. 'I feel in control,' she says now. She looks radiant . . . and has a body that is perfectly toned, her arms now showing the benefits of years of weight training and a new emphasis on physical fitness, even a passion for golf.

'I love the game because, you know, I spend all my life inside recording studios, TV shows . . . I'm a very nervous person,' Celine confesses. 'The stomach problems are because I'm nervous. Golf calms me down.'

But Celine drives herself hard, even in her leisure pursuits. For instance, her golf instructor recalls, 'Celine wasn't herself one day and I asked her what was wrong. She told me that she had a fever. "Why didn't you just cancel the lesson?" I asked her. "Oh, no. I (almost) never cancel. Even if I am sick," she said. 'There were so many instances when Celine did not cancel, even if she wasn't feeling well. She pushed herself to the limit, and exhaustion became a way of life.

There have been other changes. 'I no longer sleep ten to twelve hours a night,' she says. 'My average now is eight to nine hours. As strange as this might seem, they say that I have less need for rest than before. I remember when, at fifteen years old, I constantly needed sleep. I once slept seventeen hours straight,' laughs Celine. 'They had to wake me up or I would spend my day asleep,' she laughs again.

'I sleep less because, maybe it's a question of age, as if through the years our body gets used to a certain rhythm of life. I also want to benefit from my days and from life.'

Due to the pace of her hectic schedule on tour, Celine was often in pyjamas, on a private jet that whisked her from one country to another.

She says she doesn't read newspapers, even less what the critics have to say. Celine doesn't watch a lot of television either – she doesn't have the time or energy for these distractions. So she doesn't know what is written about her or what people have said about her. 'I don't live with success. I don't wake up in the morning asking myself how many albums I've sold. I want to lead a normal life. I don't live with the critics. I don't want to know what they say about us. I know who we are.'

And, above all, Celine's dream includes having a baby. Despite comments on her weight dropping to what some have called waif-like thinness in past years, Celine has persistently denied rumours of anorexia. 'Today my dream is just to be healthy and happy. There are other priorities, that include having a baby.'

A television interviewer once introduced Celine by saying, 'Behind the veil, behind the fairytale façade, is the deep yearning for something very fundamental.'

Celine was candid. 'For two years I've been trying to have a child. It doesn't work. If I can't get pregnant today, I'm sure it's because I'm constantly working. If ever I get pregnant – if ever I have the chance of being pregnant – I'll stop, no doubt. But, we're working on it. If it happens, it happens.'

Celine's dream of motherhood grew more pressing with every passing month. She knew that stress was making it harder for her to conceive, and she begged for a break. They promised her a year off – to begin right after the *Falling Into You Around the World* tour was over.

'I was giving an interview,' she recalls, 'and a reporter said, "Have you thought of going to a fertility clinic or something like that?" I said, "Sweetheart, have you ever thought that if my husband would be on tour every time with me it would be easier to get pregnant? I'm on tour all the time and he's not always with me." '

Coming from a family of fourteen children, Celine often joked about wanting to have fifteen children. But her heart was on her sleeve when she said, 'To be honest, if . . . we can have one it would be magic.' It was the only dream left in her heart.

CHAPTER 22

The Rich List

*'The fifteenth highest-paid entertainer in the world? Hmmm . . .
I'm used to being the fourteenth.'*

– CELINE DION

C eline could well afford to take a year off by the summer of
1997. Having earned 65 million US dollars, she was now
fifteenth on the Forbes Top Forty list of the world's highest-
paid entertainers. First on the list was Steven Spielberg with 313
million, then George Lucas of *Star Wars* fame with 241 million, and in
third place Oprah Winfrey with 201 million. Celine's earnings even put
her ahead of Michael Jackson and John Travolta.

How did she respond to this distinction? Tongue in cheek, she said,
'Fifteenth? Well, I don't know. I'm used to being fourteenth, [in the
family].'

Celine's story was that of the duckling who emerged a swan. She was
now the picture of class, dominating the pages of fashion magazines
and tabloids, wearing any one of a thousand designer outfits. Fashion
editors salivated over every new creation she wore. She somehow stood
out without being showy – bare midriff, gold metallic fishnet exposing
her minuscule waist, everything from rich creams and reds to elegant
blacks. Celine wore gold lamé and pulled off the look. She put on a
sparkling silver gown and made it look sophisticated, with a new level

of glamour the world seemed to hunger for. She had become a fashion icon.

True to all her girlhood fantasies, Celine was definitely rich and famous. As for houses, in 1997 Celine and René set out to build not one but *two* mansions. The first would be a magnificent haven for the times when Celine wasn't living in hotels, which she sometimes had to do for months at a time.

After the incredible success of the *Falling Into You* album, Celine was acknowledged by the media as not only the most popular singer in the world but the hottest star on the planet. But acclaim from others wasn't enough. As Celine said, 'I want to prove this to myself. I want to be able to amaze myself. Money is secondary.' Now she was determined to *live* her dream.

Celine chose her mansion carefully, loving the sun and warmth of Florida and also highly valuing her privacy. She chose to build a fabulous mansion, at an estimated cost of 10 million dollars, in an affluent area of Jupiter Island, near Palm Beach, Florida.

The house had a spectacular view, facing the Loxahatchee river on one side and the Atlantic ocean on the other. Privacy was a big plus on Jupiter Island, and there was no access to the island unless you were one of the millionaire homeowners or an invited guest. Celine and René's neighbours were Tom Cruise and Nicole Kidman on one side and Mike Schmidt, an ex-baseball player for the Philadelphia Phillies, on the other.

It was not surprising that Celine loved the warmth of Florida so much. Her native Quebec had long cold winters (from October to March) when the temperature could dip as low as 30 degrees below zero, and 15 to 20 inches of snow could fall in no time.

Celine and René had owned a home in Florida for years, and had often retreated to what they called their 'winter home' in Palm Beach Gardens, a gated community in West Palm Beach, Florida. They loved it.

Celine was also a sun-worshipper from way back, believing that the sun did wonders for her looks. 'When I'm exhausted I have a complexion that is almost olive green,' she has said. 'The sun relaxes me.'

By the summer of 1997, work was going well on the dream house on Jupiter Island, with almost 20,000 square feet of luxurious living space, and Celine's distinctive choice of European-style décor combined with a spectacular, futuristic sound system, over forty televisions, and a magnificent wall of twenty-four video/TV screens forming one spectacular image.

Celine loves her privacy, and needs to follow her own rhythm. For this reason, Celine and René also had separate rooms, at opposite ends of the house. While she usually sleeps till noon when she's able to, René is up early at 6 a.m. and is always on the phone. This way they could both have their own space, though they have a magnificent shared bedroom as well.

The house also included a recording studio – every singer's dream – and a guest house for friends. A particular feature was a wall that transformed into a 'tower of water' with fountains and cascades.

Several months after work had begun on their Jupiter Island mansion, Celine and René announced that they were building a second mansion – this time in Quebec.

The newest home, or collection of homes, included a 10 million dollar investment in construction and improvements of their privately owned *Le Mirage* golf club, forty-five minutes from Montreal. For Celine and René it wasn't *all* work and no play. The fruits of Celine's success had enabled them to buy their own private golf course, in December 1996. With René's long-standing passion for golf, and Celine's new-found enthusiasm for the sport, it was a great Christmas present.

They had purchased the golf club outright from partners within a year. According to a close friend of the couple, Celine and René still wanted to keep a strong foothold in Quebec, but they had a difference of opinion as to where. At one time, Celine wanted to build a luxurious house on the waterfront in the Laurentians, an hour north of Montreal, where she could really enjoy the quiet, peaceful rustic surroundings.

Meanwhile René wanted a Montreal home off the golf course. Fortunately, when Celine also discovered that she loved the sport, the choice was unanimous. 'I was looking for something where I could just have some fresh air and be in competition – but not with another person. With myself. That's why I love showbusiness so much. Because you are in competition with yourself. When you are on stage, you want to beat your last performance. You want to beat your last record. And golf is the same thing. You can just go out there and be in competition with yourself. It's wonderful.'

They had to arrange special permits to build not just one mansion, but three additional homes on the land – for members of Celine's family. Looking out over lush grounds, the mansion was to be decorated in an English manorhouse style. According to Celine, 'There will be beautiful bound books, big fireplaces everywhere and comfortable leather sofas.'

Above all, there had to be magnificent bathrooms. 'I remember [as a child] sitting on the edge of the bathtub, watching my eight sisters get ready. I couldn't wait to do my hair. That's why I love bathrooms so much today.'

Celine also remembers the hand-me-down clothes that were always too big, too frumpy, or too matronly looking. The days when Maman sat and sewed her fingers to the bone to make a pretty pink dress for Celine's first television appearance are now a distant but still vivid memory.

'I am a shopaholic,' confesses Celine. She has a passion for expensive footwear and has been know to buy twelve pairs at one time. Even in her first years of success as a teen, Celine was so fond of bathing suits – and sunglasses – she had them in every colour. In one of her homes, Celine has an enormous closet (of 300 square feet) with a heated marble floor.

Celine once participated in a fashion show called *Defile Chanel*. (She loves Chanel and the perfume Chanel No. 5.) She was backstage, getting ready for her walk on the runway, when she suddenly realized that her skirt was made of completely transparent tulle. 'It's see-through,' squealed Celine. 'You see everything!'

At least this time it was for the sake of glamour and not an unfortunate mistake like the one on Grammy night. But, in reality, Celine was not at all shy about her body.

In fact she was very proud of her physique and admitted, 'When I wear something revealing, it's not for the goal of showing off my body. When I wear something sexy, I do it, above all, for me. It's got nothing to do with exhibitionism.' Celine adored photo sessions, just as she had loved having her picture taken as a young girl. Cameras, spotlights – 'I love it when I'm photographed!' she openly exclaims. 'I am not ashamed of any part of my body. However when the lights are shut off – (and when the session is over) I am more reserved. It's bizarre!'

If Celine's fashions were a hot topic, the size she wore was an even hotter one, especially for talk-show host Oprah Winfrey who had finally succeeded in finding the 'recipe' of success for her own health and body image.

'I want to know, can I ask you, what size are you?' Oprah asked Celine.

'I think it depends, you know, at what size [what I want to buy] starts at. There's size two or size four, so I always take the smallest. If it's size two I'll take size two but if it's five I'll take size five. You know what, honey? I'll tell you something. When I like something, Oprah, it doesn't matter the size. I take it because I love it. I want it,' Celine said emphatically.

She even confessed to her obsession with shoes. 'You know when the salesman asks me, "What size of shoe do you want, mam?" I reply, "What size do you have?" [Sizes] five to ten – it all fits me!'

In 1997 *People* magazine listed Celine as one of the ten best-dressed women in the world, in the category of Most Elegant. 'She is sophisticated with a very European taste,' commented the magazine. 'I agree with that,' said Celine. 'At the prices it cost . . . at least it's recognized!'

Celebrities were now admired, not just for their talent, but as leaders of fashion. And Celine, Mariah Carey, Janet Jackson, and a host of entertainers and starlets, were constantly featured in designer fashions, in magazines like *People*, *Us*, and *In Style*.

As one of the best-dressed women in the world, Celine feels that, 'The most important thing is to be good in your own skin or feel good about yourself.' To get to her shopping destination she only travelled in the most fashionable of vehicles. Celine drove a BMW Z3 roadster (the car made famous by the James Bond movie *GoldenEye*); she also had a chorus line of limousines always waiting to take her and her entourage wherever they wanted to go; and a private plane that helped her visit the best designer houses in the world.

Celine's shopping sprees are a worldwide adventure that offer her true pleasure while she is on all those exhausting tours. When she does get a chance to see her sisters back home, it's shop talk all the way. 'We don't talk about showbiz,' says her sister Denise. 'We talk about her latest shopping spree.'

Of all her transformations, her hair has seen perhaps the greatest number of changes – long, short, slicked back, crimped, frizzed, layered, or curly. Over the years, she has changed hairstyles as often as she has changed her look in clothes. She explains it like this: 'I don't have a lot of space. Everything I do is carefully calculated, prepared and worked on, so that all that is left for me in life is the freedom to brush my teeth with the toothpaste of my choice and to have my hair cut if my heart tells me to.'

Once, in her mid-twenties, Celine even went through a Cher phase. Her almost jet-black, straight hair was parted in the middle, and nearly reached her navel. She wore a black lace beaded top, tied in a knot just under her chest, and tight black hipster stretch pants exposing her perfect bare midriff. Her 5-inch platform-sole shoes brought her height to 6 feet.

Her looks are almost as versatile as her voice. She has a real passion for fashion and a stylist of hers once summed Celine up this way: 'Out of control. A fashion victim, but a good one.'

Celine's famous wardrobe was even mentioned in a scene on the American television sitcom *The Nanny*, in which Celine made a guest appearance on 21 May 1997. 'Ooooh, would you look at these gorgeous clothes,' remarks Nanny, played by that fashion maven Fran Drescher, as she goes through Celine's rack of clothes backstage.

'I wish I had a job where I could change into designer clothes every five minutes!' whines Nanny.

Celine (who plays herself, while on tour in London) replies: 'You know this is the only time I'll have in London to really indulge my passion for shopping.'

'Oh, you *got* a passion for shopping?' says Nanny. 'I swear, if you weren't Canadian, internationally successful and could carry a tune, I'd swear we were separated at birth.'

In Paris, Celine frequents the Chanel house whenever she gets a chance. And on visits to New York, she takes time to shop around the clock for her favourite brands, Chanel, Gucci, Ralph Lauren, Versace and Givenchy, to name only a few. Even though her closets are overflowing with designer ensembles, she jokes, 'I *still* have nothing to wear.' Celine travels with Louis Vuitton luggage and there always has to be room for her shoes. She confesses that she owns more than a thousand pairs of shoes.

'Shoes are my drug,' Celine reveals. 'I love high heel shoes. They're very feminine and sexy and you walk differently than when you wear running shoes.' She loves her black Gucci stiletto boots and Chanel slingbacks. And her steel-heeled Rudolphe Menudier shoes are a must. She even adores wearing the designer brand Celine footwear and fashions (no relation to her name). Celine explains: 'I buy the shoes and then I buy the outfits to go with them.' Indeed, her collection could rival that of Imelda Marcos.

Celine is a self-confessed fashion junkie. She admits that clothes are her one and only vice: 'I love beautiful things. There are so many styles in me.'

Being the tallest of the Dion sisters (who average around 5 foot 3), Celine has always loved showing off her body. 'I like anything fitted,' she says, having once had to squirm her way out of her seat at the Grammy Awards because her dress was so tight. 'My mother told me that when you think of comfort, you're getting old.'

Celine has no trouble making fashion decisions. She is the fastest shopper on Fifth Avenue and she is known for buying multiple outfits. Whether it's Gucci or Christian Dior, if she likes it she buys a rainbow of colours in the same style.

As for her passion for golf, she jokes: 'I love golf so much that I bought my own course.' She also loves golf wear by Ralph Lauren and two-tone Ralph Lauren golf shoes. Even her golf cart is the epitome of luxury.

Whether she's in a figure-hugging black Christian Dior gown (so tight at the knees she looks almost mermaid-like) or scintillating in the five-pointed star diamond stud earrings which Chanel gave her as a gift, Celine is always the height of classic elegance. She adores Christian Dior satin evening bags and stiletto heels. Another trademark are her gowns – often revealing and sensuous, created by such designers as Chanel, Versace, Valentino and Yves Saint Laurent.

She wore a watch by Cartier, called the 'Panthere', (also worn by Princess Caroline of Monaco) which retailed for around 10,000 dollars. Celine also has Cartier earrings and her diamond eternity wedding band was a Cartier.

In fact, Celine has quite a choice of watches, including a magnificent diamond- and gem-encrusted Piaget Swiss timepiece . . . valued at 600,000 dollars!

'Every day is my birthday,' she believes. 'I say, treat yourself.' True to her word, she once gave herself a magnificent Breitling gold watch adorned with sapphires and diamonds.

Over the years, clothes have even been a type of therapy. 'Shopping relaxes me,' admits Celine. When loneliness overwhelmed her or she was swept away by a wave of homesickness, Celine always had a remedy.

'When I feel like this, there are only two things that help,' she said. 'One thing is cleaning out my closet.' (Celine then gives the designer fashions to her sisters.) The other is giving my mom or my sisters a facial or a manicure.' And nothing was too good for René. Celine gave him regular pedicures and manicures. She loved him right down to his toes.

Looking good is a full-time preoccupation for Celine, who says she puts on make-up for just about everything. But the feature she least likes about herself, Celine confesses, is her mouth. 'My mom has no lips and I have my mom's lips.' But that doesn't faze her. 'I'm a great kisser anyway.'

Between those lips are beautiful teeth, that have been painstakingly fixed and capped several times over the years. Despite all that Celine has gone through to look good, when a Canadian television interviewer commented on how beautiful the singer looked, she sensed Celine's hesitation. 'Celine, I bet you don't think you're beautiful,' she said astutely. 'I just have this feeling that you still feel that you look like that,' she said, pointing to a picture of Celine as a teenager with crooked teeth. Celine grimaced.

'Do you think you're beautiful now?' asked the talk-show host.

'Well, I feel better. I feel better about myself. Don't think I don't like myself, because I think you have to like yourself to like someone else. Don't worry, I'm okay. Not like when I look at myself in the mirror,' answered Celine.

'Do you think you're beautiful?' she asked again.

'No, I don't think I'm beautiful,' replied Celine, candidly.

'Do you think she's beautiful?' the talk-show host asked the audience. They responded with applause and cheers.

'Stop it,' said Celine, as she smiled.

Celine really needed to relax. When the *Falling Into You* tour ended, in July 1997 she and René went to the spectacular Atlantis Hotel in Paradise Island, Bahamas. They were in the Bahamas for three days, and then left for Florida. The following week, they were going to London to begin recording Celine's next album set for release by November.

In the Bahamas, Celine was suntanned and glowing – spending a lot of time on the beautiful beaches bordering the Atlantis hotel. But, for Celine, there was no time like night-time. She was like an owl that woke up at dusk.

It was 8 p.m. The wonderful French cuisine of Café Martinique was matched only by the quaint charm of its décor, overlooking the calmest of waterfronts. A group of eight walked in, single file. They were a happy, suntanned group and Celine was among them. Ben Kaye, René and Celine's business associate, was there as well. There were no bodyguards, and only a discerning eye would have recognized the superstar. Her hair was pulled back in a tight bun, she wore little make-up and seemed completely relaxed. Her suntanned face was glowing. A short black leather mini skirt and a black V-neck T-shirt were all she needed this evening, a welcome change from the stage outfits she had been wearing for the past months.

A little bonde-haired girl of around five years old came over to say hello to the star, and Celine took time to talk to her. The little girl's face lit up as Celine told her that she liked her jade-coloured dress and that it was a pretty colour, the colour of the ocean.

René (wearing black as usual) sat at the head of the table. He ordered red wine for the whole table, and meals for everyone as well. They talked for hours and if René was a little subdued that night (Lady Luck was keeping him up all hours of the night), Celine was animated and talked away, stopping to take a bite, now and then, of her Caesar salad.

René had asked for the restaurant's specialty, the sumptuous roasted rack of lamb, to be followed by the irresistible chocolate soufflé that had to be ordered an hour in advance. Celine had a sweet tooth and this was a pleasure she was not going to miss.

Celine chatted away, breaking out into spontaneous bursts of song now and then. By the end of the meal, René was definitely showing signs of fatigue. He slumped down in his chair and fell asleep twice during the meal.

Celine, exhibiting her well-known sense of humour, snapped her fingers three times, saying 'one . . . two . . . three' in an effort to gain his attention, but after a while René, who had only been taking a cat nap, awoke and was ready for a night of action at the casino.

At the end of the night, the *maître d'* came over to wish them well, and Celine autographed dollar bills for the waiters. After the meal, she took a limousine back to her hotel, while René stayed on to try his luck at the Atlantis Paradise Island Casino, just across the way. René loved to gamble. Kenny Rogers' song 'The Gambler' could have been written for him. He bet on just about everything. It was even reported that he had once won a Cadillac in a blackjack tournament.

Smiling, jovial Ben Kaye sauntered over to the casino as well. He had a business relationship with René Angelil that stretched back over thirty-five years. Ben is small in stature but big of heart – one of the nicest men in showbusiness. And no one should underestimate his influence in handling Celine's career alongside René. Talking of Celine, he remarks that, 'Many people don't know the real Celine Dion. She is kind, gentle and she doesn't feel or think she is "A Star". Celine loves it when someone comes over for an autograph or photo. She feels good if she can make someone else happy.'

Above all, Ben Kaye is modest and says, laughing, 'I'm the man behind the scenes', despite his new official title of International Consultant. However, in the early years, Ben was always the one who was quoted in the English media on Celine's career, while René was the high-profile manager in the Quebec media. Ben Kaye has a home in the Bahamas, but is not a resident. (As a Bahamian, you aren't allowed to gamble in any casino there.) And he visits Montreal from time to time as a consultant.

'We love it here in the Bahamas,' comments Ben Kaye. 'It's a great tax haven.'

It was just before midnight. René was at a blackjack table, playing one on one against the dealer, as he kept raising the wager on his original 500-dollar bet. He doubled it . . . then tripled it . . . raising the ante with almost every hand. As a true gambler, he kept on building up his bets, his gold and black wedding ring on one hand and a gold and black bracelet on the other shimmering in the sparkle of the casino lights, as he built up a tower of chips. He kept winning. Within ten minutes, he had parlayed several thousand dollars into almost 30,000 dollars. Before leaving the table, he left the dealer a 300-dollar tip.

René was an intense, quiet gambler who was very kind to and supportive of other players when he played with them. He was always ready with a 'Yes!' or a 'Good' when another player hit a black jack.

On subsequent nights that trip, René lost some money, only to win it back literally minutes before having to leave. Half an hour before his plane was due to depart, René told Ben Kaye: 'If Celine is looking for me, tell her I went to the washroom.' He went back to the tables to play.

When Celine asked Ben where René was and he gave the agreed answer, she said, 'He's not in the washroom. I know where he is!' However, a victorious René emerged just in time – with a 26,000-dollar win. 'He was so relieved,' commented Ben Kaye. 'He gets very sad when he loses.' After all, no gambler like to lose. And René has never lost on Celine.

CHAPTER 23

My Heart Will Go On and On . . . Across the World

'Even though I've heard it a thousand times, it still breaks my heart.'

– JAMES CAMERON, DIRECTOR OF TITANIC

C eline had achieved her greatest success and was ready for a break. She had become the queen of the movie theme songs. But, just when it seemed that she could not possibly equal the success of 'Because You Loved Me', she did even better with 'My Heart Will Go On'.

'My Heart Will Go On' was the theme song of *Titanic*, the most expensive movie in motion picture history. It was a soulful ballad about love, loss and inspiration, written by James Horner and Will Jennings. A song that gives you goosebumps.

Yet, amazingly, 'My Heart Will Go On' was never supposed to be in the movie. Initially, director James Cameron had not seen any need for a popular song in the movie and had instead opted for melodic background vocals and instrumentals.

'He was strictly opposed to the idea of a pop song on the sound-track,' according to the song's composer James Horner. But Horner had composed what he thought was the perfect 'love theme' for the movie and he wasn't about to give up. What's more, he knew exactly who should sing it – Celine Dion. But how could he convince James Cameron that this was what *Titanic* needed?

Horner went on a mission. He flew to Las Vegas where Celine and René were staying, and told them about 'My Heart Will Go On' and the *Titanic* movie, which still wasn't finished. He did not hide the fact that Cameron was opposed to the song.

'His honesty to Celine was touching,' recalls René. After all, James Horner had always regretted the fact that things had never worked out when Celine was originally supposed to sing his song in the movie, *American Tail: Fievel Goes West*, years before.

Then Horner went over to a piano, and just started playing the song. At this point, doing another theme song was the last thing on Celine's mind, but when she heard the melody she loved it! The next step was a surprise. They would have to do a demo in order to try and get James Cameron to change his mind and use the song. For a superstar to do a demo tape was almost unheard of. Demos were for hopefuls who hadn't quite made it, not superstars!

Yet Celine and René both believed in the song. As René put it: 'Well, if Marlon Brando had to do an audition for *The Godfather*, we could do a demo for *Titanic*.'

The demo was recorded at New York City's Hit Factory, but it was another six weeks before Horner finally gathered the courage to present it to Cameron. 'I just kept waiting for him to be in a good mood. Then one day, I just put it on his desk and played the song. He loved it! He couldn't believe that it was actually Celine Dion!' The song was in.

Celine was now the acknowledged queen of romantic theme songs, after 'Beauty and the Beast', 'When I Fall in Love', 'Because You Loved Me', and 'To Love You More' (from a Japanese drama series). 'When people do a romantic movie, they come to me because they know that what I love most is emotion and love songs,' she explains.

Of course there were risks for Celine as well. As the costliest film in history of cinema, *Titanic's* release date had just been postponed from July to December. 'There were bad vibes about *Titanic* at the time,' explains René, referring to the *flood* of media reports on the 'overflowing' budget. 'But these people hadn't seen the film. We saw it and we cried. We believed in it.'

Celine and René saw a copy of the film in July. It was an incredibly emotional experience for Celine. 'Imagine, a young mother singing lullabies to her baby, knowing that they would die together, a husband and wife who did not want to be separated and went down together. It was all so moving,' she says, with tears in her eyes.

'My Heart Will Go On' translated that emotion into song, along with the incredible flute accompaniment. But Celine was feeling another type of emotion the day she recorded the song. 'I wasn't feeling well. I had nothing to eat and all I drank was two-and-a-half cups of coffee. I usually drink water. I was shaking and sweating. My stomach was hurting and I was worried because I felt that I wouldn't be able to control my voice,' she remembers.

But that fragile physical state helped give her performance just the edge it needed. 'I'm glad I had felt that way,' says Celine, 'because look what happened.' The song 'My Heart Will Go On' played over the closing credits of the movie and Celine was swept away on the greatest tide of success she had ever known.

James Cameron (famous for *Terminator*, *Aliens* and *True Lies*) wrote, directed and co-produced the movie that is reported to have had the biggest budget of all time. Originally estimated at 200 million dollars, it topped 285 million by the time it was complete. The astronomical budget included a whopping 40 million dollars on special effects to recreate the world's most infamous disaster.

It took not one but two Hollywood studios, Paramount Pictures and Twentieth Century Fox, to fund the movie.

The actual *Titanic* was a luxury vessel, over 880 feet long, which left on its maiden voyage from England to New York on 14 April 1912. Despite being supposedly 'unsinkable', it hit an iceberg and sunk two and a half hours later. The ship went down several hours after midnight.

Out of the 2,200 on-board, about 700 survived . . . mostly women and children.

The movie focuses on the shipboard romance between Kate Winslet, who plays the young Rose DeWitt Bukater, a society girl from Philadelphia, and Leonardo DiCaprio who plays Jack Dawson, a poor artist. It was essentially a Romeo and Juliet story set at sea.

The wreckage of the *Titanic* was found in 1985, just southeast of the province of Newfoundland, Canada. Tremendous effort was put into replicating every possible detail of the real ship.

'I decided I was going to use every tool in the service of re-creating an historical event. Take it from me, this is the real deal,' says Canadian James Cameron.

Released on 19 December 1997, the three hour and ten minute film required the making of a 775-foot *Titanic* model to nine-tenths of scale and a small-scale model used for digitally created special effects.

But, beyond all the special effects and computer wizardry, is a story of love and courage in the face of death that is very real. And who could have brought that emotion to life better than Celine? The song's popularity would certainly go on and on.

The entire *Titanic* soundtrack was produced by the Sony Classical label. Originally, James Horner had begged Sony's rival record label, PolyGram, to take on the *Titanic* soundtrack. They rejected the offer. It was reported that the asking price was a million dollars, and they had felt that it was too much to pay for a soundtrack – a Titanic mistake!

Even before the film's official release date, the song had already been nominated for a Golden Globe Award for Best Original Song. And *Titanic* had swept away a total of eight nominations, including Best Director, Best Motion Picture and Leonardo DiCaprio for Best Actor. 'He is so handsome, so *good*,' said Celine, who felt that he had a real James Dean quality. It would be months before he became a teenage heart-throb and months before Celine's glory would reach all four corners of the world. In the meantime, another boat was coming in for her.

★ ★ ★

When Celine ended her *Falling Into You* tour in the summer of 1997, the last thing she expected was that she would be asked to delay her proposed one-year break. Celine had never had a 'normal' life and she had begged for time off.

She now had everything she could ever have dreamed of – except a child. Her face adorned the walls of the biggest multinational music label in the world. Her songs were played around the globe, and another movie theme song was about to be launched when *Titanic* was released, that December. She had vast wealth, all the designer clothes she could ever wear, a golf course, her own plane – what was there left for her to do but have a private life?

Then Sony Music Entertainment President Tommy Mottola called to speak to Celine and René. The conversation moved at a dizzying pace. As René recalls, 'Tommy asked, "How would you like to do another album?" ' He knew that they had planned to stop recording for a year. But this had to be an exception. 'My Heart Will Go On' would be a feature on the album – but there was more . . . This album would be different – something that Celine had never done before. It would be an album that included not just one duet with a music idol, but five star collaborations. It was like a dream. But could it be done?

René knew how important it was for Celine's career to maintain her pre-eminent position in the world marketplace. And it was essential to have a gap between albums and tours. Plus she needed the rest. She was stressed, and she believed this was the main reason why she could not get pregnant. 'How would *you* feel if you had to be in a different country almost every day on tour?' Celine replied to curious journalists when they probed her on her difficulties in getting pregnant. Celine had begun to yearn for a normal life.

Even if she agreed to do another album, followed by a whirlwind tour, would the public be ready for another Celine Dion album, so soon after the 26 million copy success of *Falling Into You*? It was a silly question. She was now the hottest star on the planet and there was a hunger and fascination for Celine, the like of which the world hadn't seen in years.

As René Angelil says, looking back, 'The Beatles came out with two or three albums a year, and they were all great. People loved it. There was nothing wrong with it then, so why not now?'

'There was one condition,' explained Celine. 'If we weren't perfectly happy with the material for the album, we would not release it. We would wait and work on it . . . coming out with an album next year like we had first envisioned.' It was agreed.

So they set out to make it happen. The album was recorded in two months, and Celine was on perfect form. There were fifteen songs on the album, but sources say that Celine recorded more than twenty, making the final selections and including some variations of songs across the continents.

Years of saving her voice before performing and her regime of self-imposed silence, plus extensive voice exercises every day, had paid off. 'Even if I was too tired, even if I thought "Oh . . . not today" my voice was ready. It was like my voice wanted to do it.'

Originally, the album was to have been called *The Reason* (after the first song on it) but when Celine heard 'Let's Talk About Love' it seemed to express everything she felt, about new places, new horizons and universal love.

The first step had been when the duet was orchestrated with Barbra Streisand. It was no secret that Celine had always adored Barbra. 'She's my idol,' Celine had affirmed on many occasions. 'When I performed Barbra Streisand's song "I Finally Found Someone" at the Academy Awards in March 1997, Barbra said to me, "Next time, let's do one together."'

The Oscar night had created controversy – on both sides of the Atlantic. When Barbra had stepped out to the ladies room while Celine sang, many wondered if it was the beginning of a feud. Were the two divas at odds?

'They don't have it printed in the programme when the songs are on, so I went, during what I thought was an intermission,' explained Streisand in ABC's 20/20 interview with Barbara Walters. 'I came back and the song was over. Why would I miss it? Is the press this cynical, to make up a story that I would have deliberately done this to her? The only thing that bothers me about these negative stories that are made up, fabricated out of the blue, is that I don't want the people who like me, who like my work, my fans or anybody actually, I don't want them saying, "She sings good but she's supposed to be this bad person or whatever." This saddens me a lot.'

Here's what actually happened. The day after the Academy Awards there was a special delivery for Celine. It was a single rose, with a note to Celine from Barbra, that read:

'I watched the tape of the show afterwards and you sang my song beautifully. Thank you. I only wish I had been in the room to hear it. Next time – let's do one together.
    Love Barbra
    P.S. I thought your song should have won. You're an incredible singer.'

'My husband took this very seriously,' recalls Celine. 'He picked up the phone and called Barbra's manager to make sure this was real. He couldn't believe it. He then called David Foster and said, "David, you have to write a song for Barbra and Celine." Immediately, David and his songwriter wife Linda Thompson collaborated with Walter Afanasieff. 'They wrote a song,' Celine continued, 'and they sent it to Barbra and myself. We loved the song.'

Years before, David had remarked that 'Celine exceeds the boundaries of talent', and even drew some comparisons between the two singing sensations. 'I had this vision for so long that these two would sing together.' The song was called 'Tell Him', and, according to Barbra Streisand, 'It was a feat to come up with a lyric for us, in terms of the mentor, the bigger sister, or the mother figure, giving advice on how to handle a relationship.'

'You know what I wished?' Celine had said to Barbra after the recording. 'That we could do a movie with that idea.'

'Never can tell,' Barbra answered. 'You can make your own fate.'

Barbra and Celine went back a long way, even though Barbra didn't know it. Celine had grown up singing to her records and standing in front of the television, imitating her every move. For Celine it was like singing with an old friend.

To produce the duet 'Tell Him', Barbra recorded her tracks first in Los Angeles and then Celine recorded hers afterwards in New York, singing along to Barbra's track. So timing, breathing and rhythm were important. 'When I sang the duet alongside Barbra's track . . . I could feel her every breath, I could follow her perfectly,' says Celine.

Afterwards, when Celine had the opportunity to speak to Barbra on the phone, she was rendered virtually speechless. René had to take the phone from her. 'Sorry Barbra,' he said. 'Celine is . . .'

'I understand,' said Barbra. 'There's no problem. I felt the same way when I sang with Judy Garland.'

When they met again, it was Barbra who was in awe this time. 'There's a lot of people out there but I think your voice is so special, so beautiful . . . a gorgeous instrument, with a great heart and sensitivity. It makes me proud to sing with you. You're *so* good.'

Celine had a tribute message to Barbra on the inside of her album cover:

'Dearest Barbra,

Having the privilege of singing with you is certainly my wildest dream come true. Since I was a child you've always been someone that I've looked up to as a model of perfection.'

Celine is disarmingly honest. 'In my life I have two idols. My mother . . . she is my idol in life. In showbusiness, it's Barbra Streisand. She is my idol as a singer, as a director, as an actor . . . as a woman. I just love her.'

★ ★ ★

She was born Barbara Joan Streisand on 24 April 1942 and grew up in Flatbush, Brooklyn, New York. In later years, she changed the spelling of her name to Barbra, leaving out the second 'a' because there was no one else in the world who spelled their name this way and she wanted to be different.

At a young age, just like Celine, Barbra knew she had a passion for singing. Poverty was no obstacle on the way to Fame. In fact, it only made them both more determined.

At thirteen years old, Barbra recorded her first demo record, on 29 December 1955. She sang 'You'll Never Know' and 'Zing! Went the Strings of My Heart'. Celine was also thirteen when she did her first studio recording of the song her mother had written.

Barbra's launch into stardom came when the motion picture *Funny Girl* was released in 1968, the year Celine was born. In her role as Fanny Brice, an awkward girl who joins a chorus line, she meets dashing gambler Nicky Arnstein (played by Omar Sharif) and falls in love.

Besides their incredible vocal talents, there was another similarity between the two singers. Celine can be really funny and she often conveys this in her shows, where she jokes easily with the audience. But, even though Celine may be a 'funny girl', acting is something she takes very seriously. 'I think that when you sing a song two hundred times, sometimes about something that never happened to you – you have to feel it. There's an actress inside of me, for sure,' she says.

After *Funny Girl*, Barbra was in fifteen more motion pictures, including *The Way We Were, A Star is Born, Yentl, The Prince of Tides* and *The Mirror Has Two Faces*. One of the world's biggest-selling artists (until Celine exploded on to the scene), Barbra has recorded over fifty albums (even a French one, called *Je M'Appelle Barbra*).

Both perfectionists, Barbra and Celine had this in common as well. 'Meeting her was the thrill. But singing with her was the best experience musically that I ever had in my life,' says Celine. 'And I don't think there will be anything that will get closer than that.'

★ ★ ★

If Celine's dream had been to sing with Barbra Streisand, René had his idols too. He had always worshipped the Beatles. Known as the 'fifth Beatle', Sir George Martin had been the legendary producer of the Beatles albums which had changed the face of music.

Now Sir George Martin had a new challenge – producing for Celine Dion.

He had intended to retire, after producing Elton John's new version of 'Candle in the Wind' in Princess Diana's memory. The song was recorded straight after her funeral . . . and it raised over 25 million dollars for Princess Diana's charities within the first four months after its release in September 1997. Celine had been part of *The Diana, Princess of Wales* commemorative album, donating her song 'Because You Loved Me'.

Sir George Martin was enamoured with Celine. She recorded at his Air Studios, in London, in August, beginning a two-month journey into new musical territory. A grey-haired, distinguished man in his seventies, George Martin produced Carole King's song, 'The Reason' for her.

'Celine is a tremendous artist,' he says. 'Always delightful to be with, always has a smile. I guess I was in love with her.' Celine, who never sees herself as an idol in other people's eyes, was intimidated as first, 'I didn't know how to act . . . how to sing, how to be with him.'

'The Reason' was a ballad with an edge. 'It's [about] a woman with strength . . . with guts,' says Celine. Carole King's lyrics were unmistakable. Carole not only wrote the song, but played piano and sang back-up vocals. 'How can anybody not like having Celine Dion sing their song?' said the folk-rock superstar whose *Tapestry* album was one of the biggest-selling records of the seventies. In fact, on the *Tapestry Revisited* album, a wonderful tribute to Carole King, released in 1996, Celine sang her famous song '(You Make Me Feel Like) A Natural Woman'.

The album's title track, 'Let's Talk About Love', was a French song written years before by Jean-Jacques Goldman, redone with lyrics by Bryan Adams (well known for his movie theme hits such as '(Everything

I do) I Do it For You', 'Have You Ever Really Loved a Woman' and his duet with Barbra Streisand in 'I Finally Found Someone').

Another collaboration on the album featured the Bee Gees, who wrote and harmonized the powerful song 'Immortality' for Celine. 'She blew everyone away!' recalls Maurice Gibb. 'When you're a songwriter and you have this happen with such a great voice like Celine's . . . it's a night you never forget.'

Brothers Barry, Maurice and Robin Gibb had moved to England from Australia in 1967 when hits such as 'I've Got to Get a Message to You' made them an international success. Years later, they became known as 'kings of disco' with their soundtrack to the movie *Saturday Night Fever*, starring a disco-dancing John Travolta.

The Bee Gees' style revolved around three-part vocal harmonies, with their unmistakable use of falsetto and vibrato.

'No party without them,' Celine recalls, always ready to make those disco moves. She had danced to the rhythm of the Bee Gees' music only months earlier, at the World Music Awards in Monte Carlo.

But their collaboration with Celine was a far cry from the pounding bass drum of the disco beat. 'We wrote a song for her called "Immortality", recalls Barry Gibb. 'She inspired the song. She inspires us. Probably the finest female pop singer in the world. So it was a dream that she might sing one of our songs one day and the dream came true.'

When Barry first heard Celine sing the song in studio, he cried like a baby. 'It was so touching,' she recalls. 'First I had met them in Monte Carlo and I was thrilled to see them. I had danced to their music so often! But then they were there . . . writing a song for me, and crying when I sang it. I couldn't believe it.'

The song had incredible meaning, about the immortality of loved ones as well as the immortality of music. For the Bee Gees, it was written straight from the heart. Their youngest brother Andy had died over fifteen years earlier.

For René, the song also meant a great deal because of the loss of his mother Alice Sara Angelil on 27 May 1997. 'It's as close to him as my song "Fly",' says Celine, referring to the one written for her niece. 'I fell in love with "Immortality" from the very first and loved recording with them,' recalls Celine. But she had to overcome her tendency to be in awe of other stars. 'When I first saw Barbra and the Bee Gees and Pavarotti, Carole King, Sir George Martin . . . I just stood there with my mouth open, gaping. I was like a groupie. But after, it was like we had known each other for years.'

She had dined at Barbra's. And when she recorded a remake of the song 'I Hate You Then I Love You' with Luciano Pavarotti, she feasted on Luciano's famous meatballs – Celine and René both loved his cooking. 'It's a very wonderful experience being able to share intimate moments along with the experience of singing with them. Having wonderful dinners, laughs and getting personal. It's wonderful luggage that you carry with you for the rest of your life.' The bond she developed with Pavarotti continued well after their recording, as Celine would later sing 'My Heart Will Go On' for a combined performance at a Pavarotti and Friends Benefit Concert in his home town of Modena, Italy. Their efforts raised money to help children in Bosnia through the War Child Foundation.

Celine's duet with the tenor illustrated the ambitious variety of musical styles she had embarked on in *Let's Talk About Love*. Luciano Pavarotti has one of the most popular and beautiful tenor voices in the world, with an exuberant personality that has changed the face of opera music forever.

'I have the greatest respect for classical music,' Celine says, admitting that she had been secretly hoping to sing a love song with Pavarotti for years. They recorded the song in the same studio. 'But he didn't need a microphone,' joked Celine.

In recording with Barbra Streisand, Sir George Martin, Carole King, the Bee Gees and Luciano Pavarotti, it would seem that Celine had spanned the entire spectrum of musical styles.

But there was still more to come. 'The one thing I never thought I would do was record a rap song,' Celine said, 'but here I was.' 'Treat Her

Like a Lady' was a reggae-influenced rap tune that was pure energy.

Corey Hart, a Montreal singer-songwriter, penned two original compositions for the new album, 'Where is the Love' and 'Miles to Go (Before I Sleep)'. Celine also did a remake of the 1977 Leo Sayer hit 'When I Need You' and a song in Spanish called *'Amar Haciendo El Amor'*.

On the version of the album released in the United States, there was also the re-release of the spectacular song, 'To Love You More', which had been on Celine's *Live à Paris* album.

In the two months that it had taken to record the album, Celine had performed miracles with the microphone, making her voice do the kind of acrobatics that have won her a world-class reputation. From London to Los Angeles, Celine was in her element. *Let's Talk About Love* was not only a challenge. It was almost the story of her life.

'This album is like an infant for me,' says Celine. For her, it was her most precious work to date, including the *Titanic* song, 'My Heart Will Go On'. 'I want to share with the world what I just did,' she announced. 'I just had a newborn. A new album and I'm so proud of that.'

Her mother understood exactly what she meant. 'Since the beginning of Celine's career, I have always tried not to publicly show my feelings but . . . as a mother, I find it extremely moving to see what my daughter has just accomplished. I know how important it was for Celine.'

Sony Music was putting all its marketing muscle behind what was the Japanese-owned multi-national's most important commercial release of the fall season. Celine and Barbra created a massive North American release of 'Tell Him' via satellite, well over a month in advance of the release of Barbra's album, *Higher Ground* on 7 November and Celine's new album on 18 November.

The album launch was one of the biggest in Sony Music history, taking place simultaneously in over sixty countries across the world. Before its actual release the company already had orders for an unprecedented 10 million copies and in its first week of release the album skyrocketed to the top of the charts around the world. It was as if

Celine had singlehandedly rejuvenated the global pop industry's slow-ing sales. The incredible thing was that, in November, *Falling Into You* was still on the *Billboard* 200 chart after sixty-five weeks!

Celine's celebrity status also led her to take part in a tremendous amount of fund-raising. Between September and November alone, she participated in a special compilation recording, *For Our Children Two*, with profits donated to the Pediatric Foundation Against Aids; the Annual VH-1 Honors to help purchase musical instruments in American schools; the André Agassi Charitable Foundation for Youth Programs; and the fund-raising gala for Aids, Leukaemia and Cancer in honour of David Foster, the man who had written and produced so many hit songs in Celine's career.

At The Time for Peace Awards, which recognizes efforts to promote peace in the world, sponsored by Concord Watches in New York, Celine was honoured, along with songwriter Jean-Jacques Goldman and pianist David Helfgott, the musician on whose life the Oscar-winning movie *Shine* was based.

Two weeks before the album's release on 18 November, a press conference was held in Montreal and was also seen via satellite everywhere from Montreal to Spain, Austria, Poland, Switzerland, England, Germany, France, Italy, Ireland, Denmark, Sweden, Norway, and all of Latin America.

However there was another technological feat that made this press conference unique. It went live interactively to London, Paris and Cologne, where moderators and fans could ask Celine questions as well. The whole thing was hosted by talk-show host Sonia Benezra and televised from the studios of Montreal's Telé-Metropole station.

A few weeks later, Celine was at another press conference in Los Angeles, where a remarkable internet launch of her album allowed fans from all over the world to go on-line with Celine and even had her talking back to them.

Everything was in place for this to be the album of all albums. Once the launch was complete, Celine would be on a series of talk shows and fund-raisers and would start a mammoth *Let's Talk About Love* world tour in the summer of 1998. With North America first on the agenda, then Europe, Australia and the Far East, the tour would continue until the end of 1999.

What did it feel like for Celine to have her idols now all asking to work with her? Tears welled up in her eyes. 'I dreamed . . . yes. But this is more than a dream.'

'I always said I wanted to go higher and farther. But I don't think I can ever do better than this album. This is it,' said Celine.

What was she saying? Was Celine really planning to retire from music? Whatever she felt, there was no time to even think about taking a break.

For now it was time to Talk About Love. The next few weeks flew by, with endless promotional appearances for the new album. With her love of children, Celine's appearance on *Sesame Street*, produced by the Children's Television Workshop and recorded on 19 November 1997, was a show she'd never forget. 'I didn't feel like ever leaving the set, after singing to the cuddly cast,' she said. Celine even joined Rosie O'Donnell and other performers for Sesame Street's *Elmopalooza* video and soundtrack celebrating the Children's Television Workshop's thirtieth anniversary.

There's a children's nursery rhyme that goes, 'I went to London to visit the Queen.' Well . . . Celine did that too. She was invited to sing before the Queen on 1 December, at a gala marking the fiftieth wedding anniversary of Queen Elizabeth and Prince Philip. Celine did a perfect curtsy for the Queen (even though Ginger Spice did not – because she had been afraid of falling out of her dress).

Celine was making headlines virtually every day. *Entertainment Tonight* featured the making of the video clip for *Titanic*, and on the day of Celine's album release she performed 'My Heart Will Go On' on *The Rosie O'Donnell Show*. 'I adore her,' said Rosie. 'She has one of the most beautiful voices ever.' Celine sang 'My Heart Will Go On' as she would on many other talk shows. *Titanic* was to be released in a month and the song was already a show-stopper.

Within a month of the movie release, 'My Heart Will Go On' had already played on the airwaves more than any other song in history. It was the song that launched an eventual 25 million sales of the *Titanic* soundtrack, and an equal number of Celine's *Let's Talk About Love*.

And, for James Cameron, the gamble had paid off. The film gained rave reviews and long line-ups from the day it came out, and its success went on and on. Box office returns totalled over a billion dollars worldwide within the first three months of its release. The public just couldn't get enough of the movie.

Industry accolades started with the Fifty-fifth annual Golden Globe Awards, voted on by the Hollywood foreign press and known as a precursor to the Academy Awards. The highly respected industry event was held on 18 January 1998 at Merv Griffin's Beverly Hills Hilton in Los Angeles. The night belonged to *Titanic*, which won four Golden Globe awards: Best Motion Picture, Best Original Song, Best Original Musical Score and Best Direction. James Horner made a point of thanking Celine and René for believing in the song and doing so much to make it happen. And James Cameron described how moved he was by it: 'Even though I've heard it a thousand times, it still breaks my heart.'

'My Heart Will Go On' had made Celine a household name everywhere. People were singing it, humming it . . . Most of all, as Celine put it, 'The song helps people express their own personal loves and losses.' With this song, Celine had sailed into the hearts of billions.

CHAPTER 24

Let's Talk About Love – A Titanic Success!

'I always said I wanted to go higher and farther. But I don't think that I can ever do better than this album. This is it.'
— CELINE DION

Celine and Barbra's duet had been nominated for a Grammy and in February 1998 there was great excitement about their headline performance of the duet at the Fortieth annual Grammy Awards on 25 February. If anticipation was building in the music industry, nowhere was it stronger than in Celine's heart. Her voice was on top form, 'But just as important was the psychological preparation,' Celine emphasized. 'I was ready and I had waited for this moment for a long time. It was a dream for me.'

As the weeks went by, excitement over the duet grew and ticket prices went from 800 to over 1,000 dollars.

But then, several days before the show, the unthinkable happened. Barbra was not feeling well. She called to say that she had the flu and was on antibiotics, and wasn't sure if she would be able to perform the song or even attend the Grammys. Barbra missed several rehearsals but Celine was still hopeful.

It was the day before the Grammy awards when the phone call came. Barbra would have to cancel. Celine was crushed. Others speculated furiously. Was Barbra jealous of Celine's popularity? Did she feel that she would be outsung? Or was Barbra really disappointed that the flu had knocked her out?

Devastated as she was, Celine took it in her stride. 'When you're sick, you're sick,' she said candidly. Yet there was no hiding her disappointment. What was she to do at the last minute? Sing the song alone? It would never be the same.

'I must admit it wasn't easy,' Celine confessed. 'Preparing to sing with her took a lot of effort on my part. Confronted by the cancellation, I was really devastated. But I called Barbra and told her: "Don't worry. Just think about getting better." I've been in that situation before and what you need is support from other people. I told her that we would find a solution. Then the idea of singing "My Heart Will Go On" came to me.'

With only twenty-four hours until the show, a frazzled-looking Celine went to her one and only rehearsal. Even though the song had come out too late to be nominated for a Grammy that year, it was already the biggest hit in the world.

It was the night of the Grammys. The show was hosted by Kelsey Grammer (star of *Frasier* and *Cheers*) who introduced Celine by explaining, 'If you ever needed proof that this show is live, watch this. At this point in the show Barbra Streisand and Celine Dion were to have performed "Tell Him", but as you know Barbra has been battling the flu for the past three days and is unable to perform. The song about to be performed is currently on both the number one album and the number one soundtrack in the world.' Before he could even say her name, Radio City Music Hall erupted in cheers.

Celine emerged and, although showing some signs of stress, gallantly sang the song that had already become the most talked-about ballad of the year. Standing on top of a circular staircase, Celine sparkled in glitter eyeshadow and a Halston gown fashionably off one shoulder.

She had a deep suntan from the promotional trip she had just been on, which saw her spend time in Hawaii. But even the glow of her suntan could not mask the stress she was under.

The Grammy orchestra musicians had a real challenge in performing the song. With time for one rehearsal, only *they* knew how tense a moment it was for them all. Celine pulled it off. A heroic effort considering what her last few days had been like.

'My Heart Will Go On' became the new staple of the talk-show circuit. The song was number one on *Billboard's* Hit Single Chart and Celine sang it everywhere. Of course she had a wonderful line-up of songs on her new album but, for the first few months, everywhere she went, people wanted her to sing what they called 'The Titanic Song'. Celine even recorded a dance-mix version!

Titanic sailed into the Academy Awards with fourteen Oscar nominations. By then, the film had already set a new record: fourteen weeks at the top of the box office charts. With a North American gross of 494.7 million dollars, it was also the all-time box office champion, shattering the 21-year record held by *Star Wars*. The worldwide takings by the week of the Oscars had reached over 1.2 billion dollars and the figure was still climbing. *Titanic* was already, without a doubt, history's highest grossing film. And it continued to bring in wave after wave of moviegoers, some for their third or fourth time. The song was almost sure to win at the Academy Awards on 23 March.

What's more, *Titanic's* soundtrack had also followed the film into the record books. Sales grossed more money for Sony Classics than the label made from its entire 1997 repertoire.

Celine appeared on the cover of *Entertainment Weekly* with the headline, 'Titanic's Celine Dion: The voice that launched fifteen million albums.' The soundtrack held the number one position on *Billboard* for sixteen weeks straight, while Celine's album *Let's Talk About Love* was close behind. In a way Celine was competing with herself.

Every aspect of *Titanic* was now in the spotlight. And, in the days leading up to the Academy Awards, a new story emerged. Asprey of London had created an exact replica of the heart-shaped sapphire and diamond necklace that they had designed for *Titanic*. James Cameron had asked the royal jewellers to create a necklace that would best reflect that time period. For the movie, the gem was made of cubic zirconium. The new necklace was the real thing, and it took a team of five people at Asprey three weeks to complete the showpiece.

The *Coeur de la Mer* ('The Heart of the Sea') necklace had come to symbolize a great deal in the movie. The Asprey necklace was exquisite. Valued at 3.5 million dollars, they planned to auction it off the night before the Oscars, with the proceeds going to the Princess Diana Memorial Fund.

Asprey had also chosen a celebrity to wear the multi-million dollar necklace to the Academy Awards. The question was . . . who? Kate Winslet was a probable choice or perhaps 87-year-old Gloria Stewart. For days, *Entertainment Tonight* recounted details of the making of the necklace . . . before finally revealing it would be none other than Celine Dion who would wear the magnificent jewel.

Celine was thrilled. 'I received the necklace three days before, so I could know what dress to wear with it. It was surprisingly heavy – 170 carat blue sapphire surrounded with dozens of carefully matched diamonds, all set in platinum.' At the auction, the necklace was sold for 2.7 million dollars to an unnamed purchaser. Was it René? 'No,' said Celine with a smile. 'It wasn't René.'

It was the day before the Oscars and, according to René, Celine was feeling the pressure. 'The whole world awaits this song. The song is not like any other and the challenge to do a memorable performance was enormous.' Over a billion people would be watching the show. There was no time for stage fright. Soon, his enthusiasm got the better of him. 'It's the biggest song in the history of music,' he said proudly. 'Never before has a song been played more on radio stations across the world.'

Strangely, by March, Celine herself still hadn't heard 'My Heart Will Go On' on the Titanic soundtrack album. 'I have not yet. Do you think I have time to go home and listen to a record? I have *no* time,' she declared.

★   ★   ★

The Seventieth Annual Academy Awards arrived with more than the usual fanfare – created by the *Titanic* tidal wave. The show was superbly hosted again by Billy Crystal at the Shrine Auditorium in Los Angeles on 23 March.

Of course Celine had already been in Los Angeles for three days prior to the show. The rehearsals started days before the final ceremony. There was even a rehearsal on the day of the awards. That night it took Celine three hours to have her hair done. 'I wanted my hair to be exceptional, because of the necklace and dress I would wear,' she said. She emerged wearing her hair in soft waves – it gave her a more classic look.

Celine actually wore two dresses at the Oscars. She arrived wearing a black dress with a plunging neckline that really showed off the diamond – and show it she did. 'Everyone who came up to me kept staring straight at the diamond as they talked to me,' laughs Celine. The jewel glittered as Celine mingled and then sat in the audience during the ceremony. The five nominated songs were all performed that night, including 'Go the Distance' from *Hercules*, performed by Michael Bolton and 'How Do I Live' from *Con Air*, performed by Trisha Yearwood. At the very end Celine sang 'My Heart Will Go On'.

Celine emerged centre stage, wearing a sophisticated sapphire-blue high-necked gown, which clung to the perfect contours of her long lean body. She stood, almost statuesque, with dry ice permeating the stage floor to set the mood. It was highly dramatic. Stars shone out above and behind her. The audience was mesmerized. But this performance had a little extra drama. 'I was very nervous and when I came to key parts of the song, for added emotion I kept banging my hand against my chest for emphasis . . . right against the heart-shaped jewel. The four bodyguards from Asprey London were so nervous,' she laughs. 'They thought that I broke the diamond!'

'My Heart Will Go On' won the Oscar for Best Original Song, which was no surprise. The night truly belonged to *Titanic*, with eleven Oscars (matching the record set by *Ben Hur* in 1959) including Best Original Song, Best Musical Score, Best Picture, Best Director and Best Visual Effects.

Who could forget James Cameron's speech in which he borrowed the Titanic line and yelled, 'I'm king of the world.' If he was king – Celine was definitely queen. It was a night of accolades for the singer as James Horner and Will Jennings accepted the award.

Afterwards, she described her feelings with her usual touching honesty. 'Winning another Oscar was great but I do it for my family. It means so much to them and I do it for them.'

It was her family that was most on her mind when she reached the next milestone in her life – turning thirty. Celine had never known a normal life and now she was being thrust into a new decade with her birthday on 30 March 1998.

Yet Celine had been saying all year that she couldn't wait to turn thirty, as if it would give her the stability she had been looking for. René had told her that they would celebrate with a romantic evening alone together. 'I didn't really believe him,' confided Celine. 'I know him well enough to know that he was up to something.'

She spent the entire afternoon of her birthday with Maman, who she had not seen for a long while due to her frantic schedule over the previous three months. Finally, at suppertime, René confessed that he had organized a *small* party for the family.

But, when Celine arrived at the reception hall in Montreal, over 200 people surprised her. They had all been waiting quietly at the top of the staircase and when she walked in they burst into a French rendition of 'Happy Birthday'. Celine was in total shock and started crying as she stared at all her family members and friends. 'I could never have imagined something like this,' she managed to say.

The room was transformed into a giant discotheque, with everyone in seventies attire, wonderfully organized by René's son Patrick. Celine had arrived wearing an elegant dress and a diamond necklace but they had a wig and outfit ready for her to change into. Celine the disco queen emerged, wearing a brown jumpsuit with white polka dots, a wild brown polka dot bandanna and huge sunglasses.

René, in white vest and pants and a black, satin, wide-collared shirt, looked like something out of *Saturday Night Fever*. And Celine's brothers and sisters looked like a seventies revolution.

When Celine had told her mother that she couldn't believe that she was thirty already, Maman replied, 'How do you think I feel? For me, Celine, you will always be the baby of the family.'

There was a giant record-shaped cake, iced in record label style, saying '30th Birthday Boogie – Celine. Duration 30 years. A Production of: Therese and Adhemar Dion.'

'Isn't thirty great?' remarked Celine. 'I feel much closer to my husband now,' referring to his fifty-six years.

It seemed as if everything Celine touched turned to gold. Even her new favourite pastime of golf translated into a lucrative deal with Callaway Golf in promoting the oversized Big Bertha golf club. The television ad had Celine standing beside an old-fashioned oversized microphone and ended with the clever play on words: 'With one of these . . . I know my drive will go on and on.'

Now well and truly in the media spotlight, Celine also needed to have a good sense of humour. The new *Saturday Night Live* skit called 'The Celine Dion Show' saw a cast member impersonating Celine. Dressed in a glittering gown, she spoke in a thick French accent and kept outsinging all her guests, all the while gesturing passionately and saying, 'I am zeee best singer in zeee world.' For Rosie O'Donnell, the spoof was incredibly funny. When Celine made an appearance on her show in May, Rosie asked what she thought of the *Saturday Night Live* skit about her. 'Oh that,' replied Celine. 'I laughed and laughed.'

'Good, because we have a clip from the skit that we'll be showing,' smiled Rosie.

'Hey . . . I didn't like it *that* much,' laughed Celine.

As Celine's fame spread, so did the satires. The infamous *South Park* television series did a show featuring an off-colour plot involving Celine, and *Mad* magazine did a satire of all the songs that Celine has recorded that have the word 'love' in them (almost twenty). Even back in Quebec, the French magazine *Delire* (Delirium) showcased Celine and René on an expensive shopping spree on which René buys a large supply of Viagra. She was in the public eye almost every day, and her schedule was as hectic as ever. With more talk-show appearances, promotional tours, interviews and articles – it was turning into 'Let's Talk About Celine'.

CHAPTER 25

Encore

'It's all about love.'

– CELINE DION

Celine had been working endlessly to prepare for the massive 100-concert *Let's Talk About Love* tour. It began in the United States in August 1998 and would continue on across Europe and Asia, until the end of 1999, just in time for the new millennium.

The show was something that Celine had never done before. It was a hugely expensive theatre-in-the-round set, with a giant heart outlining the stage. It was truly a concert about love, as Celine described it.

In the months leading up to her massive premier show in Boston on 21 August, Celine was busy rehearsing. In April, she did a pre-show at Caesar's Palace in Atlantic City. It was a three-day event and it was as if Caesar's had turned into 'Celine's Palace'. They even created a special casino chip with Celine's photo on it, which was randomly interspersed amongst all the others.

All three performances were sold out, at 150 dollars a ticket, and the Circus Maximus theatre hall was crowded with players and non-players alike from three states (New York, New Jersey and Pennsylvania) who had come in to see Celine that first weekend in April.

Patrick Angelil, René's son from his first marriage, was now actively involved with the Celine team and he was at the theatre entrance. 'The shows are sold out but everyone wants to see Celine,' said Patrick, almost matter-of-factly. 'It's like this everywhere. I don't think that there's a more popular star in the world.' The tall, dark and solidly built Patrick kept amazingly calm in the face of the crush of high-rollers begging to get into the show.

All the Sony executives had come in for the Saturday night perform-ance, led by company president Tommy Mottola, plus all the producers and naturally the trusted Ben Kaye, who was always entertaining everyone with a new joke or two.

But René was serious – studying everything. He needn't have worried. Celine's one-hour performance raised the roof. Clad in a backless leather jumpsuit that reached way below the small of her back, Celine was at her best – funny, confident, sexy and a little wild, with enough energy to light up all the casinos in Atlantic City. This was a side of Celine that the Academy Awards viewers, only weeks before, had not seen.

Celine came back to Canada quite seldom now, since *Titanic* had swept her all over the world. But when she came back at the end of April it was for a very important reason. She had been chosen to receive the Order of Quebec. Celine was to be honoured for her outstanding achievements as a native French Quebecer. But that wasn't all. She was also chosen to receive the Order of Canada, at the nation's capital in Ottawa. Both were the highest medals of achievement, honouring Canada's own heroes and heroines.

Yet Celine was modest. 'I have the feeling that I've lived many lives, but yet the feeling that I've done practically nothing. I simply received a talent that was free to me. I've worked hard, but it was all really a gift of nature.'

The Quebec medal was awarded on 30 April, and the Order of Canada on 1 May. Celine found herself in the middle – on the line. And, by accepting both awards within twenty-four hours of each other, somehow a political equilibrium was reached.

In presenting the award to Celine, Quebec Premier Lucien Bouchard said, 'You are just thirty and already your talent and incomparable voice have reached the summit of song. You are our biggest ambassador.' The crowds cheered, but when some criticized her for also agreeing to accept the Canada award, her reply was to the point. 'We are in a free country. For me, today's event had nothing to do with politics. We elect governments and they represent the people. So, to receive these honours, it comes from the people. Whether it's the government of Quebec or Canada it makes no difference,' she emphasized. 'I sing. It's my profession. Talk to me about showbusiness.'

Later, when questioned on *Larry King Live on CNN* about the issue of Quebec separation, Celine gave a carefully neutral answer, saying, 'I hate politics. I think politics destroy a lot of things.' Her lesson had been learned long ago, and she wore her ambassadorship well.

In *People* magazine's readership poll in April 1998, Celine was voted the Favourite Female Pop Performer in the world by a landslide with her *Titanic* hit. As *People* said, 'The unstoppable ballad saw Celine easily top fellow pop divas such as Mariah Carey, Whitney Houston, Barbra Streisand and Madonna.'

Celine won the most votes for Best Diva, Best Soundtrack for *Titanic* and best Female Artist during the VH-1 Viewers' Vote on 25 July 1998. *The Daily News* joked that Dion's records 'have been selling faster this year than Clinton rumours'.

On a television special called *Divas Live*, also on VH-1, Celine was one of the star divas performing alongside Carole King, Mariah Carey, Gloria Estefan, Aretha Franklin and Shania Twain. 'I wanted to share the stage with great voices. You should see the ambiance on stage! I don't care if people believe what I say, about competition. But I am very honest. I am in competition, yes, but with myself.' Celine sang several numbers, including 'My Heart Will Go On', and for the grand finale they all sang Carole King's '(You Make Me Feel Like) A Natural Woman'. Afterwards, Celine was the only 'diva' who stayed around signing autographs long after the show was over.

Celine had now cultivated a whole new following – a teenage generation of *Titanic* fans who idolized her. Her fan base was now as diverse as her talent. And *Titanic's* popularity was so strong that, even twenty-five weeks after the film's debut, the movie continued to remain on the top ten list at the box office. (Takings had now reached 1.8 billion dollars worldwide.) With the *Titanic* video release on 1 September 1998, the money just kept flooding in.

A sequel to the *Titanic* soundtrack was released on 1 September called *Back to Titanic*. This had more original music by James Horner and a new version of 'My Heart Will Go On', with movie dialogue interspersed throughout the song. Now there were three new albums featuring Celine on sale at once.

Celine then created a new French album, called *S'il suffisait d'aimer* (If Love Was Enough), released on 8 September. Like her previous French album *D'eux*, this was almost entirely written by Parisian songwriter Jean-Jacques Goldman. The album was a hit in Quebec and France as soon as it was released. But there were more albums to come. The *Divas Live* album, from the television special, was released on 6 October. Now Celine had five new albums on the market.

Celine also sang on the album *In My Life*, produced by Sir George Martin as a 'salute' to the Beatles. Celine sang 'Here, There & Everywhere'; other participants were Goldie Hawn, Jim Carrey, Robin Williams, Sean Connery and Phil Collins.

On 3 November, Celine released her twenty-second album, *These are Special Times*. This Christmas album was a blend of new and traditional, seasonal and inspirational songs. Duets included the song 'I'm Your Angel' with R. Kelly (Grammy Award winner for 'I Believe I Can Fly') and the Dion family singing 'Feliz Navidad', plus one of Celine's own compositions.

The *pièce de résistance* was 'The Prayer' with Italian tenor Andrea Bocelli. 'The Prayer' was another hit movie theme song, from the animated Warner Bros. film *Quest for Camelot*. Three weeks later, the album was already in first place on the *Billboard* Top Christmas Albums chart and in third position on the *Billboard* 200 Top Album chart.

Now the 1998 Forbes Top 40 list of highest-earning entertainers had Celine in twelfth position with earnings of $55.5 million. She was everywhere, on every show, and making almost every hit list: *The Today*

Show on 18 November, *Late with David Letterman* on 19 November, promoting *These are Special Times* all the while, making constant appearances on *Extra* and *Entertainment Tonight*.

On 25 November Celine not only appeared on *The Rosie O'Donnell Show*, but also in her first CBS network television special, *These are Special Times*. The one-hour extravaganza, with a stage set in the round, was slick and polished, produced by Pierre Cossette who also produced the Grammy Awards. But, on the second night of rehearsing, Celine was so frustrated by the cue cards, that she threw them away! She had always preferred casual banter. 'I love to sing – but I love to talk too,' she joked.

On the show, Celine performed renditions of new and old Christmas songs, duets with Rosie O'Donnell and Andrea Bocelli, plus some of her greatest hits, interspersed with old film footage and video clips of milestones in her life.

Between all the records and the performances, Celine somehow still found time to sing 'My Heart Will Go On' for the Carousel of Hope benefit at the Beverly Hilton, a night that raised 6.2 million dollars for research into juvenile diabetes.

It took almost a hundred people working behind the scenes to put together the tour, and a caravan of trucks to transport the stage and lights from city to city. The Boston concert, on 21 August, was the first on the *Let's Talk About Love World* tour and, although Celine had a chance to rehearse the new show, new staging and new choreography in Montreal, before 150 invited guests, she was scared to death.

'I could hardly sleep,' admitted Celine. 'Neither could René.' The first show was terrifying for them.

At all concerts and all the performances through the years – despite the adoring fans that always awaited her – Celine was still prone to bouts of stage fright before each show and was almost too nervous to face the crowd. 'I'm never going to get used to this. Never,' she confessed, outside her dressing room.

★ ★ ★

A central hydraulic platform elevated Celine up from below floor level, in one of the most dramatic stage entrances of her entire career. Four other pods also rose up, shared by her six musicians and three backing singers.

'I'm so scared,' Celine cried to a cheering audience, who melted with those words. 'This is my first show.' She had a huge surprise in store – long hair extensions! They went way down her back, and were almost in ringlets, and her hair was much lighter than before.

Celine also wore outfits designed by haute-couture Parisian designer Christian Lacroix, who had submitted fifty sketches to her. The stage outfits Celine had chosen had a matador theme, with pants reaching just below the knee. The ultimate costume was the 50,000 dollar early 1900s style red gown that Celine would wear as she sang 'My Heart Will Go On'.

The concert was energetic and fast-paced, with Celine dancing, and running back and forth, from one part of the circular stage to another.

Afterwards, during a press conference organized by Barry Garber, International Tour Producer and Agent with Celine and René's new company CDA Productions, reporters clamoured to find out about her hair extensions and Celine joked that she had cut off René's ponytail and added it to her own hair. Actually Celine *had* asked him to cut off his decade-old trademark. Reluctantly, he had agreed.

After the fascination with her hair wore off, Celine admitted that, 'The first show had some mistakes. The pacing was off. It takes a while to get familiar with the new stage. We'll have to take one show at a time.'

Sponsors of her shows included Ericsson telecommunications and Proctor & Gamble, as well as Avon Cosmetics. Merchandising had been well thought out, with souvenir programmes, a Celine plush frog, caps, golf shirts and T-shirts, not to mention the other items not at the show, such as Celine's celebrity caramel-filled hearts and musical shaped chocolates, as well as a whole selection of specially designed Avon products.

A week after the Boston show, Celine gave three performances in the New York area.

It was opening night and Madison Square Gardens was a frenzy of fans. Within hours of the tickets going on sale, the shows had sold out.

Celine was still nervous, but in control. Gone were the long hair extensions. 'It took my sister Manon hours to do my hair,' said Celine. And Celine had changed her stage outfits. Says her stylist Annie Horth, 'People didn't seem to like the matador pants, and Celine prefers to wear second-skin, mostly super-stretch clothes on stage, and always prefers to wear pants while performing.' Her stylist had a trick, 'I put small weights in the hem of the bottom of her pants, and, that way, they don't rise up when she's moving or dancing.'

The opening act was Quebec's André-Philippe Gagnon, who warmed up the audience with his vocal impressions, especially of Sinatra and his rendition of all of the voices on the song 'We Are the World'.

There were four large raised screens at each corner, and a huge neon-lit version of Celine's signature: 'Celine x x . . .' As Celine magically rose up on the pedestal, the 20,000 spectators gave her a standing ovation. Celine sang 'Let's Talk About Love', and was joined by dozens of children who surrounded her on stage. She then sang 'Declaration of Love', and 'Because You Loved Me'.

'What a thrill,' Celine told the New York City audience. 'I gotta tell you. I'm scared to death,' she said earnestly. Someone from the audience brought her a stuffed animal frog. 'That's my lucky charm!' she smiled, taking time to sign autographs even though her show had already begun. There was a procession of kids bearing flowers at the side of the stage.

While singing 'The Reason', and 'It's All Coming Back To Me' (one of her favourites), Celine energetically swept around the stage making sure that she 'connected' with everyone around it.

Her talks with the audience are one of her favourite parts of the show. 'You just can't sing one song after another,' says Celine. 'Well, I've had quite a year. I sung a few songs, I went on a boat . . .' Her banter also included references to her weight. 'Some people think I never eat and they call me "Slim Dion". But I do eat.' With a grin, Celine said that she had almost called her album 'Let's Talk About Lunch.'

A highlight came when Celine sang 'To Love You More', with the violin accompaniment of Taro Hakase, which drew a standing ovation. When Celine sang 'Tell Him', Barbra Streisand appeared on all the screens, and Celine sang in duet with the video.

A comical incident happened with the *Saturday Night Live* cast member, Ana Gustafson, who does such infamous impersonations of Celine on the show. Ana appeared wearing the same outfit and red cummerbund ensemble that Celine had on. She pretended she was 'the star' but she was soon lowered down on the pedestal, and disappeared from view.

Celine sang the French song, '*S'il suffisait d'aimer*' (If Love Were Enough), and then did a medley with her band of her favourite songs: Roberta Flack's 'First Time, Ever I Saw Your Face', the Beatles' 'Because', Eric Clapton's 'Tears in Heaven', and then, one that she and René both cherished, Frank Sinatra's 'All The Way'.

After 'Love Can Move Mountains' Celine did a disco routine, wearing a white blazer and pants, singing and dancing to the Bee Gees' *Saturday Night Fever* hits 'Staying Alive' and 'You Should Be Dancing', ending in a John Travolta pose.

For her encore, the stage was set with added props to recreate the bow of the Titanic. The flute began and then Celine came out in her dramatic red ball dress. She stood at the railing, and, once again, sang the song that had sailed into millions of hearts.

With so many concert performances, there were bound to be some amusing mishaps. At the Philadelphia concert, for instance, Celine started singing 'Love Can Move Mountains' and gestured so wildly that the spaghetti strap of her black top broke. Trying not to lose the rhythm of the song, she kept on singing, holding onto her top to cover her breast. Suddenly a fan threw a baseball cap up to her. She caught it, and covered her chest, completing the song! The audience loved it!

Another incident took place in Calgary during Celine's encore. She was wearing her magnificent period dress, and was about to sing her grand finale, when suddenly the centre platform stopped dead. Celine was stranded in the hole, with just her head sticking out. She shrugged her shoulders, and lost no time in climbing out. The show must go on!

Four days later, Celine was off to Toronto, for two scheduled performances and a private benefit concert that raised a million dollars for research into a cure for cystic fibrosis.

The weeks were made up of endless concerts and talk-show appearances. Amidst it all, she had made a point of hosting the twentieth anniversary of the Quebec music awards (L'ADISQ). Celine was the pride of Quebec and, having received thirty-five awards since the age of fifteen, hosting the show was her way of giving something back to the Quebec music industry. They had watched her grow up and now she belonged to the world. It was only fitting that Celine should start off the show while suspended high in the air inside a giant globe.

The thirty-city North American tour was exhausting: Boston, Philadelphia, Washington, East Rutherford, Nassau, New York, Toronto, Chicago, Cleveland, Cincinnati, Detroit, Chapel Hill, Charlotte, Nashville, Tampa, Fort Lauderdale, Calgary, Vancouver, Seattle, Oakland, San José, Las Vegas, Los Angeles, Anaheim, Phoenix, Halifax and seven concerts in Montreal, all in a four-month period.

It's another day, another concert, in another city. Celine is in the dressing room and René walks over. Celine thinks she's heard that she's having two days off after the concert she's about to give.

'Two days off, for real?' she begs René.

'Yes, two days off,' he says. Celine seems relieved.

'Wait a minute, I'm wrong, you have only one day off,' he says. She stares at him. In her eyes, there is a look – somewhere between sadness and desperation.

The albums keep selling, and the honours keep coming. On 7 December Celine wins six *Billboard* Music Awards, and, on 14 December the entertainment industry's *Variety* magazine hails Celine Dion for having sold 90 million albums to date.

New concert dates for Asia and Europe are announced: Japan,

Germany, Sweden, Austria, Holland, Belgium, France, Portugal, Spain, England, Scotland . . . the list is endless.

Celine looks over at René and seems forlorn. 'The years pass, and in reality, I don't know him. We gave so much that we forgot ourselves. I want to begin to know him. Know the sensitive man, the lover, and have his children.' She knew the 'manager' but not the husband.

Celine was getting more and more concerned about losing those she loved. 'The people we love die. When they leave us, you see your platinum records, trophies, and see that the things that we value the most, we miss. It has to stop one day.'

'One day, we will try to live a normal life,' says René. 'Because it is not normal, the life we live. We can't go on all our lives like this. We wouldn't be complete.' They have seen the greatest success the world has ever known together. But there has been a price to pay. 'A big price,' says René.

There was a memorable occasion where her album was first released, when Celine appeared on *Good Morning America* to perform her song 'Let's Talk About Love' with six backing singers. Her guitar player, piano player, percussionist and bass player were with her. As she sang, Celine kept looking back at her musicians and particularly her singers. Something was wrong, but it was hard to tell what.

The audience applauded as Celine finished but seemed perplexed. 'Right now, I have made a mistake and I wish I could start all over again,' she said, in front of the millions of television viewers, not even trying to hide her disappointment. At that moment she was so earnest, even childlike. Wanting another chance to do it right.

'I'm so sorry. Can we start the show over? Can I sing another one?' begged Celine.

'No one would know,' said co-host Lisa McCreed.

'I didn't know,' agreed Charles Gibson. 'It sounded great to me.'

But there was an audience that was even more important to Celine. 'I'm sure my thirteen brothers and sisters were watching this morning,' she said.

After the commercial, before the show finished, Celine was up at the microphone and this time she sang the song again – perfectly, with all the right modulations and all the harmonies. Her voice soared, just like her heart. Celine – so sensitive, so simple. All she wanted was perfection, and her family's approval, and, of course, René's. But most of all, it was for herself.

Later that night, back in Montreal, René reminisced about that morning's performance. 'She made a mistake,' he said, looking sad for a moment. The he brightened. 'At least it shows that she's human.'

Celine is candid when she talks about René: 'He brings the best out of me . . . all the time. He's not satisfied when it's *good*. But that's great, because *I'm* that kind of person. It is not easy for me to be satisfied.

'I want the best of me and he helps me to be. I don't know, he's very sensitive, emotional, I go crazy for that. And he loves me very, very much. And I do too. I think we complete each other. He feels strong when he's with me and I feel strong when I'm with him. Finding a person that loves you and that you can satisfy in showbusiness – because he loves showbusiness – so I can satisfy him in showbusiness as an artist, in the kitchen, and at home. He's happy with me as a wife. He's proud of his wife. Me having the best manager and best man in the world, it is incredible what we have for each other. We are each other's fantasies in a way. I look up to him, he looks up to me. He thinks I'm beautiful and I think he's gorgeous. You know what I mean. I thinks he's like a wonderful wild horse. A black one. Very strong.'

In the sleeve notes for *Let's Talk About Love* Celine dedicates a love poem to him:

René mon amour,
　　Through the wind I can feel your strength,
　　Through your emotion I can feel my music.
　　Love, je t'aime, Celine x x . . .

The thing about Celine is that she's a super megastar in both languages.

Celine is like the exception, basically. She's done so much, I think,' says Marc Langis, Celine's bass player. 'Only a few artists have been able to do this, establish herself in both French and English, and it takes talent. It takes a genius like René. Oh, he's a genius, definitely. No doubt about it. To bring Celine to that level, when she was born in Charlemagne and speaking only French, that's not typical. Not Celine, she's by herself over there. She's incredibly talented but René, he just did everything right. Basically from over fifteen years ago, that's why they're there now. There's always a price to pay I suppose, right. That's probably part of it. She can't hang with everybody, like going out with everyone to have a beer. I mean, she can't do that.

'She started doing this at twelve years old. It's been her life. She doesn't know much about anything else than what she's doing,' he adds.

'In terms of success . . . it takes a lot of money. It paid off for Sony but they spent a lot of money in the beginning, as Celine wasn't known outside Quebec. They had to push it from the very start. They're making a lot of money. You know René risked his house? He's a player. He loves to risk money. He loves to gamble. That's what he did for Celine, and most of the time he wins. He worked to have George Martin and all [those talented superstars] to come and work with Celine. That's what he did this year. That's what he likes to do.

'Now I'm telling you, René is the guy. He's brilliant. He knows what he wants and he knows how to get it.

'I wouldn't do what Celine has to do, even for all those millions. Basically you don't belong to yourself. You belong to all these people. I think she's happy. Nothing's perfect. But I hope she's happy because that's what she really wanted to do.'

Celine is as human as you can get. And it was suddenly time for her to think about her own needs.

'My mom is the person that I look up to in my life because she has, first of all, the soul of an artist. She gave her life instead of having her own life. She spent all her life between four walls raising fourteen children – with nothing. It takes a lot of courage, a lot of strength. We never had money but we were never poor. I have all the respect in the world for my mom.'

Years before, Celine had said: 'The way I see my life and my career – there is no limit. I want to continue to go farther, higher and greater.' These words, 'always higher . . . always farther,' seemed to sum up her career. But something changed as the years of fame and glory passed. Celine lost sight of herself.

'My mom, she just gave her whole life to her kids. I already gave my life to music.' Celine still wanted children desperately. 'I would love to have a child or many children. I would like to have a few. We're trying, we're trying for a long time now. It doesn't seem to want to happen. You know I say to myself: Celine, you're so lucky. There are so many things happening to you now. You can't have it all. Don't push your luck. If it happens, it happens. If it doesn't happen, it doesn't happen.

'We're working on it. The rehearsals are going very well,' Celine would say to a roaring audience. She wanted it that way. The laughter masked the pain. In the past thirty months, Celine had sold 60 million albums. She had now sold over 90 million albums in total, and the world wanted more.

While promoting Let's Talk About Love in Europe, Celine had announced that she might play the role of Edith Piaf, the legendary French singer, in a motion picture. Another dream. It was the life of a French legend, the great woman of chanson, who lived a brief and passionate life, leaving a legacy of 200 recordings. By coincidence, Celine had also done just over 200 songs when she considered doing the role.

Perhaps no other interview has more candidly brought out Celine's true feelings of depression and anxiety than the one with her close friend Sonia Benezra, a Quebec talk-show host, who met up with her in Las Vegas.

It was a time when Celine should have been rejoicing over the success of both her Titanic love theme and her hit album Let's Talk About Love. The interview took place at Celine and René's lavish penthouse in

Caesar's Palace. Celine had all the fame in the world . . . but Sonia knew she had paid a high price for it.

'It is easy to sit back and say, "Oh my goodness. How wonderful. How happy she must be." There are a lot of people . . . Once they make it, they go through periods in their lives where they say, "I don't know why I'm so depressed. I shouldn't be depressed. I have everything I ever hoped for." And then they feel guilty on top of it all. Do you ever go through periods like that? Where you think, oh my God, I'm feeling lonely or I'm feeling down. I shouldn't be,' asked Sonia.

'Yes. When you're on stage to perform, the pressure is on you. And, with the years, there is more pressure. And, once in a while, I would break down into tears, without knowing exactly why. It's hard to understand. You can't even understand your own feelings. Or, once in a while, you'll go to bed at night and you would have this kind of elevator in your stomach. And it's very painful. It's like you have something inside of you in your stomach that goes up and down, said Celine candidly.

'You can't breathe well. And you feel like screaming or crying. And then you wake up your husband and you would just like this person to look at you. Not to sleep. You just want a person to go like this [extending a reassuring hand] and just look at you without saying anything. But it's hard when somebody is in the middle of their sleep.

'It always happens in very difficult moments. In the middle of the night or when you are alone. It's scary sometimes. I think it's anxiety. It's scary. But normally, with breathing, I go through it nicely.'

'When you go through these periods, where you're saying to yourself, "This is too much", "There is too much work", "I don't have time to breathe . . .", are there times when you ever think, "Maybe I'll just stop for a while? Maybe I will stop?"'

'I can't wait to stop,' answered Celine without hesitation.

'Really?' asked Sonia.

'Yeah, I do. Look at René,' Celine talked of her husband who was getting on in years. 'I can't wait to drive in a car with him, open roof. Go for a picnic. Go to the movies. Or have four days in a row wearing a bathrobe, and say okay, I think I'll get dressed now. Like . . . he's not young any more. I would love to have the years with him now. When he'll be sixty-something, hopefully . . .' Celine paused. 'He's not getting any younger and he'll be more tired. And now I'm thirty. It's now.'

And, as she looked back over her life, knowing where it had taken her. Celine stopped and thought: Would she do it all again? She took a deep breath and sighed.

'I would say no. I would not do it again. But I don't know. Maybe, because I've touched it all, I've had it all. Maybe that's why I can say, I would not do it again. It's like . . . if you see all the fruits in the world right there and you have tasted everything, and whatever happens you say, "No, I don't need anything" because you have tasted everything. And you went through everything. And I've tasted and I've looked. You don't need it any more, maybe.

'If we put all our energy in showbusiness and make all the money, and have all the success and travel all over the world . . .' Her voice suddenly rose, as if she was almost angry, 'And perform for more and more and more people, I will look back and I will look at my husband who is getting old, and I would say to myself, "God, what is showbusiness? Why do all this" I want to have a life . . . you know, a normal life. I can't wait to stop. *Really*.'

Celine still had a time to achieve her dreams. But, for now . . . the show had to go on.

The curtain closes and the concert hall pulsates with emotion.

The fans stand . . . clapping . . . cheering. Minutes go by as the sound builds to a deafening crescendo.

René Angelil is seated in the audience, behind the sound man. He listens to the roar of the crowd, with a manager's pride and a husband's heart. There are tears in his eyes. Standing ovations often make him cry. To René, she is the most beautiful woman in the world. Sincere, sensitive, she does not think of herself as a star . . . but equal to everyone else. This is what he has always admired and loved about her. And every time he watches her on stage, it is like falling in love with her again.

Almost twenty years ago he took a child out of oblivion and made her a superstar. And, even knowing the sacrifices that have been made in the process, if he had to do it all over again . . . he would.

Celine emerges on stage for her last song and the audience goes wild. She stares out and feels their love. She sits down and motions for them to sit as well. Like obedient children, they do.

She looks out as a young girl waves to her. She waves back. Another fan screams out, 'I love you'.

'I love you too,' she answers. The love is real.

There would always be an encore but, for now, Celine ends with the song 'Immortality'.

'This is the song that I'd like to be remembered by,' she says as she speaks the first lines:

'So this is who I am,
And this is all I know.'

And flashbacks of her life roll past vividly, from the song she sang standing on top of the kitchen table at five years old . . . to the first song her mother wrote for her and the start of an international career at thirteen.

She has spent her life on stage. It is all she knows. It is her home.

In her thirties now, her teen years and twenties have flashed by fast, too fast. Now Celine is ready to start a new chapter in her life.

She wants the things most people take for granted. A child. The lost years. Time for Celine, for René. Time that she feels is running out as the years fly by.

A hush falls over the audience as she sings the moving lyrics of 'Immortality', a hush that covers the room like a warm blanket right up until the last line of the song.

'We don't say goodbye.'

And, as the cheers become deafening, she is one with the audience.

There is no greater feeling. No greater power.

It is the power of love.

Celine's Prayer

'Thank you for your prayers, and your energy. It helps a lot.'
– CELINE ADDRESSING THE 90,000
CROWD AT THE STADE DE FRANCE IN PARIS

The fairytale had gone terribly wrong. On 30 March 1999, the day of Celine's thirty-first birthday – a birthday that had once seen her enter a fairytale career when she performed and won her first Oscar for *Beauty and the Beast* seven years before – her world fell apart. In Dallas to perform at a sold-out concert, Celine awoke to discover a lump on the right side of René's neck. He had been complaining of pain in his throat, and had been finding it difficult to speak. Panic-stricken, Celine insisted that René go to a nearby hospital. The diagnosis was devastating. Cancer. Emergency surgery was performed to remove the cancerous tumour that had metastasized in his neck.

René was diagnosed with squamous-cell carcinoma, a malignant tumour that arises from the mid-portion of the epidermal layer of the skin. Metastatic meant that the cancer had spread from another area in his body.

Celine was heartbroken, but she fought her deepest fears and became the essence of strength and optimism. She surrounded René with the best medical team and then, drawing on her deep faith, put his health in God's hands.

Celine's parents were on their way to celebrate her birthday in Dallas when they heard the shocking news. They met Celine in the hospital waiting room as René underwent the surgery. 'Life isn't easy for anyone, even if you have money,' said an emotional Maman. Celine fought her sobs with courage as she became the tower of strength for family and friends. René's three children were overwrought with sadness and his many close friends were in shock.

'This is not the time to cry. We have to be strong,' Celine had said. Celine would be his guardian angel now, as he had been for her throughout her career. Celine reassured everybody that René was surrounded with a wonderful medical team. Her words 'gave courage to everyone', according to Maman.

Performing in Dallas during this devastating time was one of the hardest things Celine had ever had to do. She did not cancel the concert but, rather, her determination would allow her to perform. Stopping to compose herself from time to time, and bursting into tears while singing 'My Heart Will Go On', Celine finished the concert, longing to be by René's side.

René was released from hospital, but six weeks of radiation treatment and fourteen treatments of chemotherapy made the nightmare of what was happening to the greatest love of her life all the more real. 'René is the biggest priority in my life and I want to be by his side as he continues his treatment. I hope my fans will understand and support me in this difficult situation,' Celine uttered. And her fans did understand.

Celine abruptly cancelled the rest of her concerts across North America, including a three-day well-publicized engagement at Caesar's Palace in Atlantic City and two concerts back in her home town of Montreal. Her early April concert in New Orleans was her last performance, marking the premature end of the tour. Instead, Celine chose to be by René's side during the agonizing months that would follow as he began treatments near their home in Jupiter, Florida. But Celine intended to resume her world tour on 27 May in Dublin, Ireland, continuing on throughout Europe. Celine's spirit was remarkable, which was very much in evidence when she spoke to a news team from Birmingham, England, who had attended the New Orleans concert and were doing a story on Celine in preparation for her concert in Birmingham at the end of May. 'I'm doing fine and we're doing fine and we are there for each other. That is why we are not stopping the tour, just postponing,' said Celine. She even commented that she might play golf at the Belfry golf course in Birmingham the next month. But it was not to be. Celine would soon cancel more concerts in her European tour.

Her world had changed drastically since the months leading up to that fateful Dallas concert. Her duet 'The Prayer', with Italian tenor Andrea Bocelli, would touch Celine's heart more than ever. A song of faith, healing and guidance, the song had meaning that was so very real to her now. The song, written by David Foster and Carol Bayer Sager, had seen Celine win a Golden Globe Award for Best Original Song for a Motion Picture on 24 January, and it had moved the audience during the live performance at the Grammy Awards on 24 February. When Celine accepted four Grammy Awards that night, she looked out at René, who was seated in the audience and said 'Everybody is now taking care of my career – producers, writers, everybody. But thank you for taking care of my heart,' she said, her voice wavering.

Celine's ultimate vision of happiness was almost in sight. She set her hopes on a future spending time with René. Celine fantasized about having a normal life; she was a star who wanted nothing more than to be with her husband. And it was almost in reach as she swept through concert tour after concert tour and award show after award show. Earlier in January, Celine added her first People's Choice award to her collection for Favourite Female Musical Performer. This was followed the next day by two American Music Awards for Favourite Pop/Rock Female Artist and Favourite Adult Contemporary Artist.

Celine showed her individuality by stunning the fashion world and wearing the off-white Christian Dior pant suit, complete with fedora, that she wore to the seventy-first Academy Awards on 21 March. She later changed into a gown as she performed 'The Prayer' with Andrea Bocelli, and moved the star-studded audience to tears. The song had been nominated for an Oscar. Just before the awards, Celine was one of the three pre-Oscar-show interviewees on the celebrated *Barbara Walters Special*. She was in good company with Elizabeth Taylor and Susan Sarandon. Celine's interview started off the show, televised from her mansion in Jupiter, Florida. Radiant, poised and articulate, Celine vowed that now in her thirties she was at her happiest yet. As Celine candidly put it: 'Young enough to start things . . . but just old enough not to be stupid. You are just starting to wake up. Maybe that's why I want to stop . . . It's so overwhelming – the success, the money – it's *much* too much. It's time for René and me to stop and have a normal life.' Yet it seemed that everything was far from normal. In the earlier moments of the interview, René had joined in briefly and his voice sounded lower and raspier than ever before. It was alarming to those who knew him. Something appeared terribly wrong – barely audible, he whispered 'Are you ready, baby?' to Celine as they golfed together in the closing moments of the show.

Only one week later, Celine was trying to be strong as René fought the battle of his life. The two had retreated to their home in Jupiter, Florida, spending every moment together as Celine showered René with love and tried to keep his spirits up. She made him laugh, and it did him a world of good. He began his first treatment on 4 May, and kept up his morale by playing golf, even though he had to protect his neck from the sun with a scarf.

Celine held off the media from making what was already a devastating situation even more painful. The world was in shock and, back in Montreal, a French magazine – on behalf of his closest friends – gave an emotional 16-page tribute of hope and encouragement to René. Despite the imposed vow of silence, and Celine's instructions for the hospital not to issue regular bulletins about his progress, rumours soon crossed the four corners of the globe. Fictitious stories abounded, from Celine seeking out a guru to help René to combat the cancer, to grim speculations on how long he had to live. And before long the story that René had donated his sperm to be frozen so that they might still have a child together if the radiation treatments made him sterile hit the headlines. Above all, Celine would protect him from scouring through the magazines, newspapers and tabloids, and concentrate on only one thing. Getting better. And Celine would not leave his side. She cancelled more dates on her European tour and did not appear in Dublin, Ireland, on 27 May, as well as cancelling concerts in Belfast, Birmingham, Frankfurt, Gothenberg, Vienna, Cologne, Lyon and Marseilles. 'I love my fans and I love performing but René is my number one priority,' she repeated again. By his side was the only place she had ever wanted to be and now, in a sad twist of fate, Celine would stop the roller coaster of fame that had been central to her life to be with René. Celine continued to pray for a miracle. Continued to believe that it was in God's hands.

In the weeks that went by, René lost 25 pounds. He had no appetite and the gruelling sessions at the hospital in Florida saw René fight for his life. He had been a born winner, a gambler who loved to win. Now the stakes were at their highest. Celine would not leave his side.

Yet it was René who persuaded her to perform at some of her European concerts. With a heavy heart, Celine went to Amsterdam on 14 June, followed only days later by Brussels and Paris. On the opening night in Paris, Celine faced a crowd of 90,000 people in one of the largest stadiums she had ever sung in, as René watched from his living room at home via satellite.

Celine was brave and optimistic as she faced the crowd, 'He's doing better than he was. I am so proud of him. He is very strong,' she said, masking the deep pain in her heart. 'Thank you for your prayers and your energy. It helps a lot.'

The thunderous standing ovation melted all the hearts in the stadium. Their tears flowed easily, as lighters flickered through the darkness and Celine's love songs took on greater meaning. Celine's courage made the giant stadium seem small by comparison. As soon as her second concert in Paris was finished, she was on a flight home, sparing no time to get back to René.

Her life would be a continuous path of flights back and forth as she completed more concerts in Zurich, Munich, Sheffield, and Edinburgh, before ending the eight-city European tour in Wembley Stadium in London on 11 July. With every return home, Celine held him, sang to him, encouraged him and above all loved him. It was her turn to be strong for René. He had taken a child from oblivion and, together, they had conquered the world. Together, Celine believed, they could conquer everything. Even this. They were bound by two hearts that had long been one. A love that would for ever be in her soul.

Celine on Celine

ON PERFORMING ON STAGE: ✳ 'I really love it, because all day long, all year long . . . everybody's always telling me what to do. "Be careful", "Don't say this", "Don't forget to talk about that", "I don't think you should wear this . . ." "It's too much", or "Not enough . . ." "It's too spectacular" or whatever . . . But immediately, when the curtain opens, this is my home and nobody will have the courage to come on stage and tell me what to do. This is the only place I can be myself.'

ON THE AUDIENCE: ✳ 'I can perform for two or two-and-a-half hours and I can talk with the audience and say whatever I want to say. If I want to cry because I feel like it, I will! If I want to laugh and tell a joke, I will! If I see a beautiful girl or a baby I will bring her on stage and dance with her. Nobody can tell me what to do. This is my home and that's why I love it – because it's the place that I feel most powerful. When you feel powerful, very secure and strong about yourself, you feel beautiful and every woman in the world wants to feel beautiful. I would love to be on stage every day.'

ON LIFE: ✳ 'I prefer to live one day, one month and one year at a time. When I want to do something, I do it.'

ON LOOKS: * 'I don't think I'm super beautiful but I'm not terrible either. My strongest physical attributes are my eyes. But people also say that I have beautiful legs.'

ON BEAUTY: * 'I want to be beautiful, I want to grow old in a beautiful way. I want to be a woman in every sense of the word.'

ON HAVING CHILDREN: * 'I'm not going to try to beat my parents and have fifteen kids, but I would love to have children.'

ON PARENTING: * 'I don't want to deprive myself of singing and I would like to have children. I grew up with parents who performed in shows. I slept in banquet halls in restaurants. I am not worse off for this. My child will grow with me, following me everywhere, getting used to my rhythm of life.'

ON SUCCESS: * 'I don't want to sell five million records and be rich, and then . . . that's it. I'm afraid of that. I want a career. I want to sing all my life.'

ON STAGE: * 'I perceive the world of stage like a universe that requires discipline and resourcefulness.'

ON ROMANCE: * 'I am a romantic – romantic dinners in front of the fireplace – no champagne because I don't drink – but the dream gets me carried away in a state of lightheadedness.'

ON IMMORTALITY: * 'I admit that I would love if one day there are posters of me in black and white displayed a little everywhere, like Marilyn Monroe, James Dean, Elvis Presley, Charlie Chaplin, Edith Piaf . . . This gives something that renders them immortal. We know these legends will never die. I know that I am not a legend, but in all honesty, I would like that after I die, I could still live on . . . that there is never an end.'

ON SUCCESS: ✳ 'I try to always give the maximum of my potential and I look to constantly surpass myself, to better my preceding performance. From the age of twelve I decided to invest myself in this career and it doesn't matter what type of obstacles that I had to overcome and the efforts that I've had to deploy. It's a pact that I made with myself at that time, and – years later, nothing has really changed. I will always be in the quest of a new challenge, a new accomplishment. For me, it's as important as breathing.'

ON PRESSURE: ✳ 'I think I am good at delivering the goods under pressure. "I can take it," as they say. When the situation is critical, I think I have proven that they can have confidence in me and rely on me.'

ON SINGING: ✳ 'When I am in full possession of all my means, singing for me is a fantastic exercise – even magical. When I'm not in my best form vocally my handicap incites me to be too careful and think about my way of singing, in brief, to calculate everything. And this is a reality which I have enormous difficulty in dealing with. I detest this because it takes away my spontaneity . . . the "feeling" that you don't calculate.'

ON INTIMATE MOMENTS: ✳ 'Once the most fulfilling moments were on stage. But now, the peak moments are much more intimate – the last seconds of the day when René turns off the TV and I curl up against his back. No noise. Darkness. Hearing his breathing. When you're in love with someone, it makes you go wild. If you put your head on his back, you hear his heart.'

ON PERFORMING: ✳ 'There is nothing more beautiful than the sound of applause, the love of the public. For that – for the public – I am ready to make all sacrifices and it's my reason for living. It's what I live for.'

ON OLDER MEN: ✳ 'I love being with an older guy. He's already done his crazy things.'

ON WISHING: ✳ 'If I had a wish it would be that I would be able to stop time. I find that everything is going very fast around me and I sometimes have the impression of not having time to take advantage of the beautiful moments.'

ON BEING ALONE: ✳ 'Being alone – and I've thought about it – makes me terrified. I don't want to finish my days alone or pass my most beautiful years as a woman without a husband and without children. I don't want to wake up and feel that I've failed my life as a woman simply because I've given everything to my career. I want to give my life a sense. I don't want to end my days like Greta Garbo or like the big female stars who finished their lives in oblivion.'

ON SACRIFICES: ✳ 'I would be misleading if I said that it's easy and I'm always on a high. I find it rough and the better my career goes, the harder I find it.'

ON PEOPLE: ✳ 'I am not a "solitary" girl. I need people. It's my security.'

ON TALENT: ✳ 'I am always amazed when people talk about my way of singing and the power of my voice. Honestly, I don't know my qualities as a singer. But I know that I work hard and that I've reached a certain maturity on the vocal plane, but the great interest of people in me surprises me every time.'

ON SHOWS: ✳ 'All I can say is that I sing with sincerity and with all my heart. In shows, for example, my only goal is to establish a kind of communion with the audience and to share with them the emotions that I have. For me, singing is this above all and, before everything, a sharing.'

ON HER VOICE: ✳ 'To be honest, I never stopped to ask myself if I have a beautiful voice or not. For me, I don't stop to think of such things. Of course it warms my heart when a person compliments my style of singing, but again, I don't lose any sleep over it.'

ON LISTENING TO HERSELF SING: ✳ 'When I hear my songs on the radio, I change the station. It's not that I don't like what I do, it's simply that I prefer to listen to what other singers are doing.'

ON THE PAST: ✳ 'Everything seemed so easy at that time. It does me good to talk about those beautiful years, because it's like I return to the source. Sometimes I have this image of myself kneeling by a stream, splashing my face with the pure clean water. I see myself as a young girl, who runs innocently in the field of wheat, hair in the wind. This is to say that the more the events jostle in my present professional life, the more I hang on to those years where I didn't realize all that was happening to me.'

ON PRESSURE: ✳ 'Today . . . it's bigger, more serious, harder. I have more pressure on my shoulders. I am more demanding on myself. Other times, if I made a mistake when I was young, people found it cute, but today, I know very well that I can no longer permit myself to make mistakes. My reality today is a lot different than what I knew when I began in this profession.'

ON STAGE FRIGHT: ✳ 'I am no exception to the rule. In my case, it's always at the moment when I leave my dressing room to go up to the stage that my stage fright comes out. Precisely in the hall, when the lights are off, and the people start to scream. I attribute this stage fright to a real desire to answer the expectations of the audience. Personally, I approach every show like it is, at the same time, my first show and my last. Since the public is different at every show, we must be motivated by a constant concern to do well, performance after performance. The only solution to stage fright is to charge ahead and climb up on stage. It's doing what I love most in the world – singing. You must conquer the fear and say: 'We'll go and have fun!'

ON HER GREATEST FEARS: ✳ 'Being alone – it's a scary thought. I don't like being the youngest all the time. I'm frightened sometimes of losing everybody.'

* DISCOGRAPHY *

1st Album, 1981: *La voix du Bon Dieu* (50,000)

2nd Album, 1981: *Céline Dion chante Noël* (25,000)

3rd Album, 1982: *Tellement j'ai d'amour . . .* (150,000)

4th Album, 1983: *Les chemins de ma maison* (150,000)

5th Album, 1983: *Chants et contes de Noël* (75,000)

6th Album, 1984: *Les plus grands success* (75,000)

7th Album, 1984: *Melanie* (175,000)

8th Album, 1985: *Celine Dion en concert* (50,000)

9th Album, 1985: *C'est pour toi* (50,000)

10th Album, 1986: *Les chansons en or* (150,000)

11th Album, 1987: *Incognito* (500,000)

12th Album, 1990: *Unison* (2,000,000)

13th Album, 1991: *Celine Dion chante Plamondon* (1,500,000)

14th Album, 1992: *Celine Dion* (4,000,000)

15th Album, 1993: *The Colour of My Love* (15,000,000)

16th Album, 1994: *Celine Dion à l'Olympia* (800,000)

17th Album, 1995: *D'eux – The French Album* (6,500,000)

18th Album, 1996: *Falling Into You* (26,000,000)

19th Album, 1996: *Live à Paris* (2,500,000)

20th Album, 1997: *Let's Talk About Love* (25,000,000)

21st Album, 1998: *S'il suffisait d'aimer* (5,000,000)

22nd Album, 1998 *These are Special Times* (5,000,000)

✳ WORLDWIDE AWARDS ✳

1982
Gold Medal at the Thirteenth International Festival of Popular Song In Tokyo
Performance of the song, 'Tellement j'ai d'amour pour toi'(I Have Love for You)

1988
First prize Gold Medal at Eurovision for her performance of the song 'Ne partez
pas sans moi' (Don't Leave Without Me), held in Dublin, Ireland

1992
Oscar for Best Song for 'Beauty and the Beast' (duet with Peabo Bryson)
World Music Award for Best-Selling Canadian Female Artist, held in Monaco

1993
Grammy Award for Best Pop Performance of the Year, by a duo or a group, for
the song 'Beauty and the Beast'
Billboard Magazine Trophy for Billboard International Creative Achievement
Award

1995
World Music Award for Best-Selling Canadian Female Artist (Monaco)
Ivor Novello Award (UK): Song of the Year 'Think Twice'

1996
World Music Award for Best-Selling Canadian Female Artist (Monaco)
World Music Award for Best-Selling Artist (All Categories)
World Music Award for Best-Selling Pop Artist
Bambi Award for Best Pop International Artist (Germany)
Knight of the Order of Arts and Letters (Chevalier de l'Ordre des Arts et des
Lettres, France)
MIDEM Award for Best-Selling French Album D'eux (France)
MIDEM Award for Combined Sales of More Than 10 million in Europe During
1995 (France)
Victoires Award: French Singer of the Year (France)
Victoires Award: Song of the Year (France)
Gala Woman of the Year (France)
Irish Recorded Music Awards (IRMA):
Best International Female Vocalist
RFI (France) Award for the song 'Pour que tu m'aimes encore' (For You to Still Love
Me)
VH-1 (US Video Channel): Artist of the Year (for 1996)

1997
Grammy Award for Album of the Year: *Falling Into You*
Grammy Award for Pop Album of the Year: *Falling Into You*

Irish Recorded Music Awards (IRMA): Best International Female Vocalist for the Album *Falling Into You*
National Association Of Recording Merchandisers (NARM):
Best-Selling Pop Recording *Falling Into You*
National Association of Recording Merchandisers (NARM):
Recording of the Year *Falling Into You*
National Association of Recording Merchandisers (NARM): Artist of the Year
Amigos Awards: Best International Female Artist
World Music Award for Best-Selling Canadian Female Artist (Monaco)
World Music Award for Best-Selling Artist (All Categories)
World Music Award for Best-Selling Pop Artist

1998
Golden Globe Award for Best Original Song from a Motion Picture for the song 'My Heart Will Go On' from *Titanic*
American Music Award for Best Pop Rock Female
Oscar for Best Song: 'My Heart Will Go On' from *Titanic*
World Music Award for Best-Selling Canadian Female Artist
Billboard Music Award for Album of the Year for *Titanic*
Billboard Music Award for Female Album for *Let's Talk About Love*
Billboard Music Award for Soundtrack Album of the Year for *Titanic*
Billboard Music Award for Soundtrack Single of the Year for 'My Heart Will Go On'
Billboard Music Award Female Albums Artists for *Titanic*
Billboard Music Award for Adult Contemporary Artist of the Year

1999
Golden Globe Award for Best Original Song from a Motion Picture for the song 'The Prayer' from *Quest for Camelot*
People's Choice Award for Favourite Female Musical Performer of the Year
American Music Award for Favourite Pop/Rock Female Artist
American Music Award for Favourite Adult Contemporary Artist
Grammy Award for Record of the Year for 'My Heart Will Go On'
Grammy Award for Song of the Year for 'My Heart Will Go On'
Grammy Award for Best Female Pop Vocal Performance for 'My Heart Will Go On'
Grammy Award for Best Song Written for a Motion Picture for 'My Heart Will Go On'

* INDEX *